The Verdict of the Court

Courts are constantly required to know how people think. They may have to decide what a specific person was thinking on a past occasion; how others would have reacted to a particular situation; or whether a witness is telling the truth. Be they judges, jurors or magistrates, the law demands they penetrate human consciousness. This book questions whether the 'arm-chair psychology' operated by fact-finders, and indeed the law itself, in its treatment of the fact-finders, bears any resemblance to the knowledge derived from psychological research. Comparing psychological theory with court verdicts in both civil and criminal contexts, it assesses where the separation between law and science is most acute, and most dangerous.

THE VERDICT OF THE COURT

Passing Judgment in Law and Psychology

JENNY MCEWAN
Professor of Criminal Law,
The University of Exeter

·HART·
PUBLISHING

HART PUBLISHING
OXFORD AND PORTLAND, OREGON
2003

Published in North America (US and Canada) by
Hart Publishing
c/o International Specialized Book Services
5804 NE Hassalo Street
Portland, Oregon
97213-3644
USA

Hart Publishing is a specialist legal publisher based in Oxford, England. To order
further copies of this book or to request a list of other publications please write to:

Hart Publishing, Salters Boatyard, Folly Bridge, Abingdon Rd, Oxford, OX1 4LB
Telephone: +44 (0)1865 245533 Fax: +44 (0) 1865 794882
email: mail@hartpub.co.uk
WEBSITE: http//:www.hartpub.co.uk

British Library Cataloguing in Publication Data
Data Available

ISBN 1-901362-53-1 (hardback)

Typeset by Olympus, India, in Minion 10/12 pt.
Printed and bound in Great Britain by
Biddles Ltd, _www.biddles.co.uk_

Contents

1

Introduction

HOW DO PEOPLE THINK?

THIS QUESTION MIGHT appear to be one psychologists, rather than lawyers, would trouble themselves with. Yet lawyers frequently are forced to ask it, and either to supply their own answer or recruit members of the public to answer it for them. In the courtroom, the 'finder of fact', who might be a member of a jury, a magistrate, or a judge, is characteristically required to identify the thought processes of another. The question may be what a specific person was thinking on a past occasion, for example, whilst causing a harm to someone else. It may be how another, ordinary, person would have reacted in the same situation. It may be necessary to assess the defendant's mental capacity, either in terms of fitness to stand trial, or, retrospectively, whether he or she can be held responsible for actions that caused harm. The fact-finder may need to form a view about the state of mind, particularly the honesty, of someone actually standing in front of them in the courtroom, giving evidence. Sometimes the fact-finder is constrained by a variety of legal rules and principles which purport wholly or partly to supply the answer to these questions. Sometimes the legal rules are themselves coloured by lawyers' assumptions as to how fact-finders themselves think.

The world in which this lawyer-psychology operates has little connection with a parallel world in which psychologists have set themselves the challenge of identifying human mental processes by scientific method. Lawyers and psychologists have differing objectives and use different kinds of reasoning. Yet it may be that psychological research results could assist the legal world, if only by demonstrating to lawyers that many of their assumptions are wrong. In certain dramatic cases, lawyers have become suddenly aware that, indeed, they have been disastrously mistaken. Fundamental changes to the legal system have been made as a result. Some of the most significant instances of this are discussed in chapter eight, such as the recognition by courts of empirical findings on the reliability of identifications by eyewitnesses. Also, the legislature has been forced to confront the problems experienced by witnesses who are expected to testify in criminal trials; some, especially children, find this particularly difficult. Further, it will be seen in chapter six that the courts have taken into account, although possibly not as much as they should, the issue of the reliability of admissions by suspects with vulnerable personalities during police interrogation.

In these areas, psychology has had impact on the legal universe. Chapter eight considers whether the law is more effective as a result. The main purpose of this book, however, is to consider whether there are other areas where the law should be listening to the findings of forensic scientists. The first chapters therefore attempt to identify areas where the law might usefully reappraise its assumptions about human behaviour. The author is a lawyer, and therefore makes no claim to specialist knowledge of the psychological literature, only rather to a developing interest in it, and an increasing conviction that greater communication between the legal world and that of the forensic psychologist would benefit both.

LAW AND PSYCHOLOGY

Lawyers are famous for their all or nothing approach to science.[1] If scientists cannot provide categorical answers they run the risk of being ridiculed in the courtroom. But while some areas of 'hard science' may be treated with a deference born of a need to exaggerate certainties and ignore any proviso unhelpful to the client in the case, the domain of the 'trick-cyclist', the psychologist or psychiatrist, is regarded with suspicion. As will be shown later,[2] expert evidence on human behaviour is subject in the legal context to tight controls. Here the psychologist and the lawyer are competing for the same territory, and, in the courtroom, lawyers are well placed to ensure that they have the upper hand. In this context, the inability of empirical scientists to be absolutely certain is an excuse for the law to claim authority. In *Wakabayayaski*,[3] an expert witness was not allowed to testify that the behaviour of the complainant in a case of sexual assault was consistent with that of women who have been assaulted. The objection was that he could not say that witnesses who have not been assaulted do not behave in the same way. Yet if the expert evidence had been to the opposite effect, and she had behaved in a way inconsistent with the behaviour of genuine victims, the defence would almost certainly have been allowed to raise the point as a challenge to her credibility.[4]

In contrast to the reification of much scientific testimony, which advocates choose to present as a set of absolutes, psychologists as expert witnesses are unlikely to find themselves afforded such oracular status. They compete with the intuitive notions of advocate, judge and jury. Psychologists who apparently fail to appreciate their humble position in the legal arena are given short shrift. In 1908 Professor Münsterburg wrote a book[5] that suggested that the findings of psychology might be of value equal with those of the other forensic scientists regularly employed by courts. The great American lawyer John Henry Wigmore responded

---

[1] See CA Jones, *Expert Witnesses: Science, Medicine and Practice* (Oxford, Clarendon, 1994).
[2] See chapter 3 and chapter 7.
[3] (1996) 47 CLR (4th) 354.
[4] See J Jackson and S Doran, *Judge Without Jury: Diplock Trials and the Adversary System* (Oxford, Clarendon, 1995).
[5] H Münsterburg, *On the Witness Stand* (New York, Clark Boardman, 1923).

in vitriolic style, with an article in the form of a libel action.[6] Some legal commentators place psychology in the same camp as astrology. Yet an uneasy truce has been reached between the rival camps in recent years, and the expert evidence of psychologists is heard in court on certain approved issues.[7] Behavioural science may be of use to a court which finds itself unable to reach a decision by the usual routes. All cases require some form of resolution. The law provides devices to resolve impasse, most importantly, by imposing a burden on one of the parties to prove the case to the required standard of proof. Another favourite device where lawyers are hard put to come up with an answer, for example, as to the meaning of 'intention', is to leave the jury with the task of working it out.[8] But another is to demand that the relevant expert supplies the answer, as with infanticide.[9]

Passing on the moral responsibility for decisions which are difficult, if not impossible, is an attractive option for a court of law. Where decisions have to made as to the future well-being of a child, magistrates and judges are understandably reassured where an expert is present to suggest what outcome would be in the child's best interests. Michael King warns that some claims to expertise in such cases are over-inflated but, inevitably, courts are tempted to believe them. Recourse to expert evidence reduces the agonising loneliness of the judicial role, and psychological theory may thus legitimate the ultimate verdict, clothing it with the mantle of scientific respectability.[10]

> Erroneous information obtained by scientific methods (and therefore having the aura of truth) is more harmful than no information at all … especially when issues as sensitive as legal ones are being dealt with, and people's futures are quite literally at stake.[11]

But where absolutes are sought, the expert will not be allowed to hedge his opinion about with qualifications, such as the lack of external validation for a technique. Where it is necessary for legal purposes, the expert may simply be forced or manipulated into a categorical assertion. Failing that, expert evidence based on inconclusive results will nevertheless be accepted if it accords with the court's intuitive notions. Hence 'fireside deductions' will lend the required plausibility to empirical findings that cannot be validated by other means.[12]

---

[6] JH Wigmore, 'Professor Münsterburg and the Psychology of Testimony' (1909) 3 *Illinois Law Review* 399.

[7] See chapter 3.

[8] *Ibid.*

[9] *Ibid.*

[10] M King, 'The Limits of Law and Psychology in Decisions Concerning the Welfare of Children' in S Lloyd-Bostock, (ed) *Psychology in Legal Contexts* (London, Macmillan, 1981).

[11] VJ Konečni and EB Ebbesen, 'External Validity of Research in Legal Psychology' (1979) 3 *Law and Human Behavior* 39, 68.

[12] RE Meehl, 'Law and Fireside Deductions: Some Reflections of a Clinical Psychologist' in JL Tapp and FJ Levine (eds), *Law, Justice and the Individual in Society* (New York, Holt, Rinehart, 1977) 10.

Meanwhile, those responsible for framing our laws are increasingly taking account of the empirical findings of psychologists. But should it be assumed that these are generalisable to the legal setting? Exact duplication of court proceedings is virtually impossible in an experimental context. In the literature there is little data obtained from witnesses to real-life crimes or from studies of real jurors. Actuality research into legal issues is difficult to arrange for practical reasons, and because of the untidy welter of information that confronts witnesses and decision-makers in real cases. Much of the experimental data comes from small-scale laboratory research. Often, the method of presenting evidence in experimental jury studies is to use transcripts which fact-finders read, whereas in court live witnesses would give oral evidence. Some experimenters use videotapes of a 'witness' giving oral testimony. In either event, the content is usually edited for brevity and the issues cut down to a minimum, so that variables can be tightly controlled. The advantage is that researchers can organise information more coherently so that the issue being investigated is clearly exposed. Simulations are more objective, the experimenter has control over the variables, and they do not require major funding. But psychologists who conduct this kind of research candidly admit those factors which might affect the extent to which their results can be generalised across to real life. For example, although some studies use subjects taken from the pool of people eligible for jury service, many are forced to use university students. They tend to be available and cheap,[13] but are hardly a typical cross-section of the population. Quite often they are undergraduates studying psychology, which begs the question whether they actually have insight into the nature of the experiment.

The need to ensure that issues are clearly identifiable for research purposes means that laboratory simulations do not reproduce the atmosphere of a trial in court, where the complexity of the evidence generally forces lawyers to frequent perusal of the paperwork, ensuring a tedious slowness. Mock jurors are also unlikely to be given the amount of time to consider their verdicts that real ones are allowed. Some research work has been done by placing shadow jurors in the courtroom itself.[14] The verdict of the real jury can be compared with those of experimental subjects who heard exactly the same evidence under the same conditions. Whichever method is selected, experimenters must decide whether or not to involve jurors in a group discussion. Real jurors would be expected to discuss the case together, with a view to reaching a unanimous verdict. Whether omission of group deliberation is crucial to the value of the research is debatable. On the one hand, it must be acknowledged that the results obtained from a group of subjects do not necessarily represent the performance of any individual person. For example, if there were forty-three per cent errors in recall across the group, this may mask the fact that some subjects were one hundred per cent accurate, while others

---

[13] M King, *Psychology in or out of Court* (London, Pergamon, 1986); S Lloyd-Bostock, Juries and Jury Research in Context' in G Davies, S Lloyd-Bostock, K MacMurran, and C Wilson, *Psychology Law and Criminal Justice* (Berlin, de Gruyter, 1996); R Hastie, S Penrod, and N Pennington, *Inside the Jury* (Cambridge, Mass., Harvard University Press, 1983).
[14] Eg S McCabe and R Purves, *The Shadow Jury at Work* (Oxford, Blackwell, 1974).

may have remembered nothing at all.[15] And in the case of research into judicial admonitions to disregard evidence, omission of group discussion would seriously distort results. In real cases, the outcome could be affected by a member of the jury mentioning the inadmissible fact to the others. But in routine cases, on the other hand, there is reason to suppose that discussion does not significantly affect the final outcome. Kalven and Zeisel reported that ninety per cent of the jurors in their survey (of real juries) had reached their decisions before deliberation.[16] It should be borne in mind, also, that the vast majority of criminal cases in England and Wales are tried before lay magistrates, who generally sit over a number of years. The group involved in the discussion is a great deal smaller, and they arrive at decisions much faster. It would be simplistic to assume that judges, magistrates and jurors, mock or actual, reason in the same way. Apart from the obvious differences in training and experience, their roles differ significantly during a trial.

It may be that the gravest problem facing simulation studies is that it is impossible to duplicate in the experimental context the weight of responsibility borne by members of a real jury. The New Zealand jury project,[17] which interviewed real jurors at the conclusion of their trials, found them to be exhausted. This was partly a consequence of having to concentrate on oral evidence taken slowly with long pauses, and partly a result of members of the jury having in some cases to catch up with their own work before or after court sittings. Some were working at night when court had risen. Most found the conditions physically uncomfortable. A considerable contributor to tiredness, however, appeared to be the nervous tension generated by the responsibility of having to decide the fate of another human being. In addition, jurors might have to contend with encounters with the defendant or his family outside the courtroom. Many reported difficulties sleeping. Feelings may run high, which is exacerbated by the fact that jurors are not allowed to discuss the case with anyone outside. In one case, the jury needed a police escort out of the building because of the extreme divisions that had arisen during deliberations.[18] In some cases, the evidence was harrowing. The case might bring back traumatic memories from the juror's own past. Cases of alleged child abuse involve considerable stress.

> With very few exceptions, jurors took their role very seriously, were extremely concerned to ensure that they did the right thing, and as a result often found it stressful and worried about it afterwards.[19]

---

[15] P Rabbitt, 'Applying Human Experimental Psychology to Legal Questions about Evidence' in S Lloyd-Bostock, (ed) *Psychology in Legal Contexts* (London, Macmillan, 1981).

[16] *Contra*, eg., VP Hans and AN Doob, 'Section 12 of the Canada Evidence Act and the Deliberations of Simulated Juries' (1976) 18 *Criminal Law Quarterly* 235; DG Morgan and MF Kaplan, 'Group-Induced Polarization in Simulated Juries' (1976) 2 *Personality and Social Psychology Bulletin*, 63 — but these were *not* real juries.

[17] W Young, N Cameron and Y Tinsley, *Juries in Criminal Trials, Part 2*, New Zealand Law Commission Preliminary Paper 37, (Wellington, New Zealand, 1999).

[18] *Ibid.*, 10.7–10.26.

[19] *Ibid.*, 7.11.

Jurors are aware that even though a heavy sentence is not inevitable following every verdict of Guilty, a conviction for a criminal offence is in itself a serious outcome. The responsibility can be heavy in civil cases, too. The award of damages, loss of a child, home, or business, can be catastrophic for the parties on the losing side. This may be the responsibility of a single judge, Bench of magistrates or a jury. Experimenters cannot reproduce the experiences of real tribunals of fact, since ethical concerns restrict the amount of stress an experimenter can generate for the participants. However, Bray and Kerr argue that mock jurors become highly involved and take their role very seriously.[20] Subjects can be led to believe that their decisions have real consequences, although it is not easy to demonstrate that the deception was successful.

The gulf between a simulation and the stresses and confusion of real life might also be thought to cast doubt on the value of research into eyewitness reliability. To what extent do the results of witness studies reflect the reliability of the memory of a shopper who observed a crime being committed in the High Street? Ideally, the results of psychological research would be subjected to external validation to determine whether they generalise beyond the particular conditions of that experiment. The problem is that external validation would require experimenters to check their results against those obtained in the real setting (for example, the courtroom or the scene of the crime). Demanding external validation of simulation results recreates the identical practical problems of cost and design that prompted the researcher to opt for simulation in the first place. Bray and Kerr nevertheless argue that while it is always possible to identify differences between the circumstances pertaining to the simulation and the setting to which it is intended to generalise, there are reasons to take laboratory findings seriously. In the absence of any direct comparison, confidence in the result depends largely on how plausible it is that those differences limit its generality, bearing in mind existing theory and data.[21] If the results do seem plausible in the light of current knowledge, they have value. Bray and Kerr deny that they advocate 'employing a method with no value just because it is all we can afford'.[22] Theory development is essential for moving beyond description to an explanation of behaviour. This will not occur without controlled research methods. Their conclusion is that results obtained in the laboratory are of use if their limitations are borne in mind. They can indicate what direction future court-based research can take and build up a background of psychological theory. 'It is the theory, not specific findings, that is generalised across a variety of settings'.[23] At least it is possible to test whether a given effect is possible.[24] King, while doubting this argument, concedes that simulations provide valuable information in relation to very narrowly defined empirical issues, such as the comprehensibility of jury instructions.[25]

---

[20] RM Bray and NL Kerr, *The Psychology of the Courtroom* (New York, Academic Press, 1987) 289–318.
[21] *Ibid.*, 310; doubted, King, above n.13, p135.
[22] King, above n.13, p316.
[23] CA Lind and TR Tyler, *The Social Psychology of Procedural Justice* (New York, Plenum, 1988) 44.
[24] *Ibid.*
[25] King, above n 13 p35.

The Bray and Kerr argument in support of simulations may seem to be undermined by the work of Konečni and Ebbesen. They conducted a study on the way judges make the decision to grant bail. They used six different data collection methods: interviewing the judges, asking them to complete questionnaires, asking them to complete rating scales, simulation, observation of sentencing hearings, and analysis of court records. The results varied with the different methodologies employed, leading the authors to doubt the validity of research by way of simulation.[26] They suspect that results may be affected by 'reactive measurement effects', in that the judges knew that they were participating in a research project and, when asked questions, answered in a way not indicative of their usual courtroom practice; they may have been anxious to deliver what they perceived to be the required or desirable response. In fact, their practice in court was to stick very closely to the recommendations of probation officers. That may be more a reflection of the pressures of a heavy workload and shortage of court time than of their opinion of the reliability of the probation report. Settling down with a questionnaire or taking part in a simulation might have given them far more opportunity to depart from the probation officer's recommendations and reflect their own views. It is possible, however, as Bray and Kerr suggest, that the same disparities would not occur with lay jurors, for whom the same expectations (in terms of professionalism) do not apply.

Meanwhile, there is a danger that the same laboratory experiments are repeated endlessly changing one variable at a time, for no reason other than that it is logistically possible to do so. Although this would allow the effects of different variables to be accurately identified, the exercise could become sterile and irrelevant if changes are minimal and of little significance to the legal world. Lawyers in any case generally want to know about the effects of a number of simultaneous changes in a number of variables.[27] Some research, although purporting to have significance in the legal context, focuses on situations that have no parallel in the real world. An example is a number of studies asking juries to determine sentence for a convicted criminal. It appears in such experiments that the methodology has determined the subject matter, which means that the results have little practical value. The dilemma is that the more reality a researcher injects into the situation, the less the precision of control and measurement possible. The converse is also true; creating contexts in which the requirements of science are met militates against accurate recreation of the stresses and complexities of the exercise in real life.[28] Sir Robin Auld[29] recommends that English law be altered to enable research into the deliberations of juries, but to date there has been no sign of enthusiasm in the legislature to lift the veil of secrecy surrounding the retiring room. The closest jury research seems to be likely to get to it is the post-trial interview, as in the New Zealand research. Here, there is

[26] Konečni and Ebbesen, above n.11.
[27] Rabbitt, above n.15.
[28] Bray and Kerr, above n.20, 309.
[29] Sir Robin Auld, *Criminal Courts Review*, (London, HMSO, 2001; www.criminal-courts-review.org.uk) paras.5.76–5.87.

an obvious risk of distortion due to misunderstanding by the juror, or to lapses in memory. Using shadow juries allows the monitoring of group discussion, but the weight of responsibility born by the real jury cannot be reproduced. King notes that researchers opting for this method tend to play down that difficulty by demonstrating that shadow juries reach decisions very similar, if not identical, to the real ones; but, as he observes, this does not mean that the real and the shadow juries used the same thought processes to reach that conclusion.[30]

It is relatively easy, then, to dismiss the efforts of scores of serious researchers by highlighting all the differences between experiment and real life. But what are the alternative sources of information employed by the legal system to resolve the inevitable questions about the memory, honesty, and the intellectual abilities of fact-finders? Psychological research may have difficulties in terms of external validation, but its practitioners recognise and strive to address them. Lawyers on a daily basis operate amidst, and inflict on others, a mass of beliefs about juror bias, its extent and effect, without a 'shred of systematic or objective evidence'.[31] In the last few years, there are signs that law reformers and the judiciary are becoming aware that there is psychological data which is so persuasive and widely duplicated that it would be unwise to ignore it.[32]

RESPONSIBILITY

Much of the content of a nation's laws is concerned with the allocation of responsibility. In an individual case, courts may have to decide whether someone was responsible for an outcome. Psychologists have examined the way in which ascriptions of responsibility are made, and shown that the process is not a straightforward intellectual analysis of action. Witnesses and courts operate within a network of social and legal rules. The basis of the judgment depends upon the nature of the rule, and, depending on that, may or may not take account of the social context, the social role of the actor, or his or her intention and motive. This work was pioneered by Heider, who developed a model containing five levels of responsibility attribution.[33] Heider's five levels consist of the following:

1—Global association.
2—Impersonal causation.
3—Forseeability.
4—Personal causation
5—Justifiability.

[30] King, above n.13, 33.
[31] AP Sealy, 'Another Look at Social Psychological Aspects of Juror Bias' (1981) 5 *Law and Human Behavior* 187, 199.
[32] See chapter 8.
[33] F Heider, *The Psychology of Interpersonal Relations* (New York, Wiley, 1958).

Continuing this analysis, Hamilton[34] adapted Heider's model to the legal context, showing that the legal approach mirrors that of the lay view of responsibility.

1 Global Association

Here individuals are held responsible for acts associated with them in any way, as when all citizens are regarded as responsible for the deeds of their nation. 'A good deal of primitive law is founded on revenge, and revenge tends to be indiscriminate.'[35] Thus in the Mosaic Code it was found necessary to state that a man should be put to death only for his own sin and not that of his father or son. Hamilton argues that the current legal analogy is with vicarious responsibility in tort or criminal law. Vicarious liability, fixing the guilt of the employee upon the employer, is not common in legal systems which favour punishment only for those who are morally to blame. The criminal law has not so far found a way of allocating criminal responsibility to corporations that sits comfortably with its retributive principles. Hence criminal vicarious liability is generally imposed only in the case of minor offences. As far as the law of torts is concerned, there are several possible justifications for the imposition of liability upon employers for the actions of employees; they must have been negligent in employing a negligent servant; or, by failing adequately to control the servant, they have contributed to the harm; or, since employers benefit from the work of employees they must bear responsibility for any damage caused in its performance; or, employers have the deeper pockets; or, since most employers tend to be large organisations, it is most effective to distribute the loss amongst all their customers, who pay for it through slightly higher prices reflecting the cost of insurance cover.[36] A strict compensation principle might be seen to be an application of the 'Just World' approach to responsibility described in chapter two.

2 Impersonal Causation

Impersonal causation is interpreted in the law as strict or absolute liability. The actor is held responsible if instrumental in producing the observed effects, even though they could not have been foreseen. He or she is judged by result. In the criminal law, it is possible to be convicted of a criminal offence without being at fault in terms of negligence. These strict liability offences are few and tend to be regulatory in nature. Penalties are generally financial. Vicarious liability may also be seen as an instance of impersonal causation.

---

[34] VL Hamilton, 'Who is Responsible? Towards a Social Psychology of Responsibility Attribution' (1978) 41 *Social Psychology* 316.
[35] WH Rogers, 16th edn *Winfield and Jolowicz on Tort* (London, Sweet and Maxwell, 2002) 593.
[36] *Ibid.*, 622.

3   Forseeability

The actor is held responsible even though the result was not part of his or her goal. In legal terms, the responsibility is in negligence. The point is that the actor should have realised that the outcome was likely to occur. The criminal law is rarely concerned with negligence, although in extreme form it forms the basis of convictions for manslaughter, dangerous driving and driving without due care and attention. More usually, crimes are thought too serious to depend on a finding of negligence. They are classified as moral wrongs. Determinism in legal morality means that courts characteristically are engaged in searching for intention or other subjective states of mind in the actor. In contrast, the law of torts, which deals merely with the liability of one citizen to compensate another, is constantly engaged in attributions of negligence, measured in terms of foreseeability of the outcome. How this is done is discussed in detail below in chapter two.

4   Personal Causation

The effects were intended. This is generally held to be the most morally reprehensible form of responsibility and is the basis of liability for the most serious crimes (see chapter three). Finders of fact must apply a subjective test to the element of fault — it is a question not of what the actor should have done, but of what he or she foresaw.

5   Justifiability

The actor's intentions and motives are part of a chain of events in which he or she was subject to preconditioning by environmental factors. He or she is held responsible only to the extent that the intended behaviour was unjustifiable. There are obvious analogies to this form of attribution in legal defences such as self-defence, duress and the prevention of crime. In chapters two and three the limited defence of provocation and its dependence on reasonableness is discussed in detail.

ATTRIBUTION THEORY

Attribution theory in psychology is concerned with the way people determine the causes of the actions of their fellow human beings. In the terms of a leading writer on the subject, it deals with the answer to the question 'Why?'[37] The issue might be, why did Peter fall from the window? Was it an accident, did he jump or was he pushed?

---

[37] HH Kelley, *Attribution in Social Interaction* (Morristown NJ, General Learning Press, 1971) 1.

The last two possibilities involve a judgment that a human agent should be held responsible for the outcome — Peter himself, or another. Attribution theory was developed by Heider[38] to explain a large quantity of experimental literature, not itself necessarily concerned directly with attributions of responsibility. Rather, it dealt with people's reactions to the behaviour of others. The question may have been whether subjects would help another person in a particular situation, or whether they would like or dislike another person. Heider realised that these reactions inevitably flow from inferences that the subjects had drawn about the actor's behaviour. In particular, at some point the subjects must have decided *why* the other person behaved in that way, what caused that behaviour.[39] Thus, in psychology, causal attribution theory identifies patterns in the way a person assigns causes to events. It measures reliance on influences such as internal and external agency, stable and unstable factors. Attribution theory questions how attributions of cause, responsibility and motive for behaviour are made. Psychology therefore shares much common ground with law, which also seeks to identify shared modes of causal attribution.

Kelley suggested that the observer, like a scientist, examines the covariation between a given effect and various possible causes. Where the observer has information over successive points in time, an effect is attributed to the possible cause with which over time, the effect covaries.[40] A series of coincidences over time will be seen to have causal linkage; if x constantly accompanies y, x will be thought to have caused y, or vice versa. He went on to develop a model of covariance, known as ANOVA, to indicate the way in which perceivers make causal attributions as if they were analysing patterns of data by means of a statistical technique. The observer is examining the event against three factors; consensus (do others react in the same way to the same stimulus?); distinctiveness (does the actor react in the same way to other, different, stimuli?); and consistency (does the actor react to the same stimuli in the same way on other occasions?) Thus, in Brown's example,[41] if the question is — Why is Rita afraid of the dog?' the observer will consider the following information:

Rita is afraid of most dogs (low distinctiveness, internal cause)
Few people are afraid of this dog (low consensus, internal cause)
Most people are afraid of this dog (high consensus, external cause)
Rita is afraid of few dogs (high distinctiveness, external cause)
Rita is not usually afraid of this dog (low consistency; is she very jumpy today?)
But combined with the following —
Rita is not afraid of other dogs today (then it is external, the dog is rabid!)

---

[38] Heider, above n.33.
[39] HH Kelley, 'Attribution Theory in Social Psychology,' in D Levine, (ed) *Nebraska Symposium on Motivation* (University of Nebraska Press, 1967).
[40] Kelley, above n.37.
[41] R Brown *Social Psychology* (New York, Free Press, 1986) 137–40.

The technique may be observed in courts of law as a way of evaluating items of evidence.

The notorious mass murderer Dr Harold Shipman was convicted in 1999 of the deliberate killing of fifteen women patients. Morphine or diamorphine was found in the bodies of the nine who had been buried rather than cremated; no morphine had been prescribed for any of them. All had been apparently in good health, and died suddenly on a day when Dr Shipman had seen them. In several cases, although the doctor had told relatives that the patient had requested a home visit, there was no record of this, nor of the calls for ambulance assistance that the doctor claimed to have made. There was no eyewitness evidence that he had administered the fatal dose of morphine to them. In the absence of any direct evidence that this apparently gentle general practitioner had been murdering his patients, the jury effectively had to apply the covariation principle. Few elderly women die of morphine poisoning (low consensus), but it appeared that quite a number of Dr Shipman's did (high consistency). Few apparently healthy people die suddenly in their living room, but a large number of Dr Shipman's did, and when he visited them. Low consensus and high consistency suggested the cause of the deaths lay with the doctor himself.[42] There was also evidence that his manner to relatives became hostile and malicious following these deaths. Normally he seemed caring and courteous. This high level of distinctiveness in his behaviour indicated a cause internal to Shipman — deliberate killing. The jury conclusion was inevitable. The link between events which so consistently persisted over time indicated homicide. The covariation was sufficiently pronounced to overcome any initial doubt that a doctor would do this without any apparent reason.[43]

The same calculus may explain the emphasis in rape cases on the complainant's previous sexual history and its presumed relevance to consent. If a woman has had numerous previous lovers, low distinctiveness gives the impression of being indiscriminate. The calculus may, however, drive towards the wrong conclusion. For this reason, fact-finders are rarely told about any earlier unsavoury behaviour of a defendant in a criminal trial. However, the jury at the trial of Rosemary West[44] was told that she was often sadistically cruel, even to her own children. This badly undermined her claim that her husband, Frederick, abducted, tortured and murdered young women, including one of their own children, in their house without her knowledge. The law has found it difficult to identify the logical relationship between allegations of earlier misconduct by the defendant and a finding of guilt. This issue is discussed in chapter six.

Attribution theory holds that the attribution of responsibility by individuals is subject to certain biases. Research has found that observers over-estimate the

---

[42] Dame Janet Smith found that at least 200 other patients had been murdered by Shipman. She applied the same reasoning, relying heavily on their good health before they were discovered dead either during or after one of his visits. *The Shipman Inquiry: First Report* www.the-shipman-inquiry.org.uk/reports.asp.

[43] Although Shipman was known as 'Dr Death' locally because of the extraordinary number of his patients who died; *Daily Telegraph* 12 October 1999.

[44] See chapter 6.

importance of internal or dispositional factors. Although people tend to attribute their own action to external situational causes, they attribute, the same actions performed by others to causes internal to the actors.[45] This, the 'fundamental attribution error', has been shown to affect an observer's assessment of another's motive. The most well-known illustration of this is an experiment in which observers of a debate were informed that speakers had been allocated a role, and had been told which cause they should promote. Although they knew this, subjects believed that the arguments employed by individual speakers were more connected with a genuine conviction than a consequence of having no choice.[46] This internalisation may partly explain the frequently articulated hostility to lawyers who represent people they 'must know' to be guilty. Lay people may regard an argument well made as an argument believed. More importantly in the legal context, overemphasis on internal factors means that although the higher the consensus the more we should ascribe causality to impersonal factors, consensus information is often ignored by perceivers. Human beings' psychological need to control the immediate environment may explain the bias towards internal causes.[47]

The under-utilisation of consensus information is one example of why lawyers should be aware of attribution theory. In criminal cases, a defendant may raise the issue of insanity. Here the jury must decide whether the defendant's actions sprang from internal disposition, or from the external cause of disease. History shows that fact-finders are not easily persuaded that the external cause is the operating one.[48] The effect of the fundamental attribution error may, however, be mitigated, according to the correspondent inference theory.[49] This proposes that fact-finders seeking an explanation of another's behaviour rely heavily on his or her power to behave otherwise. In this respect, they will analyse any restriction of choice imposed by environmental factors. The more the observer knows about the surrounding circumstances, the less likely he or she is to make a correspondent inference, that is, to ascribe the behaviour to the disposition of the actor. In a well-known example, experimental subjects were required to take part in an activity with two other persons, who had been in reality 'planted' by the experimenter. One of these was more obviously in a superior social position or University post to the other. Subjects would find themselves needing to ask for help from these 'plants'. Afterwards, they were asked why these other people assisted. They attributed an internal cause (disposition) to the higher status helper, as there appeared

---

[45] ML Snyder and EE Jones, 'Attitude Attribution when Behaviour is Constrained' (1974) 10 *Journal of Experimental Psychology* 585.

[46] EE Jones, KE Davis and KJ Gergen, 'Role-Playing Variations and their Informational Value for Person Perception' (1961) 63 *Journal of Abnormal and Social Psychology* 302.

[47] See below, defensive attribution.

[48] R Smith, 'Expertise and Causal Attribution in Deciding between Crime and Mental Disorder' (1985) 15 *Social Studies of Science* 67.

[49] EE Jones and KE Davis, 'From Acts to Dispositions: the Attribution Process in Person Perception' in L Berkowitz, (ed) *Advances in Experimental Social Psychology Vol 2* (New York, Academic Press, 1965).

to be no external pressure to assist. The lower status helper was thought more likely to be doing it out of obligation or pressure.[50]

The correspondent inference theory[51] holds that attributions of responsibility take account of environmental factors[52] that limit the actor's freedom of choice. Internal attributions are made if there are few noncommon effects, that is, those produced by the action that could not be produced by alternative courses of action.[53] Weiner and Small suggest that jurors base their judgments of negligence on the ease with which they are able to imagine alternative outcomes, independent of the probability and seriousness of the risk of injury. If jurors could easily imagine a large number of alternative actions on the defendant's part that would avoid injury to anyone, they will find the defendant negligent. The authors suspect that lawyers would do the same.[54] In a much-publicised trial in 2000, Tony Martin, a Norfolk farmer of reclusive habits, was accused of murder.[55] He shot and killed a young burglar who broke into his house, with another, in the night. Martin claimed that he fired his shotgun in fear of his life. Although he lived in the countryside, there had been a large number of break-ins locally. He himself had suffered ten thefts and burglaries over the previous ten years. Therefore there was evidence of considerable consensus; householders locally had reason to fear intrusion. Yet the jury rejected Martin's argument that he was defending himself and his property. Part of the evidence against him suggested that the victim had been leaving the premises when he was shot. The defence had failed to persuade the jury that external causes such as the behaviour of the particular burglar on the occasion in question, and the ineffectiveness of police in the area were responsible for the shooting. The bias towards internal attribution was probably aggravated by the range of non-fatal options available to the defendant in order to protect himself.[56]

If observers do not have enough information to make inferences based on the covariation model, they will rely on causal schema or general beliefs about cause and effect developed from a lifetime of observations of people in various situations, a collected pattern of experience which has produced an interpretational framework.[57] Script theory[58] may offer a more likely account of the reasoning

---

[50] JW Thibaut and HW Riecken, 'Some Determinants and Consequences of the Perception of Social Causality' (1955) 24 *Journal of Personality and Social Psychology* 113.

[51] Jones and Davis, n.49.

[52] As well as factors such as motive and the observer's own role.

[53] F Heider, above n.33.

[54] RL Wiener and MA Small, 'Social Cognition and Tort Law' in DK Kagehiro and WS Laufer *Handbook of Law and Psychology* (New York, Verlag-Springer,1991) 443.

[55] *Daily Telegraph* 14 April 2000.

[56] On appeal, a plea of diminished responsibility was accepted and a verdict of manslaughter substituted: *Martin* [2002] Crim LR 136.

[57] HH Kelley 'Causal Schemata and the Attribution Process' in EE James, DE Kanouse, HH Kelley, RE Nisbett, S Valins and B Weiner, (eds) *Attribution: Perceiving the Causes of Behaviour* (Morristown, NJ, General Learning Press, 1971).

[58] RP Abelson, 'The Structure of Belief Systems' in K Colby and R Schank, (eds) *Computer Simulations of Thought and Language* (San Francisco, California, Freeman, 1973).

processes than the systematic and logical mechanisms suggested by attribution theory. A script is a kind of story grammar that defines the type of characters that are necessary for the plot to proceed and the relationships between the characters and the accompanying circumstances.[59] Nisbett and Borgida[60] argue that observers attempt to construct or imagine a scenario or causal script into which the event can easily fit. Selection of a script causes material to which it is salient or is of high associative value to be used extensively, whereas more logically significant material may be largely neglected. Script processing is a conceptual approach, which depends on the proposition that a variety of behaviours may be carried out or understood by virtue of a common sequence. Meaning is derived from the context or social situation in which the event occurs. For example, Jane gives money to a stranger — why? What action would follow? If she is in a grocery shop, the observer assumes a purchase and would expect exchange of goods. If Jane is in church, no exchange of goods would be expected. This aspect of attribution theory anticipates the narrative models of jury decision-making discussed in chapter three.

If behaviour is inconsistent with prior expectation, it will be attributed to external causes.[61] The expectation will be based on the observer's own experience. Prior information may activate a cognitive scheme. For instance, mock jurors reading transcripts of evidence in a rape case were asked to adjudicate. Subjects who were acquainted with victims of rape judged the defendant to be highly culpable, and tended to dismiss subsequent testimony for the defence. Subjects not acquainted with a rape victim at first formed strong attributions of attacker responsibility, but adjusted their ratings of liability downward once they read defence evidence.[62] One hypothesis is that the former group activated rape scripts when the case began, and found only support for them in the defence evidence. The others found the defence evidence disconfirmed the rape scripts and therefore they selected other schemata to explain the events depicted in the transcript. Cross-examination gives lawyers every opportunity to suggest a script different from the one originally offered by a witness. Drew has shown that however hard a witness tries to persist with his or her script during cross-examination, questioners can allow their own script to become apparent. The technique comprises a refusal to acknowledge the witnesses' responses, and continuing with questions suggesting, by implication, the rival version of events.[63]

[59] Wiener and Small, n. 54.

[60] RE Nisbett, E Borgida, 'Attribution and the Psychology of Prediction' (1975) 32 *Journal of Personality and Social Psychology* 932.

[61] JA Kulik, 'Confirmatory Attribution and the Perpetuation of Social Beliefs' (1983) 44 *Journal of Personality and Social Psychology* 1171.

[62] RL Wiener, AF Weiner and T Grisso, 'Empathy and Biased Assimilation of Testimonies in Cases of Alleged Rape' (1989) 13 *Law and Human Behavior* 343.

[63] P Drew, 'Strategies in the Contest between Lawyer and Witness in Cross-Examination' in JM Levi and AG Walker, (eds) *Language in the Judicial Process, Vol 5 in Law, Society and Policy*, (London, Plenum, 1990).

COMMON SENSE

In case after case, we find judicial appeals to common sense. It is the underlying principle of causation.[64] Juries and magistrates are constantly described as the embodiment of common sense. In that capacity they may resolve conflicts in scientific evidence, or even disregard it entirely.[65] What is common sense? To a psychologist, lawyers are simply ascribing some kind of rationality to the operation of heuristics. Heuristics are reasoning mechanisms commonly employed by people who find themselves required to interpret the behaviour of others.[66] They are employed because they are, generally, useful.[67] They serve valuable social functions. They prevent a paralysis of decision-making, which could happen if every possible contingency is agonised over. They drastically cut down on the costs, in terms of time and effort, of mental searching. They can be constantly revised with repeated experiences but without expensive conscious effort. They allow people to make relatively quick judgments where information is limited. Whether we are attempting to negotiate the physical world, or to form and preserve relationships with others, we need to interpret and predict events and behaviour. However, heuristics encourage people to develop stereotypes. They may lead to the exclusion of other, relevant, information from consideration, if it is less psychologically meaningful and less arresting. The effect of heuristics on decision-making in court may clearly be seen in illustrations throughout this book.

The operation of heuristics in law is most apparent in the kind of case where the tribunal of fact is required to assess how likely an outcome was to occur. The court is likely to succumb to the 'availability heuristic'. This is a method of estimating probability. The frequency and therefore the probability of events is measured by the ease with which instances or associations come to mind.[68] An event is therefore regarded as more likely or frequent if it is easy to imagine or recall instances of it. In general, it is easier to recall instances of frequent, rather than infrequent events, and so normally this heuristic works quite well. Here the common sense notion of coincidences, likely and unlikely, comes into play. In one case of obstruction of the highway, the plaintiff's daughter was killed by a passing car while she was walking in the road around the obstacle. He recovered damages.[69] But in a similar case, where the pedestrian was forced to detour close to a landing ground, he was struck by an aeroplane trying to land. No damages were awarded;

---

[64] See chapter two.

[65] See chapter seven.

[66] A Tversky and D Kahnman, 'Judgment under Uncertainty; Heuristics and Biases' (1974) 185 *Science* 1124.

[67] HJ Einhorn and RM Hogarth, 'Behavioral Decision Theory: Processes of Judgment and Choice' (1981) 32 *Annual Review of Psychology* 53.

[68] A Tversky and D Kahnman, 'Availability: a Heuristic for Judging Frequency and Probability' (1973) 5 *Cognitive Psychology* 207; D Kahneman, P Slovic and A Tversky, *Judgment under Uncertainty* (Cambridge, Cambridge University Press, 1982). The availability heuristic may explain the hindsight effect; Nisbett and Borgida, above n. 60.

[69] *O'Neill v City of Port Jervis* (1930) 253 NY 423.

the outcome was considered too improbable, and was dismissed as coincidence.[70] Problems arise when media coverage influences this process of recall and produces utterly inaccurate predictions. For example, subjects asked to make frequency judgments of causes of death, for example, by cancer, flood, fire, or motor vehicles, were badly wrong, but very confident they were right.[71] Recent events or horrific events may cause exaggeratedly vivid memory, and therefore are perceived as being more frequent. The sense of danger may have nothing to do with the actuarial risk of the harm. Thus the figures on deaths travelling by air, land or sea, do not explain fear of air travel, nor do the number of nuclear accidents explain the hostility of the public to nuclear power stations. While experts take no account of the effect of dread', in the assessment of risk, it is a factor regularly employed by non-experts.[72]

The 'representativeness heuristic', according to Tversky and Kahnman, is the basis of argument by analogy.[73] The estimation of how probable it is that an object or event belongs to a certain category is based on how prototypical the event is of that category, regardless of how common it is in fact.[74] With this cognitive shorthand, people assess cause and effect; they estimate the likelihood that event x caused effect y by recalling how often x causes y. But they ignore the base rate (how often x does *not* cause y). The 'representativeness heuristic' thus accounts for the inability of most people to assess probability accurately. If a physician is told that a treatment is seventy per cent successful, he is likely nevertheless to abandon it if it failed his patients the last three or four times he used it.[75] Thus applicants to a law school might be admitted on the basis of their similarity to others who were successful in the past, even though the similarity may not be influential. Saks and Kidd[76] argue that in the United States at any rate, courts are ignoring base-rate information in a growing number of scientific and technological cases, such as antitrust, product liability, and pollution. They claim that the problem is worst in the decisions of regulatory bodies, where, typically, although base-rate information is provided, it carries less weight than case-specific information. Over-prediction of dangerousness in offenders, despite the very low base rate of violent behaviour either in the population at large or in a particular individual, is another example of the effect of the representativeness heuristic.

---

[70] *Doss v Town of Big Stone Gap* (1926) 134 SE.

[71] S Lichtenstein, P Slovic, B Fischhoff, M Layman and B Combs, 'Judged Frequency of Lethal Events' (1978) 4 *Journal of Experimental Psychology, Human Learning and Memory* 551.

[72] C Perrow, *Normal Accidents* (New York, Basic Books, 1994); On the disaster potential of 'tightly coupled' activities affecting perceived risk, see P Slovic, B Fischhoff and S Lichtenstein, 'Characterising personal risk' in RW Kates, C Hohenemser and JX Kasperson, (eds) *Perilous Progress: Managing Hazards of Technology* (Boulder, Westview, 1985).

[73] D Kahnman and A Tversky, 'Subjective Probability: a Judgment of Representativeness' (1972) 3 *Cognitive Psychology* 430; Tversky and Kahnman, n. 68.

[74] *Ibid.*

[75] LR Goldberg, 'Man versus Models of Man; a Rationale plus some Evidence for a Method of Improving Clinical Inference' (1970) 73 *Psychological Bulletin* 422.

[76] MJ Saks and RF Kidd, 'Human Information Processing and Adjudication: Trial by Heuristics' (1980–1981) 15 *Law and Society Review* 123.

Expert witnesses commonly are forced in the courtroom to extrapolate from the general to the particular, with insufficient case-specific information to do this accurately. Lawyers are heavily influenced by the fallacious belief that a small sample of the population represents characteristics of the whole population. In *Phelps v Hillingdon LBC*[77] an educational psychologist employed by the defendant local authority failed to diagnose dyslexia in a twelve year old who was achieving little at school. Garland J noted that dyslexia was at the time a well-recognised condition and therefore held the defendant to have been negligent. But he may have ignored the base-rate and therefore under-estimated the difficulty of diagnosis amongst a large population of children who are unsuccessful at school.

The representativeness heuristic can be seen at work also in cases concerning 'similar facts' evidence. Evidence of the defendant's misconduct on other occasions is admissible if it is more probative than it is prejudicial.[78] But how probative it is often depends on whether the similar circumstances can be attributed to coincidence or bad luck. For example, in 1999, Sally Clark, a solicitor, was convicted of murdering her two children. Her son, C, was aged eleven weeks when he died, and H was eight weeks old. There was statistical evidence, hotly disputed by the defence, that the probability of two 'cot deaths' in one family with this profile was one in seventy-three million. The other evidence in the case was not particularly probative; there were some coincidences of fact between the two deaths, and Clark's personality became an issue. The statistical evidence was dismissed as unreliable on appeal, although the Court of Appeal thought the rest of the case sufficiently strong to uphold her conviction.[79] Irrespective of the misleading probability given at trial, it was considered a rare thing to have two natural deaths in the same family with those features present. She seems to have been convicted by the representativeness heuristic. In reality, little is known of the number of cases where two 'cot deaths' do occur within the same family. For it is often difficult to be sure, in any given case, whether the death of an infant is natural or not. The effect of this kind of thinking was even stronger in the case of Angela Cannings, convicted of murdering seven-week-old J in 1991 and eighteen week old M in 1999. There was no clear proof of suffocation. She had also lost a child aged twelve weeks in 1989.[80] Here heuristics filled the gap left by forensic science. It seems that like jurors, paediatricians rely on the maxim 'Two is suspicious; three is murder'.[81]

Heuristical assumptions may become enshrined in the law. Courts can take judicial notice of an obvious fact.[82] Jurors may also take note without proof of

[77] (1997) *The Times* 10 October.

[78] See chapter six.

[79] *Clarke* Court of Appeal (CD) 2 October 2000 www.lexis-nexis.com/professional. In 2003 her conviction was overturned in the light of the non-disclosure by prosecution experts of material evidence, *R v Clark*, 11 April 2003, www.inference.phy.com.ac.uk/sallyclark/judgment03.html.

[80] *Daily Mail*, 17 April 2002.

[81] B Mahendra, 'Science in the Miscarriage of Justice' [2001] *New Law Journal* 1686.

[82] This means that there is no need to call a witness to establish facts such as the location of the Rocky Mountains or the date of Christmas Day. *Brandao v Barnett* (1846) 12 Ch & F 787; *Taylor v Barclay* (1828) 2 Sim & Sim 213.

well-known facts.[83] But heuristics may become part of judicial notice, then becoming part of the law, so becoming very difficult to refute. For example, judicial notice has been taken of such generalisations as electrical storms being hazardous to livestock, and camels being domesticated beasts. In *Mullen v Hackney London Borough Council*,[84] the defendant was accused of being in breach of an undertaking to the court to repair a council house. The judge observed that this was one of 'numerous failures' by the Council to take promises made to the court seriously, and, in consequence, he fined it £5,000. There was no evidence before him of other failures to honour undertakings to the court, but the Court of Appeal held that he was entitled to take judicial notice of how the council had conducted itself in regard to undertaking to the court in similar cases he had heard. Thus one judge's memory of his own experience of a particular defendant was crystallised into incontrovertible fact. Similarly, MacCrimmon argues, judges have now heard so much expert evidence in cases of domestic violence against women, that a new stereotype of the battered woman, which operates irrespective of the evidence in the particular case, has been created. The battered woman is perceived as victimised, helpless and dependent. This could mean that a woman who fails to fit this mental picture will be penalised.[85]

As representatives of the community, it appears to be legitimate for jurors to employ general knowledge. Accordingly, they can take account, in driving cases, of what usually occurs on a highway.[86] Otherwise, triers of fact are not supposed to act on their own personal knowledge, other than local knowledge.[87] But there seems to be little hope of enforcing this rule in the jury room. The New Zealand research found jurors adopting each other's expertise on such matters as the signs of schizophrenia, the street value of cannabis, financial procedures in the construction industry, and the legal procedures for buying and selling property. Some even knew the defendant locally.[88] MacCrimmon gives examples of reasoning based on racial stereotypes.[89] Jurors have ample opportunity to apply their own heuristical structures when assessing probabilities. They also make value judgments as to which is the best out of various possible outcomes. They must decide whether the scale of the defendant's retaliation to provocation was reasonable.[90] They must decide whether material is obscene, applying the standards of 'ordinary, decent, right-minded people'.[91] In the United States it has been decided that they should base this decision on local standards of tolerance. Yet individual

---

[83] *Hoare v Silverlock* (1848) 12 QB 624.

[84] [1997] 2 All ER 906.

[85] MT MacCrimmon, 'Fact Determination: Common Sense Knowledge, Judicial Notice and Social Science Evidence' in S Doran and J Jackson, (ed) *The Judicial Role in Criminal Proceedings* (Oxford, Hart Publishing, 2000) 31.

[86] A different category from judicial notice; *Burns v Lipman* (1975) 132 CLR 157.

[87] *Reynolds v Llanelli Tinplate Co* [1948] 1 All ER 140.

[88] Young et al above n.17.

[89] MacCrimmon above, n. 85.

[90] See chapter two.

[91] *Elliott* [1996] 1 Cr App R 432.

jurors may have little knowledge of these and employ instead their own moral standards, raising the issue of how representative the jury is in demographic terms. Jurors have been found to believe their own personal standards to be the community standard, whether they are tolerant or intolerant.[92] Research shows that the best predictor of attitudes to allegedly obscene material is age rather than social background; not only are young people more tolerant than older ones, but they also presume the community to be tolerant.

We all have to make judgments as to whether or not people are likely to behave in particular ways. These assessments are based on a mixture of folklore assumptions derived from media and everyday stories, and our own professional and personal experiences. Seldom are they subject to the kind of scrutiny and criticism attracted by decisions reached in courts of law, At the hearing of the libel case brought by former MP and best-selling author Jeffrey Archer against the Daily Star newspaper in 1987, the central issue was his payment of £2,000 to a prostitute. He admitted paying her the money but denied any sexual relations with her. The trial judge, Caulfield J, famously drew the attention of the jury to the testimony of Archer's attractive wife, Mary. He asked whether she was not 'fragrant, elegant and radiant?' He observed that a man with such a wife surely had no need of the services of a prostitute. The jury clearly agreed and awarded substantial damages against the newspaper. However, the verdict has since been proved to be mistaken; in 2001 Lord Archer[93] was convicted of perjury in relation to his testimony at the libel hearing.

In family cases, judges and magistrates may have to decide what is in the best interests of a particular child — how to allocate happiness. It has been said that welfare decision-making in family cases forces judges into 'predictive, person-specific, relational determinations that their legal training ill equips them to provide',[94] leaving a vacuum in which heuristical idealised images of family life may affect judgment.[95] Frequently, the court is presented with disconcertingly contradictory evidence from and about the parents and their relationship with the child. The increasing emphasis on grandparents' rights, involving an extended vision of the family, makes the task even more difficult. There is evidence that judges regard contact with grandparents as a positive thing;

> a grandmother is not a frail old lady cut off from the world making lace ... Grandparents ordinarily play a very different role in the child's life; they are not authority figures and do not possessively assert exclusive rights to make parental decisions. At best, they are generous sources of unconditional love and acceptance ...[96]

---

[92] JE Scott, DJ Ellis and SE Skovron, 'Is it Possible for a Jury to apply Contemporary Community Standards in Determining Obscenity?' (1990) 14 *Law and Human Behavior* 139.
[93] As he had become.
[94] RA Thompson, MJ Scalora, L Castrianno and SP Limber, 'Grandparent Visitation Rights' in DK Kagehiro and WS Laufer, *Handbook of Psychology and Law* above n.54.
[95] HL Collier, 'The Analysis of Family Dynamics in Child Custody Cases' in G Davies, S Lloyd-Bostock, K MacMurran, and C Wilson, (eds) *Psychology Law and Criminal Justice* (Berlin, de Gruyter, 1996).
[96] *Mimkon v Wood* 66 NJ 426, 332 A 2d 199 (1975).

Research based on one hundred custody cases, in which judges were required to identify the best interests of a child, showed two considerations to be of paramount importance: the extent of discord between parents and grandparents, and whether the child's relationship with the grandparents was 'very close'. None mentioned the child's wishes, preferring broad generalisations of unproven validity, which may not have applied to the particular family. Contact with grandparents was perceived as a positive thing. Anyone seeking to prevent it must produce significant evidence to the contrary.[97]

The image of the close and loving family is so strong that a father who wishes to disinherit his children would normally be advised to leave them a tiny amount so that it is clear that the failure to leave provision is not an oversight. The legal presumption is that a father would wish to provide for his children.[98] Judges have said that to have a child is always a blessing, so parents cannot be compensated even where a birth follows an incompetently performed sterilisation procedure. The judicial view is that it would be damaging for a child to learn that a court has publicly declared his or her life or birth to be a mistake, being unwanted.[99] And the 'traveller on the London Underground' apparently would consider that

> the law ... had no business to provide legal remedies upon the birth of a healthy child, which all of us regard as a valuable and good thing.[100]

Perhaps it is significant these views emanate from male judges. In a recent case,[101] the Court of Appeal departed from this principle to award substantial damages to a visually handicapped mother whose child had been born notwithstanding a sterilisation procedure carried out by the defendant. The Court acknowledged the difficulty the claimant would have in coping with a young child. The leading judgment was given by Lady Justice Hale, a mother herself, the sole dissenting opinion being given by a male judge.

The judicial picture of relationships between siblings is less clearly defined. In *R v M*[102], several adults were tried for offences connected with the serious and systematic sexual abuse of children. M, a boy of fifteen, was accused of involvement, including a vicious rape against his young sister. Evidence that he had been 'educated and encouraged' by his father to watch and commit acts of sexual abuse was admitted, despite its prejudicial nature. For otherwise, her testimony, which

---

[97] RH Mnookin, 'Child Custody Adjudication: Judicial Functions in the Face of Indeterminacy' (1975) 39 *Law and Contemporary Problems*, 226.

[98] *Commissioner of Stamp Duties v Byrnes* [1911] AC 386. Mothers traditionally were thought not to have the means to do so.

[99] Jupp J in *Udale v Bloomsbury Area Health Authority* [1983] 2 All ER 522, cf Dr Stuttaford: 'The assumption by children that they were wanted at birth and childhood is essential to the sense of belonging, an important element in the formation of identity on which self-esteem depends.' *The Times* 15 February 2002.

[100] *MacFarlane v Tayside Health Board* [1994] 3 WLR 130, per Lord Steyn at 977.

[101] *Rees v Darlington Memorial Hospital NHS Trust* [2002] 2 All ER 177

[102] [1999] Crim LR 922.

described violence, verbal abuse and misogyny would have been 'barely credible in the behaviour of a brother'. But judges will not always presume affection between siblings. In proceedings which followed on from the disaster[103] at the Hillsborough Football Stadium in Sheffield in April 1989, relatives of some of the victims sought damages for psychiatric damage they had suffered. The House of Lords held that, in order to succeed, 'bystanders' must show that there was physical and temporal proximity to the event, but also a 'close relationship of affection between the plaintiff and the primary victim'.[104] Close ties of affection could be presumed in some relationships, such as between parent and child, spouses, and possibly fiancé(é)s.[105] There was, however, no automatic presumption as between siblings, so a sibling plaintiff would have to bring specific evidence of a close relationship with the deceased victim. 'The quality of brotherly love is well known to differ widely — from Cain and Able to David and Jonathan'.[106] What might this specific evidence be? A close relationship apparently is not established by the fact that psychological damage has been caused by the death, nor that two brothers were together at the same football match. The Law Commission has suggested the introduction of a fixed list of relationships where such ties can be irrebuttably presumed — namely between parents and children, spouses and co-habitees of different or similar gender. Siblings would be included.[107] Other claimants would have to produce specific evidence.

The law has shown disapproval of the use of stereotypes in police work:

'Reasonable suspicion can never be supported on the basis of personal factors alone ... nor may it be founded on the basis of stereotyped images of certain persons or groups as more likely to be committing offences'.[108] The law of evidence prevents the use of stereotypes to some extent, for example, in excluding evidence of the defendant's bad character and criminal record,[109] even though criminal record is a good predictor of future criminal behaviour and is of high diagnostic value. The levels of probability are not high enough to justify findings of guilt.[110] Judges do, however, make use of heuristics, or, in their own estimation, the fruit of their experience. In *Shonubi*,[111] the defendant was arrested at John F Kennedy airport. He had swallowed a hundred and three balloons. The prosecution offered chemical analyses of the contents of only four of them. Nevertheless, the Judge declared that all the balloons contained heroin, observing, 'No one carries sugar in balloons from Nigeria to New York'.[112] Also, 'common sense' suggested that a

---

[103] 95 people crushed to death and over 400 injured in a crush at a football match; supervising police allowed an excessively large number of people to enter pens from which there was no escape.
[104] *Alcock v Chief Constable of South Yorkshire* [1992] 1 AC 310.
[105] *Ibid.*
[106] *Ibid.*, per Lord Ackner at 406. But see Law Commission 'Liability for Psychiatric Illness, *Report*, Law Com No 249 (1998).
[107] A list suggested by the Commission's consultees.
[108] Police and Criminal Evidence Act 1984, *Codes of Practice*, A1.7A.
[109] See chapter six.
[110] S Lloyd-Bostock, 'Attributing Causes and Responsibility' (1979)143 *Modern Law Review* 152.
[111] 1993, *US v Shonubi* (Court of Appeals): 998 F.2d; 1993 US App.; Referred for sentence: 895 F. Supp 460; 1995 US Dist.
[112] Transcript, 10.

smuggler would carry at least the minimum quantity required to make him a profit, and so expert evidence was heard from an FBI witness on the economics of heroin smuggling. This was amplified by information derived from years of experience on the Bench. It concerned drug dealers in general, and, more specifically, dealers from Nigeria, their relationship with their 'mules', and their methods of recruitment and training. Undeterred by his extensive reading of psychological literature, particularly that on heuristics, Judge Weinstein commented that 'Every sentencing judge receives daily education in criminology'.[113] From this heuristical apparatus some key facts were held to be proved on the balance of probability. The first was that the inflexibility of most criminals causes them to repeat the same crime committed in the same way. Hence Shonubi, who was carrying heroin on his eighth return from Nigeria to New York, would have been carrying it on his earlier journeys. In addition, it was held that he had been smuggling large quantities from the outset. The opinion of local judges (contained in replies to a questionnaire distributed for this purpose) was that 'mules' are pressured by their associates into swallowing as much heroin as possible early in their careers. The sentence, therefore, could legitimately be fixed on the basis that the defendant had smuggled substantial amounts of heroin on the earlier journeys, about which there was no direct evidence whatever.

[113] Transcript, 21.

2

Responsibility

T HE OPERATION OF the legal system demands on a daily basis the making of judgments on questions of responsibility. Civil and criminal cases frequently involve attributions of responsibility for harm done. It is acknowledged that arriving at attributions of responsibility requires a decision-maker to reason across a series of given steps, as will be seen below. The conclusion that someone is legally responsible for a harm is therefore generally governed by the answers to a series of several questions, the content of which is a matter of law. Law determines which are relevant inferences and which are not. The finder of fact must produce the required assessments of fact from as neutral a position as possible, basing the decision solely on the evidence adduced. Estimation of probabilities may be involved, however, in the final determination of fault, and the calculation required in that case could only with difficulty be described as a value-free factual exercise. Thus the decision-making process may involve assumptions, prejudices and bias. There may be preconceptions common to all human beings who have to evaluate the behaviour of others.

FINDINGS OF NEGLIGENCE — HEIDER'S THIRD LEVEL

Although there are criminal offences where ordinary negligence is a sufficient degree of fault, for instance, dangerous driving, they are unusual. Since we know little of the basis of jury verdicts, the best illustrations of how fact-finders make assessments of likelihood or probability are found in civil cases on negligence in the law of tort. Here the fact-finder, the trial judge, articulates his or her reasoning in the course of giving judgment. The tort of negligence requires that the defendant should owe the claimant a duty of care. That duty should have been breached in a manner that caused the claimant injury. The existence of a duty of care, in broad terms, depends upon a finding that, in the circumstances, the harm was reasonably foreseeable as a consequence of the defendant's act or omission to act. Once the duty to take care is established, it must be decided whether the defendant's acts or omissions were negligent. This question similarly is answered by evaluating the forseeability of the harm. The language of forseeability has dominated the duty of care issue for many years since the famous judgment of Lord Atkin in *Donoghue v Stevenson*:[1]

> The rule that you are to love your neighbour becomes, in law, that you must not injure your neighbour; the lawyer's question, 'Who is my neighbour?' receives a restricted reply. You must take reasonable care to avoid acts or omissions which you can reasonably foresee would be likely to injure your neighbour. Who then, in law, is my neighbour? The answer seems to be — persons who are so closely and directly affected by my act that I ought reasonably to have them in contemplation as being so affected when I am directing my mind to the acts or omissions which are called in question.

This test proves Hamilton's point[2] that responsibility is inevitably a social judgment to some extent. In fact, an actor will be held more or less responsible according to the nature of the role he or she occupies at the time of the event. The inputs to the decision, according to Hamilton, are the rule itself, the actor's deeds and the expectations of others as to what the actor should do. These are defined by social roles. In fact, the *Donoghue v Stevenson* test in practice was found to push back the boundaries of liability too far, creating the spectre of a flood of potential litigants. To stem the flow, judges sought to justify reduction or denial of the duty to take care, and a counter-reaction was begun. The position now is that even when the harm was foreseeable there may be no duty of care, either on grounds of 'policy' or because of a lack of 'proximity' between the parties.[3] Nevertheless, forseeability must be established in every case. In non-lawyer language, this asks the question, how probable was the harm? that is, would the ordinary person have thought it was likely to occur? [4] Judges or juries are expected to provide an answer to this question of probability. In the absence of expert evidence, which will be available in some cases involving technical issues, such a judgment could amount to a wild stab in the dark. The basic question, 'Was this outcome forseeable to an ordinary person?' led to the birth of that renowned legal paragon, the 'Reasonable Man.'

The Reasonable Man

The question of forseeability, which governs both the imposition of a duty of care and whether there was a negligent breach of duty, depends very heavily upon the concept of the reasonable man and the standard of behaviour he employs himself

---

[1] [1932] AC 562, 580.

[2] VL Hamilton, 'Who is Responsible? Towards a Social Psychology of Responsibility Attribution' (1978) 41 *Social Psychology* 316.

[3] *Leigh & Sillavan Ltd v Aliakmon Shipping Co* [1988] AC 175: see also *Alcock v Chief Constable of the South Yorkshire Police* [1991] 4 All ER 907—a wide class of potential litigants whose loved ones suffered death or injury at the Hillsborough football ground in 1989 was dramatically cut down by the 'proximity' test.

[4] *Blyth v Birmingham Waterworks Co* (1856) 11 Ex 781.

and expects from others.[5] He is frequently described as 'ordinary' — 'the man on the Clapham omnibus.' More recently, he has been updated to become the gender-neutral 'traveller on the London Underground.'[6] In the United States, he has been described as 'the man who takes the magazines at home, and in the evening pushes the lawn-mower in his shirt sleeves.' Whether or not the American version incorporates not only gender, but also class hierarchies,[7] he does appear to have rather more economic substance than the English embodiment of normality. The diet of the Reasonable Man, however, is difficult to identify. When it was argued that a reasonable man does not eat raw kipper, Donovan J replied that when it came to an article of food, it was 'impossible to conceive of a reasonable person.'[8] In temperament, however, it is well–known that he is 'free both from over-apprehension and from over-confidence.'[9] Within the complicated rules which govern compensation for psychiatric injury, we find all kinds of judicial conceptions of 'customary phlegm'[10] or 'a normal standard of susceptibility.'[11] Exposed to unpleasantness at the scenes of accidents, apparently the 'ordinary frequenter of the streets has sufficient fortitude to endure such incidents as occur from time to time in them.'[12] On the other hand, 'suppose, for example, that a scholar's life's work of research or composition were destroyed before his eyes as a result of a defendant's careless conduct'; he might well sustain psychiatric illness as a result.[13]

The reaction of Reasonable Men to traumatic events is therefore difficult to predict. They are likely to offer assistance after accidents, but should not expect damages for psychiatric injury unless in physical danger themselves. In general,

> the law must take us to be sufficiently robust to help at accidents that are a daily occurrence without suffering a psychological breakdown.[14]

Even when the accident amounts to a 'disaster', psychological trauma would not be a foreseeable outcome in every case. Thus in *McFarlane v EE Caledonia Ltd*[15] a suit brought in the aftermath of the Piper Alpha disaster, where an oil rig in the North Sea caught fire, the plaintiff failed to recover compensation for his post-traumatic stress disorder. He had been in a vessel that went to help, but had not seen the explosion. He fetched blankets for the injured taken on board. It was held that it was not foreseeable that his 'very limited activities' as a rescuer would cause

---

[5] *Ibid.*

[6] *MacFarlane v Tayside Health* Board [1994] 4 All ER 961, 977.

[7] NS Ehrenreich, 'Pluralist Myths and Powerless Men: the Ideology of Reasonableness in Sexual Harrassment law' (1990) 99 *Yale Law Journal* 1177.

[8] *Newberry v Cohen's (Smoked Salmon) Ltd* 1956 *The Times* 27 April.

[9] *Glasgow Corporation v Muir* [1943] AC 448, 457.

[10] *Bourhill v Young* [1943] AC 92, per Lord Porter at 117.

[11] *Ibid.*, per Lord Wright at 110.

[12] *Ibid.*, per Lord Porter at 117.

[13] *Attia v British Gas plc* [1988] QB 304, per Bingham LJ at 320.

[14] *White v Chief Constable of South Yorkshire Police* [1999] 1 All ER 1, 6.

[15] [1994] 2 All ER 1.

this injury. Yet damages were awarded to some of the police officers who assisted at the Hillsborough disaster and suffered psychiatric illness as a result. At first instance, Waller J thought professional rescuers to be persons of 'of extraordinary phlegm'[16] and therefore their illnesses were not foreseeable. Indeed, it was possible, he thought, that a sense of 'professional shame' at being so affected might have exacerbated the officers' stress. But the House of Lords did not consider that the training and experience of police officers would protect them from psychological injury sustained as a result of their very direct involvement in the disaster, given the 'nature and scale of the catastrophe.'[17]

The Reasonable Woman would be upset and intimidated by sexual harassment at work,[18] suggesting that she is both passive and delicate. However, a woman who behaves like a man at work, swearing and making dirty jokes, falls outside the feminine stereotype, and may be thought to have brought even extreme abuse upon herself.[19] But in adversity, the reasonable woman behaves with a mixture of daring and caution. In *Sayers v Harlow Urban District Council*[20] the plaintiff was waiting for a bus, due in about twenty minutes, when she visited the public lavatory, leaving her husband at the bus stop. She found herself unable to get out of the cubicle as the door handle was missing. She tried unsuccessfully to attract attention, and then considered the possibility of climbing over the door. Her initial move, to stand on the lavatory seat, was considered by the Court of Appeal to be entirely foreseeable. It would be asking too much to require her to wait for fifteen minutes for her husband to come, without making any attempt at escape. The Court of Appeal contrasted this case with *Adams v Lancashire and Yorkshire Railway Co*,[21] where the passenger on a train noticed that the carriage door kept opening and tried to close it three times. He then rested his whole weight on it as the train was moving and fell out. He got nothing for his injuries, since his behaviour was unreasonable. 'It might be irritating to see a door open, but it was summer and it was not suggested that he was cold.' However, Mrs Sayers, once standing on the lavatory seat, went on to place one foot on the toilet roll and its holder in order to test the feasibility of climbing over the gap over the door. Realising that she still would not have enough leverage, she began to climb down; the shift in her weight caused the toilet roll to rotate, and she fell, injuring herself. This was a step too far for the Court, who dismissed counsel's claim 'that it was perfectly reasonable for a lady of thirty-six with a skirt, and, no doubt, high heels, to do it.' She should have known that to climb out was a very hazardous undertaking, and therefore she was twenty-five per cent contributorily negligent.

The actions of the reasonable man or woman are not, then, those of someone blessed with near-perfect patience. Judges claim that the person envisaged is only average, with all the usual shortcomings and weaknesses tolerated by the community.

---

[16] *Frost v Chief Constable of South Yorkshire* [1997] 1 All ER 540, 547.
[17] *White v Chief Constable South Yorkshire Police* n.14, 29.
[18] *Ellison v Brady* 924 Fed Rep 2d Ser 872 (9th Cir 1991).
[19] *Carr v Allison Gas Turbine Division* 32 Fed Rep 3rd Ser 1007 (7th Cir 1994).
[20] [1958] 1 WLR 623.
[21] (1868) LR & CP 739.

It has been claimed that the reasonable man is 'neither a perfect citizen nor a paragon of circumspection.'[22] Yet they are generally unpersuaded by any arithmetic which suggests that 'normal' behaviour is far from ideal, and may even be dangerous. For every accident on the roads there are a hundred and twenty-two near misses,[23] and, in an American study, even 'good' drivers committed an average of nine driving errors every five minutes in normal conditions.[24] Nevertheless, the number of road accidents is proportionately very small, and the average car driver may expect to be involved in one that causes personal injury only once in twenty-five years. 'Thus, it seems that whether an act of negligence ends up in the accident statistics or as a near miss is almost pure chance; it has little to do with the defendant's culpability.'[25] Jørgensen studied driving behaviour when traffic lights switch to amber. There is a moment when clearly drivers will not brake; it is too late, and they are going too fast. There is a later moment when they will brake, just as the light is about to change to red. Between these moments is the 'dilemma zone', which includes non-obvious factors such as time/distance relationships, and how long these particular lights stay on amber. Of all the motorists whom Jørgensen observed approaching amber lights in the 'dilemma zone', not one applied the brakes.[26] Researchers at the University of Nottingham,[27] also found drivers to be remarkably casual. Fewer than ten per cent of them adjusted their actions in any way to allow for the fact that there were children crossing a road. Accidents were avoided only because the children got out of the way.

It seems, then, that drivers are unwilling to deviate from a fixed course of conduct unless there is certain to be an accident.[28] This may be statistically common behaviour, but it hardly conjures up the picture of the Reasonable Driver. The Reasonable Driver does not make basic errors, and almost any mistake made whilst driving is treated as negligence without argument.[29] Thus courts are willing to find fault despite the absolute ordinariness of drivers' behaviour; this might support defensive attribution or just world theories, discussed below. The achievement of perfection is an unrealistic goal to set drivers; but courts perhaps recognise the unusual social phenomenon of almost universal access to potentially lethal machinery, and of almost universal insurance cover.[30] In other contexts, where the same social necessity is not so apparent, courts do resort to headcounting

---

[22] *AC Billings and Son Ltd v Riden* [1958] AC 240, 255 per Lord Reid.

[23] M Austin, *Accident Black Spot: an Analytical Study of Road Safety Policy and Practice* (Harmondsworth, Penguin, 1966) 33.

[24] Automobile Insurance and Compensation Study *Driver Behaviour and Accident Involvement: Implications for Tort Liability* (Washington US Government Printer, 1970) 176–80.

[25] P Cane, *Atiyah's Accidents, Compensation and the Law* (London, Butterworths,1999) 146.

[26] NO Jørgensen, 'Risky Behavior at Traffic Signals: a Traffic Engineer's View' (1988) 31 *Ergonomics* 657.

[27] CI Howarth, 'The Relationship between Objective Risk, Subjective Risk, and Behaviour' (1988) 31 *Ergonomics* 527.

[28] WA Wagenaar, 'Risk-Taking and Accident Causation' in JF Yates (ed) *Risk-Taking Behaviour* (Chichester Wiley 1992).

[29] *Ibid*, 421.

[30] See discussion below of just world theory and the compensation principle.

to define reasonable behaviour. In *Harlow v Forklift Systems Inc*,[31] the plaintiff failed in her claim of harassment against a fellow manager who was, in fact, the son of the President of the Company. Her reaction was held to be unreasonable, given that other female employees did not object to the 'jocular work environment.' But in *EEOC v. Sears*,[32] the plaintiff argued without success that she had been rejected for a post because of her gender. For the defendant, two feminist historians gave evidence that the company's history of not employing women in highly-paid commission sales jobs was a consequence of women lacking interest in such competitive work.

Perceptions of the Reasonable Man therefore appear to shift from one context to another. Atiyah concludes that liability in negligence does not depend entirely on fault.[33] 'This contention gains strength from the courts' apparent unwillingness to take account of the personal limitations of defendants, even where it is impossible for them to achieve the required standard of performance. Learner divers are expected to drive to the standard of an experienced driver at once,[34] and the courts have an erratic policy on physical disability.[35]

> If, for instance, a man is born hasty and awkward, is always having accidents and hurting himself or his neighbours, no doubt his congenital defects will be allowed for in the courts of heaven, but his slips are no less troublesome to his neighbours than if they sprang from guilty neglect. His neighbours accordingly require him, at his proper peril, to come up to their standard, and the courts which they establish decline to take his personal equation into account.[36]

It is scarcely surprising that courts are unsympathetic in cases where a person with physical or learning disabilities has chosen to engage in an activity, which endangers the safety of others. In respect of more everyday pursuits, they will take account of any limitations on the defendant's power to exercise normal standards of care. For example, a blind man is entitled to walk along the street, but not to drive a car.[37] And if a driver is suddenly overtaken by a sudden, unexpected, and disabling illness, he is not liable for the damage he does.[38] Even the reasonable man can have a heart attack. Fleming can see no difference between that situation and the onset of an insane delusion which causes a driver to cross red traffic lights to escape an imagined enemy.[39]

---

[31] *Westlaw* 487444 (US Supreme Court 1993).
[32] R Milkman, 'Women's History and the Sears Case' (1986) 12 *Feminist Studies* 375.
[33] Cane, n. 25.
[34] *Nettleship v Weston* [1971] 2 QB 691; an approach rejected by the Australian courts.
[35] JG Fleming *An Introduction to the Law of Torts* (Oxford Clarendon, 1985) 27.
[36] OW Holmes, 'Lectures, III: Torts, Trespass and Negligence', *Collected Works of Justice Holmes* (Chicago, University of Chicago Press, 1995) Vol 1, p170.
[37] Fleming, n. 35 27.
[38] *Waugh v James K Allan Ltd* [1964] 2 Lloyd's Rep 1.
[39] Fleming, n.35 225.

Children receive rather different treatment from the law. A young child may be incapable of the necessary mental state for liability;[40] the claimant must show the defendant's behaviour would be unreasonable for a child of his or her age;[41] Thus in *Mullin v Richard*[42] the court had to think itself into the shoes of a fifteen year old schoolgirl playing during a mathematics class. Two girls, the plaintiff and the defendant, had been 'fencing' with plastic rulers when one snapped, so that a fragment of plastic entered the plaintiff's eye. She lost all sight in that eye, and sued her friend. The Court of Appeal dismissed the claim. On the subject of the defendant's youth, Butler-Sloss LJ said: 'I would say that girls of fifteen playing together may play as somewhat irresponsible girls of fifteen.' As Fleming observes, it is curious that the law is flexible in its approach to children who cause harm but judgmental where the defendant is handicapped by mental illness or learning disability:

> We are prepared to tolerate the mistakes and failings of childhood as a condition to which everyone is heir in contrast to insanity, which, besides being rare and creating administrative difficulties enough in the criminal context, is perhaps still beset with an atavistic attribution of sin from which modern man has not yet succeeded in emancipating himself.[43]

If the person who caused the harm did so whilst exercising any calling, the test is not that of the actions to be expected from the reasonable layman. The relevant standard is the degree of skill or competence normally associated with efficient discharge of that profession. This standard is absolute; in medical negligence cases, it does not depend on the skill or experience of the particular doctor, nor the pressure long hours place upon him. It depends on the qualities normally associated with that post.[44] Again the reasonable man test of negligence is out of step with perceptions of moral fault. It also is out of step with lay perceptions. In Lloyd-Bostock's survey of accident victims, context was found to be an important factor in the blaming process.[45] The criminal law has made a greater effort to adjust responsibility to context. In *Prentice*,[46] two junior doctors were pressed by their employer to perform a difficult medical procedure despite their protestations that they were unqualified to do so. In the absence of anyone more experienced being available, they carried out the treatment, made a mistake, and the patient died. The Court of Appeal considered that the test for gross negligence in manslaughter cases must take account of any excuse or mitigating circumstances rather than simply make objective measurement of the scale of the error.

---

[40] Ibid., 26; WVH Rogers, *The Law of Torts*, 16th edn (London, Sweet and Maxwell 2002) 712.
[41] *Gough v Thorne* [1996] 3 All ER 398.
[42] [1988] 1 All ER 920.
[43] Fleming, above n.35, 26.
[44] *Wilsher v Essex Area Health Authority* [1988] AC 1074.
[45] S Lloyd-Bostock, 'The Ordinary Man and the Psychology of Attributing Causes and Responsibility' (1979) 42 *Modern Law Review* 143.
[46] [1993] 4 All ER 935

To insist, in civil cases, on perfection in the Reasonable Medical Practitioner could be counter-productive to the interests of patients. The increase in the number of negligence actions in the medical context in the USA and the United Kingdom has caused some alarm. One anxiety is that fear of suits for damages will deter clinicians from any course of conduct which is neither ultra-cautious or not approved by some judicial pronouncement. 'Crystallised standards' have been said to cause some clinicians to regard the avoidance of liability as their main concern, irrespective of the best interests of their patients. These standards may be found in a body of case law which has evolved in the United States, and embodies the judicial concept of best practice. Judicial observations on conduct have, because decisions are reported, become 'endowed with pervasive generality.' They thus provide complex and detailed guidelines as to what is reasonable in a given context.[47] Professionals attempt to help themselves in this climate through guidelines issued by professional bodies. Together with the reported decisions, these direct the law towards set standards which enable clinicians to predict tort liability.[48] Critics complain that the law at one and the same time imposes on the clinician a fiduciary duty to consider only the patient's interests, while creating an incentive structure that promotes violations of that duty. Sceptics may feel that the courts' dependence on experts to explain what standard is to be expected in the context already provides clinicians with very valuable protection against unfairness.

A final point is that the Reasonable Person, against whose standards risk, and therefore foreseeability, is assessed, bears virtually no resemblance to the Reasonable Person who features in criminal law cases dealing with the defence of provocation. Since the basis of the defence is that the defendant has retaliated to acts or words of provocation by killing someone, and that the Reasonable Man would have done the same thing, a far more passionate and imperfect human being presents himself to the imagination. Further, and also unlike the civil version, the criminal-law Reasonable Man may suffer from mental illness or personality disorder, in which case the fact-finder will have to consider how this disturbed or inadequate (but reasonable) individual would have responded to the provocation. This is discussed in chapter three.

Defensive Attribution

We have seen that the ascription or responsibility is affected by the erratic effect of heuristics on perceptions of likelihood. We have seen also that the human representation of normality, the Reasonable Man, is a somewhat unpredictable construct. Why do courts take account of the inexperience of childhood but not the limited abilities of the mentally ill or learning disabled, in deciding responsibility?

---

[47] Fleming, n.35, 24.
[48] RF Schopp and DB Wexler, 'Shooting Yourself in the Foot with Due Care: Psychotherapists and Crystallized Standards of Tort Liability' in DB Wexler, BJ Winick, (eds) *Essays in Therapeutic Jurisprudence* (Durham NC, Carolina Academic Press, 1991).

The fundamental attribution error could play a role in this; it would cause the role of an external cause such as the onset of a mental illness to be underestimated. Another explanation might be that adults, whatever their intellectual limitations might be, are more likely than children to have the financial means to compensate their victims. The temptation to find responsibility in the person with the greatest potential to compensate will be discussed below: it is suggested here that it could be regarded as a form of defensive attribution.

The theory has been advanced that, in experimental situations, people are more likely to attribute blame to the actor where the harm caused is serious. In a study by Walster,[49] subjects were told of a young man, Lennie, who left a car at the top of a hill. The handbrake failed and the car rolled downhill. From that stage the scenarios were varied so that seriousness of the outcome might be great or minor. Significantly more responsibility was assigned to Lennie for the severe accidents than for the mild ones, even if only he suffered harm. Walster attempted to explain these unexpected results with a theory of defensive attribution. This suggests that if the damage caused by an accident is trivial, the observer can feel sympathetic toward the victim, whilst attributing his misfortune to chance, that is, ascribe less responsibility to the actor, whether or not he is the victim. But if a serious harm occurs, merely to view the victim as unlucky carries the threatening implication that the observer too by bad luck may suffer a grave accident. It is possible that we need to reassure ourselves that we are in control of the world. If so, we would have to balance our choices between what can be controlled (but may be unimportant) with what is important (but may be impossible to control). Defensive attributions would be made only when the importance of preventing such accidents is more salient than the infeasibility of trying to prevent them.

It would be clearly unwise to argue straight from this piece of research to an analogy with court decision-making. For there, the attribution of responsibility frequently involves visiting a sanction upon the culprit. Walster's study presents another problem, as far as the court analogy is concerned, in that her subjects did not consider Lennie to be more *careless* in the severe examples, even though they held him *responsible* in those cases, throwing into doubt what Walster and her subjects meant by responsibility. In law, the seriousness of the harm should have no effect on the decision whether a duty of care exists,[50] although, it does have a role in the evaluation of whether the defendant was negligent. The nature of the risk being run depends partly on the extent of the possible damage. The more serious the damage which will happen if an accident should occur, the more thorough are the precautions which should be taken.[51] The scale of the potential damage is weighed against the cost and practicability of preventing the risk.[52] Where it is

---

[49] E Walster, 'Assignment of Responsibility for an Accident' (1966) 3 *Journal of Personality and Social Psychology* 73.

[50] *Hill v Chief Constable of West Yorkshire Police* [1988] 2 All ER 238; *M (a minor) v Newham London Borough Council* [1995] 4 All ER 602.

[51] *Paris v Stepney Borough Council* [1951] 1 All ER 42.

[52] *Wagon Mound (No 1)* [1961] 1 All ER 404; *British Railways Board v Herrington* [1972] 1 All ER 749.

feared that a process could lead to major harm, but scientific evidence on the point is inconclusive, any claimant alleging that injury has resulted is unlikely to succeed in a compensation claim. This has led one commentator to argue that the burden of proof on the causation issue should shift to the defendant, or that the damages should be divided. This 'would increase the incentive for the makers of potentially toxic substances to investigate the substances' causal powers more carefully before distributing them widely.'[53] Where large-scale harm is caused by such a process, however, courts may be over-generous to litigants.

There are signs of defensive attribution in the public reaction to disaster. The danger is that the need to find someone to blame will result in scapegoating. After a nightclub fire that killed nearly five hundred people, the citizens of Boston seemed determined to impose responsibility on someone, rather than accept that it might have been a pure accident.[54] Wagenaar accuses judges of being too quick to find liability in cases of industrial accident and disaster, such as the capsizing of the Herald of Free Enterprise, or the stranding of the Esso Valdez.[55] He argues that often it would have been impossible to assess risks at the time of the initiation of a procedure, because the situation is too intricate to be analysed. The systems themselves are so sophisticated that errors can cause problems only when unforeseen coincidences occur, thus in a manner with which operators inevitably have not been trained to deal. He concludes from this that there is little or no conscious risk-taking in these cases. Thus the huge accidents, which lead to 'disaster' mass claims in the courts, are the impossible ones that no one foresaw. Foreseeable consequences are avoided because the system takes care to avoid them.[56] Yet judges, according to Wagenaar, frequently ascribe foreseeability where a complex system has broken down with catastrophic results. Whether or not this is a fair description of judicial reasoning in disaster cases, experts have been castigated for erring in the opposite direction. Perrow[57] argues that scientists are conservative to a fault when required to estimate risk. He points to the increase in the number of potentially dangerous complex processes set up by scientists who fail to accept the inevitability of 'normal accidents.' Internal safeguards designed to deal with anticipated faults mean that when things do go wrong, the cause was a chain of coincidences which were not predicted by the designers. Scientists deny that the disastrous consequences were foreseeable, tending to place any blame on operators, who inevitably, were not trained to deal with the unexpected combination of problems that occurred. Perrow argues that in fact the very complexity of the systems makes such accidents entirely foreseeable, and concludes that scientific estimation of risk is unrealistic; it assumes that only one thing at a time goes wrong, and this inspires the regular production of misleadingly optimistic figures on safety.

---

[53] HL Feldman, 'Science and Understanding in Mass Exposure Litigation' [1995] *Texas Law Review* 1, 45.
[54] HR Veltford and GE Lee, 'The Coconut Grove Fire: a Study in Scapegoating' (1943) 38 *Journal of Abnormal and Social Psychology* 138.
[55] WA Wagenaar and J Groeneweg, 'Accidents at Sea: Multiple Causes and Impossible Consequences' (1987) 27 *International Journal Man-Machine Studies* 587.
[56] WA Wagenaar above, n.28.
[57] C Perrow, *Normal Accidents* (New York, Basic Books, 1994).

Efforts to replicate Walster's findings have been numerous. Variations of her method, introducing new variables, has generated an impressive volume of literature, but without consistent results. Shaw and Skolnick failed to find a correlation between the seriousness of an accident and ascriptions of responsibility. Their subjects ascribed the more serious accidents to chance, and the minor ones tended to be regarded as the actor's fault. But there was a difference between male and female subjects, the latter having a tendency to claim that they would have made the same judgment, suggesting, perhaps, lower self-esteem in women.[58] Shaver adapted Walster's methodology to include a new issue, similarity between the actor and the subject. The results contradicted defensive attribution; the greater the similarity between subject and actor, the less responsible the actor was thought to be. Where fault was a virtually inevitable conclusion, the subject tended to deny the similarity. Thus it may be, as Shaver concludes, that the greater concern is to avoid blame for the accident rather than to avoid the accident itself.[59] A parallel may be seen in the notorious historical unwillingness of juries to convict of motor manslaughter cases. Most jurors drive cars and are aware that sometimes they make mistakes.[60] Yet there is evidence that people take fatalities in road accidents very seriously. Respondents to a survey thought killing a pedestrian very serious and argued that it should be treated as manslaughter. It is possible that attitudes to bad driving have changed.[61] Certainly, there has been criticism of sentencing in cases where bad driving has caused death. In 2001 there was an outcry at the fine of £100 levied against Steven Atkinson in respect of a car accident that killed the parents of six children.[62]

The apparent contradiction in defensive attribution research may spring from the theory's inability to predict with whose fate (actor or victim) the subject will identify. The experience with motor manslaughter prosecutions suggests that jurors identify with the car driver. Respondents to a survey, where the defendant is only a hypothetical individual may identify with the victim. Class, age or gender might affect this process,[63] but what explains the apparent readiness of jurors to award damages against psychiatrists should their depressive patients commit suicide?[64] Defensive attribution researchers have been accused of supporting the theory even though their own results cast doubts on it and provide better support for

---

[58] JI Shaw and P Skolnick, 'Attribution of Responsibility for a Happy Accident' (1973) 18 *Journal of Personality and Social Psychology* 380.

[59] KC Shaver, 'Defensive Attribution: Effects of Severity and Relevance on the Responsibility Assigned for an Accident (1970) 14 *Journal of Personality and Social Psychology* 101.

[60] S Cunningham, 'The Reality of Vehicular Homicides; Convictions for Murder, Manslaughter and Causing Death by Dangerous Driving' [2001] *Criminal Law Review* 679; B MacKenna, 'Causing Death by Reckless or Dangerous Driving: a Suggestion' [1970] *Criminal Law Review* 67.

[61] B Mitchell, 'Further Evidence of the Relationship between Legal and Public Opinion on the Law of Homicide' [2000] *Criminal Law Review* 814.

[62] *The Times* 13 August 2001.

[63] But see Lloyd-Bostock, n.45, on 'situational relevance' — the perceiver is anxious that in such an accident he be not blamed.

[64] BB Wexler and RF Shopp, 'How and When to Correct Errors of Juror Hindsight Bias in Mental Health Malpractice Litigation' in BB Wexler and RJ Winicke, (eds) *Essays in Therapeutic Jurisprudence* (Durham NC, Carolina Academic Press 1991).

other explanations.[65] Certainly, they can be terminologically imprecise; 'cause', 'blame', 'responsibility' and sometimes 'sanction' are lumped together in these studies, so that it is impossible to say what it is that is being measured.[66]

Just World

Defensive attribution suggests that subjects identify themselves as potential victims of a harm similar to the harm done. In contrast, the Just World theory detaches the subject from both victim and actor, in the sense that it holds that attributions of responsibility are affected by a more fundamental issue. Lerner[67] posited the theory that for sanity's sake, people need to believe that the world is a just and predictable place; they anticipate a reasonable fit between merit and reward. Thus one might be able to tolerate the prospect of minor accidents befalling people at random, but the possibility that one could suffer a severe accident without somehow being responsible threatens the belief that the world is just. This may be seen in the reaction of experimental subjects who were asked to observe an individual apparently being punished severely. Unable to prevent this, the observers tended to reject the victim and find her unsympathetic.[68] Kalven and Zeisel found[69] that jurors in rape cases often nullify the law of rape by blaming the victim, prompting the suggestion that an unabridged portrait of the defendant, criminal record and all, might counter any risk of juries operating just world against a rape complainant.[70]

Evidence for the just world hypothesis is said to derive from victim studies. Genuine victims of permanently disabling accidents (such as diving, football or car accidents) which all had the elements of chance but which are classed by them as having been avoidable, tend to blame themselves for their injuries.[71] If they do blame themselves they appear to have a greater chance of psychological survival. This effect is most marked in cases where the injury occurred during a leisure activity and absolutely no one else could have been involved. The explanation for this phenomenon may be that it would threaten the conception of a just world held by these victims if the person responsible for harming them has escaped injury.[72]

[65] FD Fincham and JM Jaspars, 'Attribution of Responsibility: from Man the Scientist to Man as Lawyer' in L Berkowitz, (ed) (1980) 13 *Advances in Experimental Psychology* 82.
[66] For example, GR Semin and ASR Manstead, *The Accountability of Conduct* (London, Academic Press, 1983).
[67] MJ Lerner, 'Evaluation of Performance as a Function of Performer's Reward and Attractiveness' (1965) 1 *Journal of Personality and Social Psychology* 355.
[68] MJ Lerner and CH Simmons, 'Observer's Reaction to the Innocent Victim' (1966) 4 *Journal of Personality and Social Psychology* 203.
[69] H Kalven and H Zeisel, *The American Jury* (Boston, Little Brown, 1966).
[70] DP Bryden and RC Park, 'Other crimes evidence in sex offense cases' (1994) 78 *Minnesota Law Review* 529 at 581.
[71] R Bulman and CB Wortman, 'Attributions of Blame and Coping in the Real World: Severe Accident Victims React to their Lot' (1977) 35 *Journal of Personality and Social Psychology* 351.
[72] Although Burger finds support for attribution theory in studies which show that victims of crimes and disasters tend to blame themselves for accidents which cause serious injury. JM Burger,

Rape victims also have a tendency to blame themselves. But their reaction does not support a just world hypothesis, and casts doubt on any support being derived from the self-blame of other victims. For although rape victims make a better psychological recovery when they blame themselves, their self-blame does not morally exonerate the rapist. Instead, it identifies those of their own actions which made them vulnerable to the rape. These might include having invited the offender in for a coffee, or having taken the late bus home. By avoiding repetition of this behaviour, the victim can feel relatively safe from a further attack.

> If a woman can believe that some how she got herself into this situation, if she can make herself responsible for it, then she's established some sort of control over the rape. It wasn't someone arbitrarily smashing into her life and wreaking havoc.[73]

Janoff-Bulman describes this reaction as 'behavioural self-blame.'[74] It is closer to defensive attribution than just world, in that the victim seeks to regain control and make the world safer, if no fairer.

Chaikin and Darley have cast doubts on the 'just world.'[75] Each of their subjects was told that, in the future, they would be assigned the roles of either worker or supervisor. Some were told that workers would be paid strictly according to output, others that the supervisor had discretion on pay. They then watched a video in which blocks, which the worker had assembled, were sent flying by the supervisor knocking the table accidentally. Future supervisors tended to attribute the accident to chance. When the consequences were severe, the accident was less likely to be attributed to chance, but was blamed on

> not the supervisor, who bumped the table, which toppled the blocks, which docked the pay of the worker; and not on the worker, who was obviously pretty innocent, but on the person who chose such a rickety table in the first place.[76]

Future workers were more likely to ascribe the accident to chance if it caused no loss to the worker, tending instead to find the supervisor at fault whether the consequences were mild or severe. These findings conflict with 'just world', in that workers should derogate victims in order to maintain a belief in justice. To blame the supervisor does not restore justice if the worker loses pay. The subjects attributed blame in a way that avoided casting it on the person with whom they identified, supporting Shaver's version of defensive attribution.

'Motivational Biases in the Attribution of Responsibility for an Accident; a Meta-Analysis of the Defensive Attribution Hypothesis' (1981) 90 *Psychological Bulletin* 496.

[73] A Medea and K Thompson, *Against Rape* (New York, Farrer Strauss and Giroux, 1974) 105.
[74] R Janoff-Bulman, 'Characterological and Behavioral Self-Blame: Inquiries into Depression and Rape' (1979) 37 *Journal of Personality and Social Psychology* 1748.
[75] AL Chaikin and JM Darley, 'Victim or Perpetrator: Defensive Attribution of Responsibility and the Need for Order' (1973) 25 *Journal of Personality and Social Psychology* 268.
[76] *Ibid.*, at 273.

If maintenance in belief in a just world is essential to well being, and generally employed in assignment of responsibility, obvious problems confront the finders of fact in legal proceedings. If all victims were thought to deserve their fate, then defendants would always win the day, irrespective of whether or not the tribunal identified with them in terms of personal similarity. In cases where blaming the victim is impossible, the problem would be solved by derogation of the victim, possibly affecting compensation levels. Since the tribunal itself will decide final outcome, imposing any penalties thought appropriate, it effectively is in a position to create a just world, where perpetrators are punished. Hence it is only rare cases that 'just world' can be seen to distort reasoning. For example, courts can be so affected by the conduct of a litigant that they slip into just world thinking. This can be seen in the 'rescue' cases, where the plaintiff or claimant is seen as a hero.

> A rescue attempt to save someone from danger will be regarded as foreseeable. A duty of care to a rescuer may arise even if the defendant owed no duty to the primary victim, for example, because the latter was a trespasser. If a rescuer is injured in a rescue attempt, a plea of *volenti non fit injuria*[77] will not avail a wrongdoer.[78]

Thus the claim of police officers for damages for post-traumatic stress disorder suffered as a result of assisting at the Hillsborough disaster succeeded. The actions of relatives to recover compensation having suffered psychiatric damage after watching those events, which they knew involved their family members, on television, were not.[79]

In *Chapman v Hearse*,[80] for example, the defendant negligently caused a road accident. A doctor stopped to help the injured. A following car negligently struck him. The defendant was liable for the doctor's death, although it would not have been a foreseeable consequence of his *driving*, and was not the risk that identified his conduct as negligent in the first place. The doctor' death become a possibility once the negligence had occurred:

> The emergency begets the man ... Public policy favours a wide rather than a narrow definition to ensure that those brave and unselfish enough to go to the help of their fellow man will be properly compensated if they suffer damage as a result.[81]

Thus, 'where ... a person has been killed in a heroic attempt to rescue another, judges will strain every nerve to find someone at fault if they possibly can'.[82] An example is the case of a heroic railwayman who sacrificed himself to save his

---

[77] 'No injury is done to one who consents'.
[78] *White and Chief Constable of South Yorkshire Police*, above n. 14 per Lord Steyn at 37.
[79] *Alcock v Chief Constable of South Yorkshire* [1992] 1 AC 310.
[80] [1951] SASR 51.
[81] *Frost v Chief Constable of South Yorkshire Police* [1997] 1 All ER 540, per Henry LJ 567–8.
[82] P Atiyah, *Accidents, Compensation and the Law* 2nd edn (London, Weidenfeld and Nicholson, 1975) 426; also, H Kalven and H Zeisel, *The American Jury* (Boston, Little Brown 1966); accidents suffered by the defendant influence jurors towards leniency.

young child.[83] The Court of Appeal held at one and the same time that the presence of the stationmaster's toddler son on the railway line at a small station was not reasonably foreseeable, but that his father's leap (at the cost of his own life), to save him from a rapidly approaching trolley, was. The child was a trespasser, but 'it is surely ... remarkable how readily the focus expanded at the sight of a rescuer'.[84]

The finding that the sufferer of a harm was contributorily negligent might be seen as a manifestation of the just world, analogous to the self-blame of accident victims. In *Jones v Livox Quarries Ltd*,[85] the plaintiff had been riding on the towbar at the back of a vehicle, when the driver behind negligently drove into it. The most obvious risk to the plaintiff from his own behaviour was that he might have been thrown off. Being negligently rammed from behind was rather less predictable, but it was held that he had exposed himself to the risk of it. His damages were reduced accordingly. Denning LJ explained that if, instead, the plaintiff had been shot in the eye by a negligent sportsman, that would have been entirely outside the category of injury that was foreseeable. In *Rose v Plenty*,[86] the plaintiff, a thirteen-year-old boy, had been illegally employed by a milkman to help him with deliveries. The boy perched on the milk float with one leg dangling off, in order to leap off the faster. The milkman negligently drove too close to the kerb, trapping the boy's foot and breaking it. The plaintiff was held to be twenty-five per cent responsible. Sometimes victims of crime are accused of 'contributory negligence'. Various studies show that mock jurors regard offences as less serious where the victim has made even a mild contribution.[87] In a hypothetical rape case, subjects selected a lighter sentence where the rapist persuaded the victim to let him in to make a telephone call, than where he forced his way into the victim's apartment.[88] In another study, subjects watched a videotaped interview by a detective, ostensibly of a crime victim. The crime described might be either rape or robbery, and the circumstances varied. Most blame of all was attached to a female victim who had been hitchhiking at the time she was robbed. The least blame of all attached to a female rape victim who had been jogging. The more likely a particular assault was perceived to be, the more blame was attributed to the victim.[89]

Hamilton[90] argues that expectations are defined by the actor's social role, and so these should be included in an understanding of responsibility judgments. Perhaps judges should articulate policy and social considerations more than they

---

[83] *Videan v British Transport Commission* [1963] 2 QB 650.

[84] Fleming, above n.35, 54.

[85] [1952] 2 QB 608.

[86] [1976] 1 All ER 97.

[87] GR Miller, GR and JK Burgoon, 'Factors Affecting Assessments of Witness Credibility' in NL Kerr and RM Bray, (eds) *The Psychology of the Courtroom* (London, Academic Press, 1982).

[88] H Field, 'Rape Trials and Jurors' Decisions: a Psychological Analysis of the Effects of Victim, Defendant and Case Characteristics' (1979) 3 *Law and Human Behavior* 261.

[89] J Howard, 'The "Normal" Victim: the Effects of Gender Stereotypes on Reactions to Victims' (1984) 47 *Social Psychology Quarterly* 270.

[90] Hamilton, above n.?

do at present. Atiyah has highlighted the problem that the urge to compensate those who have suffered harm has encouraged the locating of fault in cases where in fact the behaviour complained of is entirely ordinary.[91] In fact, harm doers are generally anxious to compensate their victims,[92] suggesting that the compensation principle is a moral one. In her study of accident victims, Lloyd-Bostock found greater willingness to blame employers and other organisations, and concluded that this was linked to some extent with their ability to compensate. It was rare for anyone to be blamed for domestic accidents or leisure or sports accidents, but more common in work and road accidents, where, of course, the victims were aware of the probability of insurance cover. Thus it seems that the lay perception of responsibility to compensate is not based on a generally held moral opinion that wrongdoers must pay wherever harm is caused. It seems rather to be influenced by knowledge of the way liability is assigned, probably in combination with assumptions about ability to find the money. Where the perpetrator of the harm has little ability to pay compensation, it appears that the victim is happy not to ascribe blame. This is more consistent with just world than defensive attribution. Hamilton suggests that large organisations are held to more stringent standards of accountability, probably because of their very diffuse array of obligations, which include the supervision of individuals. But Lord Templeman reacted to a plaintiff's argument that manufacturers of audio systems with tape-to-tape copying facilities should be liable to compensate recording companies who lost revenue as a result, as follows:

> The pleading assumes that we are all neighbours now, Pharisees and Samaritans alike, that foreseeability is a reflection of hindsight and that for every mischance in an accident-prone world someone solvent must be liable.[93]

Hindsight

Psychologists have shown that hindsight tends to produce inflated perceptions of foreseeability. Where mock jurors were asked in hypothetical cases whether there had been reasonable and probable cause to justify police search, their assessments were dramatically affected if they knew the results of the search. If the plaintiff had in fact been implicated in crime by what had been found, jurors were more likely to consider there to have been probable cause for the search, irrespective of judicial warnings to ignore its product.[94] Fischhoff[95] found that subjects who

---

[91] Atiyah, above n. 82.

[92] S Lloyd-Bostock, 'Common Sense Morality and Accident Compensation' in DP Farrington, K Hawkins and S Lloyd-Bostock, (eds) *Psychology, Law and Legal Processes* (London, Macmillan, 1979).

[93] *CBS Songs v Amstrad Computer Electronics Ltd* [1988] AC 1013, 1059.

[94] JD Casper, K Benedict and JL Perry, 'The Tort Remedy in Search and Seizure Cases: a Case Study in Juror Decision Making' (1988) 13 *Law and Social Inquiry* 279.

[95] B Fischhoff, 'Hindsight and Foresight: the Effect of Outcome Knowledge on Judgment Under Uncertainty' (1975) 1 *Journal of Experimental Psychology, Human Perception and Performance* 288.

were told that an outcome had occurred viewed that outcome as far more likely than did those subjects who were not told of the outcome but were asked to predict the likelihood of its occurrence. Merely admonishing people to disregard the hindsight effect does not eliminate it; and all subjects failed to predict that hindsight would affect their own judgment. Judges, however, appear to be alert to the danger — 'After the event even a fool is wise'.[96] *Walker v Northumberland County Council*,[97] illustrates the way judges try to locate themselves psychologically at the place and time of the alleged negligence and project forward from that point the likelihood of the harm being caused. Colman J held that the defendant Council knew that social work is particularly stressful and that personnel were overstretched and under-resourced. It did nothing to relieve the load this placed upon the plaintiff, despite his pleas for assistance. However, in the judge's opinion, there was no reason initially to believe that the plaintiff's mental health would be damaged by the admittedly intolerable load he bore. Once he had had a breakdown, however, the risk of further mental damage resulting from the continuing lack of support was eminently foreseeable.

In general, judges' do not allow hindsight to distort their perception of risk. But Wagenaar[98] accuses judges of being excessively influenced by hindsight in cases of catastrophe. In combination with the availability heuristic, which distorts estimations of probability, defensive attribution allows the magnitude of the disaster to affect judgments of frequency. The use of hindsight to some extent is inevitable, however. Courts cannot decide whether a particular harm should have been foreseen as a likely consequence of an action without knowing that it did occur.[99] The hindsight test was specifically included in the American *Restatement of the Law of Torts*, allowing recovery even where abnormal coexisting circumstances contributed to the harm, so contemplating almost unlimited responsibility: 'Negligence is tested by foresight, but proximate cause is determined by hindsight'.[100] The defendant is liable for all the consequences which the reasonable man, knowing all the facts whether they could have been known at the time or not, would have thought at the time of the negligent act as reasonably likely to follow if they had been suggested to him.[101]

Juries have been accused of applying hindsight to the forseeability issue. In Britain there are no jury trials of negligence actions, but in the United States, jurors are alleged to be far too ready to believe harms to be reasonably foreseeable. Wexler and Schopp[102] contend that juries are over-eager to award damages against psychiatrists whose patients commit suicide subsequent to treatment. Also it was found in a study using simulated trials, that knowledge of the outcome of

[96] *Wagon Mound* above n. 52, Viscount Simonds at 414.
[97] [1995] 1 All ER 737.
[98] Wagenaar, n.28.
[99] *Page v Smith* [1995] 2 All ER 736. It is certainly legitimate to do so where psychiatric damage is suffered by a secondary, as opposed to primary, victim of the defendant's negligence.
[100] *Dellwo v Pearson* (1961) 107 NW 2d 859.
[101] *Butts v Anthis* (1937) 181 Okla 276, 73 P 2d 843.
[102] Shopp and Wexler, above n.48.

illegal police searches affected the level of damages, particularly of punitive damages. This occurred irrespective of judicial warning to ignore the guilt or otherwise of the plaintiff.[103]

> Magical thinking by jurors in suicide malpractice cases involves a conception of foreseeability which is absolute, in yes or no terms opposed to the more probabilistic, risk-benefit reasoning in which the clinician must engage; the use of hindsight rather than reconstruction of the conditions under which the clinician exercised foresight; failure to acknowledge the uncertainty that surrounds clinical judgment; unicausal rather than multicausal explanation for the suicide...[104]

Schopp and Wexler accept that the effect of hindsight is not easy to eradicate. They suggest some strategies to reduce it. The first is bifurcation of trials. Trials would be divided into separate hearings concerned with different issues so that outcome information would be withheld from the finders of fact. The danger would be that they inevitably know something happened, and might guess the harm to have been worse than it actually was. Also, it is not clear that issues are separable in practice. In many cases the finder of fact must know the outcome in order to judge whether the defendant was negligent. The second proposal is to amplify the judicial warning by calling expert testimony on the hindsight bias. However, there is no evidence that this would have greater success than a judicial warning on its own.

CAUSATION

Legal causation is to be understood as the man in the street, and not as either the scientist or the metaphysician would understand it.[105] In negligence, defendants are responsible only for such harm as they could reasonably have foreseen and prevented.[106] In criminal law, the defendant's act causes a harm of which it is a foreseeable consequence.[107] A foreseeability test for causation allows the courts some flexibility in the allocation of blame. Blame is partly a function of belief and value systems; therefore these have a vital role in findings of causation. Hart and Honoré's example shows how perceptions of cause are affected by normative systems. The cause of a famine in a third world country might to a peasant appear to be drought, to a relief worker, corruption in government, while to a charity it might be the product of meanness in developed countries.[108]

---

[103] Casper, Benedict and Perry, above n.94.
[104] H Burstztajn and T Gutheil, 'Magical Thinking: Suicide and Malpractice Litigation' (1988) 16 *Bulletin American Academy Psychiatry and Law* 369.
[105] *Yorkshire Dale SS Co Ltd v Minister of War Transport* [1942] AC 691, per Lord Wright 704.
[106] *Wagon Mound* above n.52.
[107] *Hayward* (1908) 21 Cox CC 692.
[108] A Norrie, 'A Critique of Criminal Causation' (1991) 54 *Modern law Review* 684, 690, modifying a scenario proffered in HLA Hart and A Honoré *Causation in the Law* 2nd ed (Oxford, OUP 1985) 37.

Causal agency can only be artificially located in individuals in abstraction from their place in social relations, structure and belief systems, and therefore the work of location must ultimately be carried out by a *fiat* based upon non-individualistic, socio-political criteria.[109]

The moral quality of causation can be seen in the criminal law cases where injured persons have died partly through the neglect of those whose duty it was to treat an injury inflicted by way of a criminal act. Even where the treatment was entirely inappropriate or non-existent, courts are reluctant to hold that medical failure amounts to an intervening cause that would excuse the person who inflicted the original injury. Hence, in order to amount to an intervening cause of death, the treatment would have to be 'so independent of [the defendant's] acts, and in itself so potent in causing death, that [the jury] regard the contribution made by his act as insignificant'.[110]

The same thinking is found in the judgment in *Pagett*,[111] a non-medical case. The defendant, who was armed, attempted to evade arrest by using his pregnant girlfriend, Gail Hitchen, as a shield against police marksmen. When he fired at them, the police responded by returning fire. A police bullet hit Gail, who died. Pagett was convicted of her manslaughter. The jury must have decided that the action of the officers, although negligent, was a foreseeable consequence of Pagett's actions, although he might have assumed that the police would not shoot back. Indeed, the police behaviour broke official guidelines on the use of firearms. However, the fact that responsibility was allotted to him is unsurprising, given that Pagett could have chosen from a number of alternative actions other than firing at the police over Gail's head, and his motives would not have attracted social approval.[112]

In *Empress Car Co v National Rivers Authority*[113] the owners of an oil tank were prosecuted for polluting a river. An unknown person had opened a tap so that diesel oil flowed into the yard and out into the river through a storm drain. Lord Hoffman drew an analogy with a man who forgets to take his car radio out of the car, following which it gets stolen at night. If the thief were on trial, he would be held responsible; if the man has already had several car radios stolen, his wife would say he is responsible. Common sense would say the car owner had a duty to take care and that his carelessness had caused the loss. Consequently, liability depends upon the extent to which there is a duty to take precautions to prevent third parties from causing damage. To the extent that there is a failure to do so where a duty exists, that person has caused the loss. In the instant case, the defendant did have a duty to take precautions against the intervention of others to the

---

[109] *Ibid.*
[110] *Cheshire* [1991] 3 All ER 670.
[111] (1983) 76 Cr. App. R. 279.
[112] Correspondent Inference Theory suggests that these factors will indicate that the cause was Pagett's disposition, rather than the officer's negligence (see chapter one).
[113] [1998] 1 All ER 481.

extent to which that intervention was within the 'general run of things'. If it were unpredictable behaviour, he did not cause the pollution. Here the effects of high consensus and high consistency are clear in the attribution of causation.

Attribution theory, particularly the covariation principle, holds that observers often see relationships between things that are unrelated and infer contingency where none exists. Where there is a frequent co-occurrence of symptom with disease, there is a tendency to assume a relationship between them, ignoring instances where this does not occur.[114] However, a statistical association between events may be insufficient to convince a judge in a 'mass torts' case. For example, it was argued for the plaintiffs in *Reay v British Nuclear Fuels*[115] that, since the occurrence of childhood leukaemia and non-Hodgkin's lymphoma tended, within populations close to nuclear re-processing plants, to be higher than the national average, the defendant's activities at the Sellafield plant in West Cumbria must be causally linked to the illnesses and subsequent deaths of their children. French J examined the epidemiological evidence with great care, but found it inconclusive. It was also substantially contradicted by other evidence. He said that it is not impossible to establish a causal relationship between an industrial operation and an epidemic solely on the basis of statistical evidence, but it is difficult, although the very notion of cause is a probabilistic one. How fact-finders are to distinguish between cases where there is sufficient evidence and cases where there is not is unclear. All empirical evidence is probabilistic.[116] Experience and coincidence may build a body of support sufficient to convince many people that it is more prudent to act as though an association were causal than to assume that it is not. It is common to find the general public being warned by the medical profession that it would be dangerous to ignore the statistical relationship between an activity and a disease. The co-variation principle was applied perfectly rationally in the Shipman case.[117]

Kelley claimed that in the absence of information to support a covariation model, the observer will rely on causal schema based on experience.[118] In *Page v Smith*[119] a minor car accident caused no physical injury to the plaintiff, but allegedly triggered the return of the chronic fatigue syndrome he had suffered from in the past. Symptoms developed within hours of the car accident. Otton J refused to dismiss that as mere coincidence.[120] An ANOVA model would not help here as consensus information was incomplete. Although it is uncommon to

---

[114] HM Jenkins and WC Ward, 'Judgment of Contingency between Responses and Outcomes' (1965) 79 *Psychological Monographs* 1.

[115] (1994) 5 *Medical Law Review* 1.

[116] D Rosenberg, 'The Causal Connection in Mass Exposure Cases: a 'Public Law' Vision of the Tort System' (1984) 97 *Harvard Law Review* 849.

[117] Chapter one.

[118] *Ibid.*

[119] [1995] 2 All ER 736 (HL).

[120] The Court of Appeal considered the return of ME unforeseeable, but the House of Lords took a different view. A person of normal fortitude could have been terrified of the event and the resultant assault on the nervous system could well have caused a post-traumatic neurosis of some kind [1995] 2 All ER 736 at 754 per Lord Ackner.

develop chronic fatigue syndrome following a minor accident, there is little information about the susceptibility of former sufferers to recurrence after accidents. Consistency was relatively high because the plaintiff had suffered from the illness earlier. However, there was little information on distinctiveness, in terms of what, if anything, would trigger a recurrence of the illness in the plaintiff. Against this, the time-scale was very short. The uncertainty allowed a good story to explain a coincidence and provide a cause. Narrative coherence is an important element in the attribution of causality.[121]

Tony Ward argues that psychiatrists, like judges, rely heavily on biographical narratives, assessments of individual credibility and analogical reasoning. In *Vernon v Bosley*[122] Mr Vernon's two daughters drowned before his eyes when the car being driven by their nanny fell into a canal. The plaintiff alleged that this experience resulted in post-traumatic stress disorder, which rendered him incapable of working or being able to look after himself. The defence claimed that much of his condition had pre-dated the accident, and therefore the accident was not its cause. Sedley J constructed a biography of the plaintiff's life in order first, to assess his personality and then to judge the extent to which any or all of his disorder was attributable to the defendant's negligence. In the Court of Appeal Stuart-Smith LJ criticised the judge for making his own diagnosis of the plaintiff's condition, but the other judges thought he was right. It was the judge's story, not the experts' stories, that had to be compared with the body of medical knowledge and the judge, not the expert, had to make the comparison. According to Ward, the narrative nature of causation is not accounted for in attribution theory.[123] An unusual story was presented by the American case, *Palsgraf v Long Island Railway*.[124] Servants of the defendant railway company negligently pushed X, who was attempting to board a moving train. Consequently, he dropped a package containing 'fireworks', leading to an explosion, which caused some weighing scales to fall on to the plaintiff, who was injured. The railway was held not to be liable. Although the defendant was negligent in relation to X, there was nothing to suggest that the package would explode and that therefore the plaintiff would be injured. The harm did occur, and but for the defendant's act it would not have done; to this extent it was a foreseeable, although not a reasonably foreseeable, consequence. The plaintiff's story, that she was injured by a falling weighing machine because someone had been crammed into a train, is not a familiar narrative.

Similarly Fincham and Jaspars doubt[125] that individuals construct their causal attributions in a systematic manner as part of their cognition, and not as part of their cultural system. They suggest also that attribution theory is unhelpful in the legal setting because it is concerned with the perceived relationship between

---

[121] N MacCormick, *Legal Reasoning and Legal Theory* (Oxford, Clarendon Press, 1994); T Ward 'Psychiatric Evidence and Judicial Fact-Finding' (1999) *International Journal of Evidence and Proof* 180.
[122] [1997] 1 All ER 577; *Vernon v Bosley (No 2)* [1997] 1 All ER 614.
[123] T Ward, above n. 121.
[124] 248 NY 339; 16 2 NE 99 (1928).
[125] Fincham and Jaspars, n. 65.

behaviour and an unspecified internal or external cause. Legal inquiry is more narrowly focussed, being concerned with the connection between behaviour and its outcome. This may be a problematic matter if other factors could be identified as causal agents. Devotees of attribution theory have tried to address this problem by investigating the effect on observers of chains of events that present multiple possible causes. Not surprisingly, observers who know there is more than one possible cause are less confident that one in particular was the operating cause.[126] Some experimental work has been carried out on the question whether perceptions of responsibility are affected by the length of the chain of events and/or the amount of time which separates the negligence and the eventual harm.

Johnson and Drobney,[127] for example, devised a study which showed that complex series of events affect perceptions of remoteness. They gave their experimental subjects various sequences of events to consider. In scenario 1A, a businessman leaves a briefcase containing handguns in an airport lounge. A maladjusted individual takes it and uses one of the guns to shoot a taxi driver. In 1B, there is one additional feature, in that a security guard takes the case to the lost property department, where a clerk steals it. The maladjusted individual steals it from him, and then shoots the victim. In 2A, an oil tanker driver falls asleep at the wheel, the tanker overturns and burning oil sets fire to a house, which is destroyed by fire.[128] In 2B, 2A is expanded; ignited petrol floats down the river for a mile, then sets fire to grass along the riverbank, and then the fire spreads to the house. The authors found a causal proximity bias — subjects ascribed responsibility more readily in the short chain scenario. They suggest this is because of the simulation heuristic,[129] for the long chain is more implausible. There was no temporal proximity bias until they mixed the long and short chains with different timescales. Shooting was seen as more likely within several minutes of the theft. In an adaptation of scenario 2, the truck accident was caused by faulty repair work. The repairers were held responsible if the accident occurred a day later, less so if it was weeks after the bad repair job, and subjects were much less sure if the damage occurred a year or five years later, even though they were told that the fault was definitely the cause. It seems that unexpectedly soon is less disconcerting than unexpectedly late. But the effect of the time lag varies from one scenario to another, suggesting that there is a built-in expectation of timescales for particular events. (The judgment in *Page v Smith* suggests that this is the case). A large number of intervening events or longer intervals of time reduced the likelihood of attributions of negligence. They created a large range of possible candidate causes and corresponding uncertainty in the observer.

---

[126] HH Kelley, *Attribution in Social Interaction* (Morristown NJ, General Learning Press, 1971).

[127] JT Johnson and J Drobny, 'Proximity Biases and the Attribution of Civil Liability' (1985) 48 *Journal of Personality and Social Psychology* 283.

[128] Based on *Kuhn v Jewitt*, (1880) 32 NJ Eq 647.

[129] The easier it is for a subject to generate that scenario the more likely it is thought to be: D Kahneman and A Tversky, 'The Simulation Heuristic' in D Kahneman, P Slovic and A Tversky, (eds) *Judgment under Uncertainty* (Cambridge, Cambridge University Press, 1982).

In law, the foreseeability test makes the length of the chain theoretically irrelevant. The issue is whether the interaction of these events is foreseeable. An unforeseeable, abnormal intervening cause that produces an unforeseeable event will relieve the actor of responsibility. In *Kuhn v Jewitt*,[130] the driver of a train which carried petrol cars negligently collided with an obstruction on the line. Cars overturned. Next, the spilled petrol ignited and poured into a river. It was carried downstream for a mile and then set fire to dry grass. The fire spread across the fields and burnt down the plaintiff's house a mile away. He recovered damages. But an almost identical set of facts in a case in Pennsylvania produced the verdict that the damage was 'too remote'.[131] Kelley's[132] discounting principle would explain findings of remoteness of consequence in the 'chain' cases. Observers discount the role of any one antecedent as a cause to the extent that other possible causes are available. Chains of events supply too many plausible alternative causes for the originator of the original event to be held responsible. And although, generally, the negligence of others is foreseeable,[133] some negligent acts will be considered unforeseeable. In *Knightley v Johns*,[134] the sheer number of negligent acts by others rendered the plaintiff's injury too remote. D1's negligent driving had blocked a busy tunnel. After much confusion, D2, a police inspector, took charge but did not immediately close the tunnel as he should have done. He ordered the plaintiff, a constable, to drive back against the traffic to close the tunnel. The plaintiff was then struck and injured by D3, who was driving too fast in the tunnel. The Court of Appeal held that D1 was not liable. While it might be natural, probable and foreseeable that the police would come and there might be risk-taking, and even errors (the police inspector's actions were negligent), there were so many of these before the incident that the subsequent collision was too remote from the defendant's negligence. This decision is puzzling; if the negligence of one other is foreseeable in the aftermath of the defendant's negligence, why is the negligence of several people not foreseeable? Each mistake on its own would have been. The decision appears to be affected by the length of the chain of events, which produced an unfamiliar narrative.

In *Wright v Lodge*,[135] D1's car broke down in fog on an unlit carriageway. She negligently failed to remove it at once, and tried instead to start it. A lorry, driving recklessly at speed, crashed into her car, injuring her passenger, P1. The force of the crash threw the lorry on to the opposite carriageway, where it collided with an oncoming car carrying P2 and P3, who were injured. It was held that D1 was ten per cent contributorily negligent as far as P1 was concerned. It was within her reasonable contemplation that leaving the car on the road might cause a collision

[130] Above, n. 128.
[131] *Hoag v Lake Shore and Michigan SR Co* (1877) 85 Pa 293.
[132] HH Kelley, 'Attribution in Social Interaction' in EE Jones, DE Kanouse, HH Kelley, RE Nisbett, S Valins and B Weiner, (eds) *Attribution: Perceiving the causes of Behavior* (Morisstown NJ, General Learning Press, 1972).
[133] *Rouse v Squires* [1973] QB 889.
[134] [1982] 1 WLR 349.
[135] [1993] 4 All ER 299.

resulting in injury to her own passenger. However, it was not within her reasonable contemplation that in those conditions another person would drive so fast that the collision would cause injury to people on the other side of the road. Hence, she bore no liability to P2 and P3. The lorry driver was a hundred per cent liable to them, because it was well within his contemplation that driving at that speed could cause injury to oncoming traffic should he hit an obstacle. By this time, P1's car had ceased to be an operating cause of the accident (although it should not have been there!). Although his brethren did not agree that a distinction between negligent third party action and reckless third party action was crucial, Parker LJ based his decision on the recklessness of D1, the lorry driver. P1 should foresee negligence by others, but not reckless conduct by others. In *Hines v Morrow*,[136] the defendant had failed to keep a crossing in repair. A truck got stuck in a mud hole on the crossing, and the plaintiff helped the driver to pull it out. The plaintiff had a wooden leg, which then became stuck in the hole. He took hold of a rope attached to the truck, hoping to be himself pulled out of the mud as the truck moved off. Unfortunately, the rope caught round his other leg and snapped as the truck drove forward. He sought damages for the injury to this leg. It was held that although the outcome was bizarre, and not at all foreseeable, it was not unlikely that people would be injured having become stuck in the mud. Not everyone crossing would be able-bodied, and some, encountering difficulty, would do unwise things.

Brickman attempted to measure attributions of causation in long chains of events. In the chains he mixed internal and external causes. His subjects were presented with counterfeit insurers' reports of car accidents. He found differences in the relative impact of immediate and prior causes in chains consisting entirely of internal causes as opposed to chains consisting entirely of external causes. He concluded that longer chains probably increase external attributions as the length of the chain itself enhances the perception of causality as complex and difficult to specify.[137] Unfortunately, the study failed to make clear distinctions between internal and external causes. Also, some of the scenarios give the impression that where there is a prior internal cause and an immediate external cause, the external cause is itself a result of the preceding act of the perpetrator, for example, the car in front swerves (immediate external) because the insured's headlamps blinded the driver (prior internal).[138] Classification of causes as internal or external is, in any event, far from straightforward. For instance, the Court of Appeal was presented with a highly problematic case when a saga of litigation followed a car accident caused by the negligence of the defendant, McCreamer.[139] Serious head

---

[136] (1921) 326 SAW 183 (Texas Civil Appeals).

[137] P Brickman, K Ryan and CB Wortman, 'Causal Chains: Attribution of Responsiblity as a Function of Immediate and Prior Cause' (1975) 32 *Journal of Personality and Social Psychology* 1060. Internal causes included the driver failing to look out, or falling asleep. External causes included steering failure or a tyre burst; this might have a prior internal cause, such as the driver's failure to keep his car maintained. Equally, internal causes might have prior external explanations.

[138] Fincham and Jaspars, n. 65.

[139] *Meah v McCreamer* [1985] 1 All ER 367; *W v Meah* [1986] 1 All ER 935; *Meah v McCreamer* [1986] 1 All ER 943.

injuries were sustained by Meah, who suffered a personality change which apparently prompted him to commit crimes, including rape. He was duly sentenced to life imprisonment. He then sued the defendant in relation to the accident. He argued that he should be compensated, amongst other things, for being imprisoned. He was successful in this, and was awarded substantial damages. Subsequently, two of the victims of his sexual assaults sued Meah. Each recovered damages from him. He then sued McCreamer again, arguing that his tortious liability to his victims arose from the accident, so he should be compensated in respect of the damages he had been required to pay the two victims. The Court of Appeal held that Meah's liability to them was too remote a consequence of the defendant's negligence.[140] Yet it is difficult to see why civil liability arising from assaults effectively caused by McCreamer's negligence was not attributable to it in the same way as his liability to criminal punishment had been. The length of the chain of events seems to have played a crucial role in the decision.

Brickman's research suggests that external causes gain prominence where uncertainty is attached to complicated chains of events, but that effect is not discernible in the Meah cases. Where the chain was longest, the court appeared to dismiss the external cause, the accident caused by the defendant. But this litigation demonstrates that internal and external causes are so closely and interactively related that they are impossible to separate. This may be seen also in *Barnett v Enfield LBC*.[141] The plaintiff had been in the care of the defendant authority. He argued that negligent decisions made in relation to his placements had disrupted his upbringing, which had affected his self-esteem and caused behavioural problems, including alcoholism. His consequential loss included his reduced employability. The Court of Appeal held that it would be impossible for the plaintiff to establish that the defendant's negligence caused or contributed to his condition. The House of Lords disagreed; although proving causation would be difficult, he should at least be allowed to call expert testimony on the question whether the negligent management of his care had been the significant causal determinant of his current psychological difficulties. The internal/external cause dichotomy seems unable to provide a useful explanation of these judgments, which may be better understood in the light of social policy. Social setting is clearly a crucial factor in the attribution of responsibility. An interpretative social psychology might be more suited to the analysis of judgments on causation than attribution theory.[142]

Third Party Intervention

We have seen that negligence law becomes confused where chains of causation involve acts by third parties. Reckless or wilful acts by others normally are

---

[140] There were public policy issues also.
[141] [1999] 3 All ER 193.
[142] GR Semin and ASR Manstead, *The Accountability of Conduct* (London, Academic Press, 1984); RL Wiener and MA Small, 'Social Cognition and Tort Law' in DK Kagehiro and WS Laufer, *Handbook of Law and Psychology* (New York, Springer-Verlag, 1992).

regarded as external causes if they amount to the introduction of abnormal conditions.[143] In *Lamb v Camden London Borough Council*,[144] the plaintiff's tenants had to abandon the house because squatters had moved in and damaged the premises. The council were held not to be liable, although squatting was a well-known consequence of their failure to provide housing in the area. The reasoning is far from clear; Watkins LJ's judgment cites his intuition, which tells him the damage is too remote. Denning LJ appeals to policy, adding that the plaintiff's insurers could pay. Fincham and Schultz[145] have attempted to measure how responsibility is allocated where a small initial harm is exacerbated by an intervening cause. They found that judgment of responsibility is mitigated when the third party intervention was entirely voluntary, and where it was unforeseeable. Unfortunately, the design of the research is clumsy, and has been said[146] to guarantee the result. However, the conflict between two cases on the foreseeability of damage arising from the activities of children might be reconcilable on that basis. In *Henningsen v Markowitz*,[147] the defendant broke the law by selling a boy of thirteen an air rifle and ammunition. The boy's mother told him to return it. He would not, so she took it and hid it. Six months later the boy found it and allowed a playmate to use it. He shot and accidentally wounded the plaintiff, who lost the sight of an eye. It was held that the chain of causation was not broken, although the mother's precautions appear inadequate. There was a break in the chain, however, in *Pittsburgh Reduction Co v Horton*,[148] where a parent allowed a child to play with a gun obtained from the defendant. Again, a voluntary act (here the parent's), which was unforeseeable, broke the chain of causation, whereas a foreseeable negligent one did not.

Although the law says that naughtiness and curiosity in children is always predictable,[149] anticipating destructive behaviour from adults is far from straightforward. In some cases it is the defendant's failure to have made that prediction that forms the substance of the claim. In *Tarasoff v Regents of the University of California*,[150] a male student was obsessed by a young woman fellow student. He confided in a University counsellor. Later, he killed the object of his obsession. The California Supreme Court, in a decision later followed elsewhere,[151] held that therapists had a duty to use reasonable care to protect third parties from the danger, which might be posed by a patient. The University reached a settlement with the victim's parents, so it is not clear whether the therapist would have been found negligent;

---

[143] *Wright v Lodge* [1993] 4 All ER 299.
[144] [1981] 2 All ER 408.
[145] FD Fincham and TR Schultz, 'Intervening Causation and the Mitigation of Responsibility for Harm' (1981) 20 *British Journal of Social Psychology* 120.
[146] J Shotter, 'Are Fincham and Schultz's Findings Empirical Findings? A Critical Note' (1981) 20 *British Journal of Social Psychology* 121.
[147] (1928) 132 Misc. 547 230 NYS.
[148] (1928) 113 SAW 647.
[149] *Hughes v Lord Advocate* [1963] AC 837.
[150] 551 P 2d 334; 131 Calif. Rpts 14 9 (1976); *No 1* 529 p 2d 553; 118 Calif Rpts 129 (1974).
[151] PC Cartensen, 'The Evolving Duty of Mental Health Professionals to Third Parties; a Doctrinal and Institutional Examination' (1992) 17 *International Journal of Law and Psychiatry* 1.

the patient had not been violent in the past. But without a reliable predictor of dangerousness, how may negligence be judged? In every case where the issue arises there is a clear risk of a hindsight effect. In *Clunis v Camden and Islington Health Authority,*[152] the plaintiff had a history of mental disorder. He was discharged from hospital and failed to keep appointments with a psychiatrist. He then stabbed a complete stranger to death. He was convicted of manslaughter, and sued the care authority on the ground that they should have taken action. The plaintiff argued that they should have known he was dangerous, since the police had informed them that he had been seen brandishing a screwdriver and talking about devils. In contrast to *Meah v McCreamer,*[153] the case was dismissed partly on the ground of that Clunis should not profit from wrong-doing.[154] But the plaintiff's reasoning was also strongly suggestive of the influence of the representativeness heuristic. It assumed that evidence of mental disorder *per se* amounted to an indicator of risk. This is to ignore the base-rate information of the number of those who suffer from mental illness who do not kill or injure people. The European Court similarly recognised the dangers posed by hindsight and the representativeness heuristic in *Osman v UK.*[155] L, a schoolteacher, became obsessed with a male pupil aged fourteen. He sent him presents, stalked him, changed his name to his, drove a van at one of his friends, daubed offensive graffiti about him near the school and vandalised his home. The police sought to arrest L for criminal damage but lost track of him. Three months later he broke into the Osman home, and shot both the boy and his father, who died. It was held that it could not be said at any stage in this sequence of events that the police knew or ought to have known that the lives of Osman and his family were at risk.

---

[152] [1998] 3 All ER 180.
[153] n.139.
[154] *Ex turpae causa non oritur actio* (no remedy for a case founded on wrongdoing).
[155] [1999] Crim LR 82.

3

Criminal Responsibility

T
HE CRIMINAL LAW contains a broad range of legal principles. Since several different degrees of fault are recognised, criminal responsibility falls within several of the various categories identified by Heider.[1] Strict, or absolute liability offences fall within the second level, 'Impersonal Causation'. Crimes of negligence are few, so comparatively little use is made in the criminal court of Heider's third level, 'Forseeability'.[2] The most serious crime in this category is manslaughter (where death is caused through gross negligence). However, all drivers are aware of offences concerning negligent driving; driving without due care and attention,[3] dangerous driving[4] and causing death by dangerous driving.[5] Some crimes involve negligence in respect of only one particular. For example, defendants accused of the possession of a controlled drug might wish to raise as a defence that they believed on reasonable grounds that the substance was not a controlled drug.[6] Offences which require proof of recklessness as a mental element are difficult to place within Heider's categories, since it is not clear whether recklessness is an extreme form of negligence, or is a subjective mental state where the accused must have actual foresight.[7] A subjective state of awareness belongs in Heider's fourth level, 'Personal Causation'. This category includes the most serious criminal offences. Moral fault is normally required because the criminal law operates in general within a framework of moral blame. The clearest manifestation of moral fault is where an action not only caused harm, but also was intended to do so. The criminal law defines crimes on the basis of a simple model of human behaviour in which people perceive facts clearly, and calculate the consequences of their actions. The definitions employed:

> have no understanding of personality, no reference to conscious motive or unconscious motivation; they allow no discount to the disadvantaged; they apply without discrimination to sudden anger or unforeseen temptation as to cold revenge or calculated profit.[8]

---

[1] Chapter one.
[2] Dominant in the law of torts: see chapter two.
[3] Road Traffic Act 1988 s. 3.
[4] *Ibid.*, s. 2.
[5] *Ibid.*, s. 1.
[6] Misuse of Drugs Act 1971 s. 28.
[7] See below.
[8] EJ Griew, *Dishonesty and the Jury: an Inaugural Lecture* (Leicester University Press, 1974) 11. Griew acknowledges that these issues have relevance at the sentencing stage.

The determinist insistence on willed consequences, the 'guilty mind', is not the only instance of moral principle defining criminal responsibility. Even matters of causation are as much a matter of moral principle as of science. Certain defences which negate or reduce criminal responsibility also largely depend upon an assessment of moral fault. But here, as we shall see, the legal system may prefer to describe these defences in scientific terms. Scientists are routinely called as witnesses into court and expected there to utilise and explain concepts which began within their own discipline but have been adapted to legal ends and may have become unrecognisable. In order to achieve its purposes, the law is willing to distort and manipulate scientific principles. Experts and fact-finders alike are expected to collaborate in this endeavour.

REQUIREMENT OF AN ACT (ACTUS REUS)[9]

In *Hill v Baxter*[10] it was uncontested that the defendant's car had passed through traffic lights showing red. He claimed to remember nothing of the incident, and suggested that he had been rendered temporarily unconscious by an unspecified illness. It was held on appeal that had he indeed been unconscious, through no fault of his own, he would have a defence.[11] The crime was one of absolute liability, in that no mental element of foresight was required, and no degree of negligence need be proved. But the prosecution would be unable to prove that the defendant performed the prohibited act if the defendant was not in fact *driving* the moving car. In law, acts involve an element of volition. Any bodily movement which is directed by a conscious brain is voluntary action:

> A criminal walking to execution is under compulsion if any man can be said to be so, but his motions are just as much voluntary actions as if he were to leave his place of confinement and regain his liberty.[12]

A complete absence of consciousness, so that the defendant's movements do not have the quality of action, gives rise to the defence of automatism. So also do those of a person who is conscious whilst unable to control movement, as when a man is in the kitchen carving meat, but is knocked sideways by his child, falls, and injures his wife with the knife.[13] Judges have made the same claim for ordinary sleepwalking[14] or small movements while completely asleep.[15] In fact relative ignorance about both the nature of sleep and the nature of movement from a

---

[9] In law, *actus reus* is broader in meaning than 'act'. It may include an act, circumstances and consequences. Indeed, the existence of a mere state of affairs may amount to an *actus reus*: *Larsonneur* (1933) 24 Cr. App. R. 74.
[10] [1958] 1 QB 277.
[11] A self-induced state of automatism is no defence: *Majewski* [1977] AC 443.
[12] JF Stephen, *History of the Criminal Law of England*, Vol II (London, Macmillan, 1883) 101–2.
[13] M Hale, *Pleas of the Crown* (London, Tonson, 1716) Vol 1 434.
[14] *Bratty* [1963] AC 386.
[15] *Boshears* (1961) *The Times* 18 February.

physiological point of view means that it is not possible to judge whether a sleeper acts purposefully.[16]

The legal dichotomy between purposeful and non-purposeful movement is simplistic. A great deal of human behaviour is not readily classifiable as willed movement or action. Most car drivers will freely admit to not thinking about their physical movements, and even to not consciously recognising the layout of the road. Some psychologists argue that, in this situation, what is willed is the 'driving', not necessarily its constituent elements of changing gear or moving the steering wheel. Changing gear whilst driving is almost a reflex action. 'Volition' therefore seems to be a blanket term for the processes of initiating, guiding and controlling movement.[17] Taylor argues that there is a distinction between active consciousness (in the frontal lobe of the brain), and passive consciousness, which takes in sensory information, (in the posterior area).[18] Hence visual awareness may be dissociated with action, and a driver may observe himself to be driving past a building without actively recording the fact, in a 'trancelike or contentless state'.[19] Hence, someone who is conscious may be unaware. Script theory in psychology also suggests that actors can perform routine tasks automatically, leaving them the cognitive capacity to focus on new and unfamiliar stimuli.[20] A script is initially a vignette, preserving prior experiences in an organised way.[21] It may consist of a sequence of actions and perceptions at different levels of detail. These form units of information for encoding efficient movement in the environment. A car script specifies how the sequence of activities for driving a car is carried out. The actions necessary to drive a car have to be learnt through practice, in the first instance, with full attentional control, but ultimately they become automatic.[22] Looking for intention in the various actions, which comprise the activity of driving, is probably unrealistic. Certainly, devising experiments to demonstrate at what point and to what extent subjects form an intention to perform an action is problematic. Libet's work has been criticised partly on the ground that he depended upon subjects to report at what stage they became aware of intention. Arguably, awareness of having an intention is not the same thing as intending the action.[23]

---

[16] P Fenwick, 'Automatism, Medicine and the Law'; (1990) 17 *Psychological Medicine, Monograph Supplement*, 13.

[17] A Gauld and J Shotter, *Human Action and its Psychological Investigation* (London, Routledge & Kegan Paul, 1977).

[18] JG Taylor, *The Race for Consciousness* (Cambridge, Mass, MIT Press, 1999) 211.

[19] *Ibid.*, 267.

[20] B Ashworth and Y Fried, 'The Mindlessness of Organizational Behaviors' (1988) 41 *Human Relations* 305.

[21] R Abelson, 'Script Processing in Attitude Formation and Decision-Making' (1976) 33 *Cognition and Social Behavior*, 33.

[22] Taylor, above n.18, 210.

[23] B Libet, 'Unconscious Cerebral Intitiative and the Role of Conscious Will in Voluntary Action' (1985) 8 *Behavioral and Brain Sciences* 529; Replies, *ibid.*, 539–66; cf RE Hoffman and RE Kravitz, 'Feedforward Action Regulation and the Experience of Will' (1987) 10 *Behavioral and Brain Sciences* 782; B Libet, 'Response' *ibid.*, 783. It has been argued that since the criminal law's sharp dichotomy between consiousness and unconsciousness does not reflect the 'more or less' nature of real consciousness,

It may be that because we are capable of conscious action we are excessively inclined to assume all action is conscious. There has been concerted action by psychologists to dispel notions of an intelligent agent lurking somewhere in the brain directing all that we do, but lawyers appear not to have noticed. Despite a wealth of evidence to the contrary, the law assumes the existence of a controlling 'executive computer system', [24] or seat of consciousness, to reinforce the dichotomy between controlled and automatic actions. In reality, it is difficult to ascertain to what extent people are aware of their actions. If by accident I put my hand into boiling water and immediately snatch it away to avoid scalding, at what level am I aware of my actions, and in control of my arm movements? It has been noted above that some mundane learned behaviour is 'automatic' in the sense that we are not aware that we willed it at all. We have all experienced the confusion that arises where an 'automatic' programme of this kind is interrupted (why have I gone upstairs?) or when we initiate the familiar pattern of movements in the wrong context (driving in the wrong direction because it is our normal route to work). Most thought processes are unconscious in the sense that the actor is unaware of them. Psychology has identified failures of the will which arise where the intention was to carry out a moderately routine series of actions, but instead, a different, even more habitual series of actions inappropriate to the occasion is performed, such as putting on a pair of pyjamas when supposed to be dressing to go out, or putting lettuce on the back doorstep and the milk-bottle in the rabbit hutch.[25]

Nevertheless, observers are reluctant to believe that a person who is not medically unconscious is unaware of his or her actions. Gauld and Shotter argue that ascertaining the volitional element is done by 'inference by analogy' — how our own behaviour has been linked with a particular intention in the past. We interpret behaviour as action unless we have a reason not to do so. There is an assumption that others 'are conscious, purposeful and rational agents' not as a matter of a series of inferences, but as the basis of our interaction with others from infancy.[26] This may explain the reaction of the Court of Appeal in a case[27] where a lorry driver veered on to hard shoulder and crashed into parked vehicles, killing two people. The prosecution alleged that he had fallen asleep. His defence was automatism. Professor Brown gave expert evidence of a condition he called 'driving without awareness'. The theory is that repetitive visual stimuli experienced on long straight and featureless motorways can induce a trance-like state; the driver's focus moves closer to just beyond the windscreen, so attention to the road ahead diminishes. Although the driver is physically in control, the steering and so forth

a category of 'semi-voluntary' acts should be created: DW Denno, 'Crime and consciousness: Science and Involuntary Acts' (2002) 87 *Minnesota Law Review* 269.

[24] S Monsell and J Driver, 'Banishing the Control Homunculus' in S Monsell and J Driver, (eds) *Control of Cognitive Processes: Attention and Performance, XVIII* (Cambridge, Mass, MIT Press, 2000).
[25] S Monsell, 'Control of Mental Processes' in V Bruce, (ed) *Unsolved Mysteries of the Mind: Tutorial Essays in Cognition* (Erlbaum Hove, Sussex, Taylor and Francis, 1996) 109.
[26] Gauld and Shotter, above n.17, 166.
[27] *Attorney-General's Reference (no 2 of 1992)* [1993] 4 All ER 684; Taylor LCJ at 689.

is done at subconscious level. The Court of Appeal upheld the view of the trial judge, that there was insufficient evidence of automatism even to put to the jury. The defence requires the total destruction of voluntary control; impaired, reduced or partial control is not enough. Similarly, in the Australian case, *Ryan v R*,[28] the defendant, who was in the process of carrying out an armed robbery, was startled by the sudden movement of one of the people he was threatening. His gun went off, and the man who had moved was killed. The defendant claimed that he pulled the trigger in a reflex action caused by surprise. Windeyer J rejected the argument that the shooting was involuntary, and said that in any event there was 'moral voluntariness' in creating the situation in the first place.

In order to provide support for a successful claim to automatism, medical evidence must indicate a complete absence of consciousness. In *Charlson*,[29] the defendant had a cerebral tumour which caused blackouts. During one of these he hit his own son, aged ten, on the head with a mallet and then threw him out of the window. He pleaded automatism and was acquitted. The well-known rock guitarist, Peter Buck, also had a sympathetic hearing when accused of assault and criminal damage on a flight to London from Seattle.[30] He produced evidence that he had lost consciousness as a result of taking a mixture of drugs and alcohol. The jury had to decide whether that was indeed the case, but if so, it would afford him a defence only if his condition was not self-induced. The jury acquitted him despite the uncontested evidence that Buck had tried to throttle an aircraft steward, manhandled a female member of the cabin staff, thrown crockery about and annoyed many fellow passengers. The defence claimed that Buck was affected by the unforeseen effects of a sleeping pill he had taken in combination with alcohol supplied during the flight. They argued the effects of the drug made him more willing to accept drinks repeatedly offered to him by airline staff. For such a defence to succeed, it would have to displace a narrative which must have been familiar to the jury; members of the public are persistently regaled with tales of rock stars behaving wildly after drinking and drug-taking sessions. This incident could easily have been perceived as Buck's normal behaviour. However, over the course of a long career in rock music, the defendant had had countless opportunities to behave in this way, and, according to a number of defence witnesses, had not done so, being a quiet and gentle man, devoted to his family. It is possible that the high degree of consistency in Buck's behaviour over many years suggested to the jury that he must have been unconscious during the violent episode. Also, increasing attention in the Press to the disruptive behaviour of airline passengers who, like Buck, are plied with free alcohol despite their increasingly intoxicated condition, creates an impression of high consensus. These factors point to an external cause, the behaviour of the airline. The intervention of an external cause would support the defence claim that Buck's automatism was not self-induced.

---

[28] (1967) 121 CLR 205.
[29] [1955] 1 All ER 859.
[30] *The Times* 6 April 2002.

In general, however, the reluctance of courts to perceive behaviour as involuntary has led them to a restrictive approach even where there is a medical condition. The law's espousal of a Cartesian dichotomy between mind and body demands that there is no middle ground between complete acquittal, where automatism is found to be present, and a finding of guilt where it is not. If an individual causes harm in a state of complete unawareness, induced by an incurable organic disease, the possibility of recurrence makes acquittal an unattractive option. The safest recourse for the courts is to classify such a person as legally insane. A physiological disorder that affects brain function causing lapses in consciousness is treated in law as a 'disease of the mind' within the definition of insanity in the *M'Naghten* Rules. *Kemp*[31] is the case that began this trend. In the opinion of all the expert witnesses, Kemp had been completely unaware of his actions when he struck his wife with a hammer. He suffered from blackouts because the supply of blood to his brain was affected by arteriosclerosis. Kemp pleaded automatism. Devlin J ruled that he was suffering from a disease of the mind, and his defence in effect was one of insanity.

Judicial decisions which followed this case have attempted to develop criteria to distinguish sane from insane automatism. In a curious parallel with attribution theory, the distinction rests on whether the condition arises from external as opposed to internal causes. Hence, where a defendant suffers from diabetes, any blackout caused by hypoglycaemia (overdose of insulin) is external and not insane.[32] If, on the other hand, it arises from hyperglycaemia, (not taking insulin at all so that the inherent condition of high blood sugar level prevails) the cause is internal, and the condition amounts to insanity.[33] In the same way, a defence based on epilepsy is regarded as one of insanity even where the condition has been successfully controlled over many years. This was the case in *Sullivan*,[34] where the court ignored evidence that the defendant's epileptic fit would not have occurred but for a misunderstanding about dosage with the hospital. An external cause was found, however, in *R v T*.[35] The defendant had been raped three days before the alleged offences, which were robbery and assault. The defence was that she suffered from post-traumatic stress disorder, which had led to a dissociative state, so that she committed the offences during a psychogenic fugue. The trial judge treated the case as non-insane automatism and left the defence to the jury.

The theory of defensive attribution could explain the apparent incoherence of the judicial approach to automatism. The need for a controlled world prevails over the moral assumption that someone behaving unconsciously should be excused. The 'somnambulism' cases illustrate the conflict between the determinist

---

[31] [1957] 1 QB 399.
[32] *Quick* [1973] 3 All ER 347.
[33] *Hennessey* [1989] 2 All ER 9.
[34] [1983] 2 All ER 673.
[35] [1990] Crim LR 256.

insistence on volition and the need for an orderly world. In *Burgess*,[36] a young man carried out a violent attack on his female neighbour, who had fallen asleep while they were watching television together. She had made it clear that she did not want to become romantically involved with him. He had not previously exhibited signs of mental illness, and claimed that he, too, had fallen asleep and had been asleep when he attacked her. There was no apparent external cause for his sleepwalking, since the Court of Appeal rejected the possibility that unrequited love could have been an external trigger. It could not be equated with something like concussion. The court therefore assumed the cause was internal, and his condition must be regarded as insanity. A Canadian court had previously reached the opposite conclusion about somnambulism in *Parks*.[37] Parks claimed that he had been asleep when he drove to the home of his mother- and father-in-law and attacked them. He was acquitted of murder and attempted murder. His condition was held to be one of non-insane automatism, although he was said to have had a long history of sleep disorder. The expert evidence was that he posed no threat in the future; there were no documented cases of repeated violent somnambulism. In *Burgess*, the Court of Appeal was unpersuaded by the reasoning in *Parks*. Although sleep is a normal condition, the evidence in this case indicated that sleepwalking, particularly violence in sleep, is not normal.

To describe arteriosclerosis as insanity may seem unwarranted and offensive, but there are other problems with these cases. They are founded on the premise that insanity can afford a defence of automatism. In cases of genuine mental illness, however, this assumption cannot be defended. It is not correct to claim that mental disorder prevents the mind from controlling the body.[38] Neither is it clear in the case of organic conditions, such as epilepsy, that the brain cannot operate independently of the mind.[39] Sleepwalking is particularly problematic in that it may be associated with organic or neurotic factors.[40] Nevertheless, the medical profession appears content to collude with courts on these issues, proba- bly as a matter of pragmatism,[41] and the apparent incoherence of the legal approach appears to cause few problems in practice. Between 1975 and 1979 there were four special verdicts (of insanity) returned on the basis of insane automatism. Three were on account of epilepsy, and one was *Burgess*, the sleepwalking case. However, this low figure may result from many defendants electing to plead guilty to the charge rather than have a special verdict returned against them.[42]

---

[36] [1991] 2 All ER 769.
[37] 95 DLR 47th 27 (1992).
[38] See below.
[39] G Fenton, 'Epilepsy and Automatism' (1972), January, *British Journal of Hospital Medicine* 57.
[40] CH Howard and PT Orbán, 'Violence in Sleep: Medico-Legal Issues and two Case Reports' (1987) 17 *Psychology and Medicine* 915.
[41] Since the Criminal Procedure (Insanity and Unfitness to Plead) Act 1991, defendants will not auto- matically be detained in a mental hospital on a finding of insanity.
[42] RD Mackay, *Mental Condition Defences in the Criminal Law* (Oxford, Clarendon Press, 1995) 66.

REQUIREMENT OF A GUILTY MIND (MENS REA)

The most morally heinous criminal offences are those where the consequences of the defendant's actions were intended or foreseen. 'Guilty mind' implies a model of behaviour that tends to be:

> largely or exclusively cognitive in nature, unitary (in relation to each defined crime) and based on a presumption of free will rather than scientific determinism.[43]

It is generally supposed to be demanded by the theory of individual responsibility. The rhetoric of the law, says Norrie,[44] is couched in universality, that individuals are the same and should be treated the same. Academic criminal lawyers have long advocated the subjectivist standpoint of the responsible individual.[45]

> Legal discourse constructs for itself a standard human subject, endowed with consciousness, reason, foresight, intentionality, an awareness of right and wrong and a knowledge of the law of the land. These are the attributes which provide the ground for legal culpability.[46]

The legal system recognises that behaviour is affected by social and economic circumstances which may reduce individual responsibility, but these are taken into account only in relation to sentencing. Attribution theory may interpret the subjectivist tradition as an application of the bias towards internal causes. The 'guilty mind' requirement identifies an active offender, a causative agent, rather than a passive victim of circumstances or physical power.[47] The outcome was within the individual's consideration, and he or she has did not attach sufficient negative value to it to avoid it. Legal indifference to external factors may be seen in the unenthusiastic reception for the argument propounded by Lady Wootton, that the mental element is important only at the sentencing stage, affecting the likelihood of recidivism. She suggested that it could therefore be omitted from the definition of the crime itself.[48] In contrast, the relationship between responsibility and intention is deeply entrenched in popular thought. Mitchell tested the reactions

[43] N Eastman, 'Psycho-Legal Studies as an Interface Discipline' in J McGuire, T Mason and A O'Kane, (eds) *Behaviour, Crime and Legal Processes* (Chichester, Wiley, 2000) 94.

[44] A Norrie, *Crime, Reason and History* (London, Weidenfeld and Nicolson, 1993) 24.

[45] G Williams, *Criminal Law: the General Part* (London, Stevens, 1961); JC Smith, Note on *Caldwell* [1981] *Criminal Law Review* 393.

[46] H Allen, *Justice Unbalanced: Gender, Psychiatry and Judicial Decisions* (Milton Keynes, Open University Press, 1987) 31.

[47] D Ruimschotel, 'The Psychological Reality of Criminal Acts' in PJ Hessing and G van den Heurel, (eds) *Lawyers on Psychology and Psychologists on Law* (Amsterdam, Swets and Zeitlinger, 1988) 83.

[48] B Wootton, *Crime and the Criminal Law* (London, Stevens, 1963). In reply, Hart argued that it deprived persons of what is most valuable to them and distinguishes them as persons — the autonomy their self-reflective personality creates. HLA Hart, *Punishment and Responsibility* (Oxford, OUP,1968).

of mock jurors to various crime scenarios. The perceived seriousness of the actor's behaviour in causing death was measured in terms of intent.[49]

'Guilty mind' is usually expressed as a requirement that the actor intends the consequences of his or her act, or that the actor is reckless as to whether those consequences follow or not. Defining those terms has proved difficult. In *Moloney*,[50] the House of Lords hazarded a model direction for judges to use to explain intention for the jury:

> First, was death or really serious injury in a murder case (or whatever relevant consequence must be proved to have been intended in any other case) a natural consequence of the defendant's voluntary act? Second, did the defendant foresee that consequence as being a natural consequence of his act? The jury should then be told that if they answer Yes to both questions it is a proper inference for them to draw that he intended that consequence.[51]

In *Hancock and Shankland*[52] the apparent incomprehensibility of this direction to the jury, who asked the judge to explain what it meant only for it to be read out to them again, led to the quashing of the defendants' convictions for murder and the substitution of convictions for manslaughter. The test has subsequently been adapted, so that jurors are now asked to consider whether the outcome was virtually certain, and whether the defendant foresaw it as a 'virtual certainty'.[53] However, if the answer to both questions is in the affirmative, this supplies only evidence from which the jury is *entitled*, but not *obliged*, to infer intention. There are no judicial guidelines to suggest when it would be appropriate not to infer intention where such a high degree of foresight exists. This leaves jurors free to take account of laudable motive, such as attempting to save a life; foresight of a high degree of risk may not amount to evidence of intention to kill in such a case.

In general, motive is irrelevant to intention in law. It creates the risk of acknowledging external causes, forcing the law to recognise the link between social disadvantage and crime.[54] The law of murder regards as equally culpable a person who performs a contract killing for reward and one who carries out the compassionate mercy-killing of an elderly relative.[55] As shall be seen below, science may be required to afford the latter defendant a medically based excuse. Even lawyers, however, are not happy to convict of murder a surgeon who performed a high-risk surgical operation which led to the patient's death, but who did so

---

[49] B Mitchell, 'Further Evidence of the Relationships between Legal and Public Opinion on the Law of Homicide' [2000] *Criminal Law Review* 814.
[50] [1985] 1 All ER 1025.
[51] *Ibid.*, per Lord Bridge at 1039.
[52] [1986] 1 All ER 641.
[53] *Woollin* [1999] 1 AC 82.
[54] Norrie, above n.44, 43.
[55] *Ibid.*

because of a remote possibility that it would save the patient's life.[56] In Mitchell's survey[57] motive did affect perceptions of intention; circumstances had much to do with the allocation of blame. However, participants also took account of pre-meditation, and regarded that as an aggravating factor. The legal definition of intention, which defines the most serious crimes, takes no account of premedita-tion. But Mitchell's subjects extended the concept of premeditation to include a case of drink driving where a pedestrian was killed, on the basis that the driver would have known about the risk when he decided to drink and drive. Fact-finders may be more willing to assume that risks were taken consciously where the out-come is serious.

Recklessness is normally defined in subjective terms as awareness of the risk that the outcome will result from one's act. However, in *Caldwell*[58] the House of Lords applied the ordinary meaning of 'heedlessness' or 'carelessness', so that defendants who were unaware of the possibility of the risk of harm are guilty if their actions create an obvious risk. According to this decision, the jury should be told that the defendant is reckless in a criminal damage case, if 'he does an act which in fact creates an obvious risk that property would be destroyed or dam-aged', if when he does it:

> he either has not given any thought to the possibility of there being any such risk or has recognised that there was some risk involved and nevertheless goes on to do it.[59]

This test resembles that for gross negligence, a plank of one form of involuntary manslaughter.[60] The subjectivist tradition in criminal law made *Caldwell* an unpopular decision.[61] However, their Lordships' view that a person could effectively choose not to know of a risk had some support. Duff argued that utter indiffer-ence to the welfare of others indicates a level of selfishness morally indistinguish-able from appreciating a risk but nevertheless continuing the action.[62] In *Hudson*,[63] the defendant was accused of rape. He alleged that he did not realise that the woman in question suffered from Downs' syndrome. It was held that the jury should consider what effect the young woman's condition, appearance and behaviour at the time would have on someone, and bear in mind that Hudson was not entitled to 'shut his eyes to the obvious'.[64]

---

[56] See Lord Hailsham in *Hyam v DPP* [1974] 2 All RE 41, 55. It is possible that this is the kind of case where a jury could properly decide that although death was virtually certain to follow, and the surgeon was aware of this, nevertheless that the outcome was not intended.
[57] Mitchell, above n.49.
[58] [1981] 1 All ER 961.
[59] *Caldwell* [1981] 1 All ER 961 per Lord Diplock at 967.
[60] *Seymour* [1983] 2 All ER 1058. But see *Prentice et al* [1993] 4 All ER 935.
[61] For example, Smith, n.45. Recklessness in most criminal offences is still defined in terms of subjec-tive awareness of risk, for example in rape: *Satnam* [1985] *Criminal Law Review* 236.
[62] A Duff 'Recklessness' (1980) *Criminal Law Review* 282.
[63] [1966] 1QB 448.
[64] *Ibid.*, Ashworth J at 455.

In crimes where the mental element is a subjective one, the court will take account of the defendant's intellectual limitations. The objective standard employed in *Caldwell* meant that even subnormality, which might suggest a reduced capacity to appreciate risk, does not prevent the defendant from being judged to have been reckless if the risk would have been obvious to the reasonable man.[65] Again, the external factor, even of a medical kind, is discounted. In *Stone v Dobinson*[66] the defendants clearly found coping with everyday life a difficult matter. John Stone was sixty-seven, partially deaf, almost totally blind and had no appreciable sense of smell. Gwendoline Dobson, who lived with him, was 'ineffectual and somewhat inadequate'.[67] Stone's younger sister Fanny came to stay with them. She was 'eccentric in many ways', frequently shutting herself in her room. She often starved herself in order to lose weight. She became unwilling to leave her bed. The defendants initially took food up to her, but stopped. It was held that she became their responsibility once they had begun looking after her, and so when she subsequently died, emaciated and suffering from toxaemia resulting from her filthy conditions, they had effectively caused her death by ceasing care. It was conceded in the Court of Appeal that neither defendant was capable of using the telephone, and that, when on one occasion they walked miles in search of Fanny's doctor, they had gone to the wrong village. Nevertheless, their limited capabilities were held irrelevant to the issue of gross negligence, and they were both held to be guilty of manslaughter. Yet insanity is a defence even to crimes of negligence; the inability to appreciate the nature and quality of one's act appears to extend to its foreseeable consequences.[68] The explanation for this apparent contradiction may lie in the restricted definition of insanity in the law.[69] Only the most extreme of mental disorders falls within it, so that the bias in favour of attributions of internal cause is displaced by the overwhelming nature of the condition.

Drawing the Inference

We have seen that a neat dichotomy between awareness and unawareness is unlikely to exist:

> Even the most reflexive behaviours (withdrawing one's hand from heat, moving one's eyes towards sudden changes in the visual field) are subject to some degree of control from advance intentions. Even the most deliberate behaviours are subject to contamination and interference, which may be subtle in its effects, from sources of information that the person is trying to ignore, or response tendencies the person is trying to suppress. In between there is a complex array of interactions between

---

[65] *Elliott v C* [1983] 2 All ER 1005.
[66] [1977] 2 All ER 341.
[67] *Ibid.*, Geoffrey Lane LJ at 342.
[68] G Williams, *Textbook of Criminal Law* 1st edn (London, Stevens, 1978) 656–7.
[69] See below.

control by goals and intentions and control by learned associations between stimuli/events/contexts and behaviours that are highly practiced as responses to them (habitual) or 'wired in' (like the tendency to orient to novel events/object).[70]

Human control processes are only beginning to be understood. Research into 'task switching' demonstrates that we do not have an absolute capacity for voluntary control over mental processes.[71] Yet criminal trials frequently confront issues arising from lapses of concentration, as with absent-mindedness in cases of alleged shoplifting. Genuine claims of forgetfulness tend to be associated with distracting factors such as children wandering off.[72] In general, lapses of attention in everyday situations are not visited by serious consequences. For example, verbal slips are rarely salacious or seriously embarrassing, possibly because there is a self-protective function being exercised even during the period of reduced attention.[73] Thus, the most common lapses in shops are shoppers forgetting what they came into the shop to buy, or leaving the goods behind after paying for them. An alleged thief's claim that he or she simply forgot to pay suggests a failure in the protective mechanism. Certainly, forgetfulness, rather than dishonesty, may explain why goods found on people who have not paid for them are usually of very small value.

Subjective recklessness and intention are based on the actor foreseeing a degree of risk, and engaging in a calculation of probability. This would involve awareness of the statistical probability (based upon the frequency of real events) balanced against the utilities associated with certain outcomes, known as the 'Subjective Expected Utility'.[74] Research shows that in fact human beings rarely assess risk in conformity with the SEU. Instead, they typically make a variety of errors.[75] Rather than make a rational assessment based on the percentage of similar cases where the negative outcome occurred, they tend to use the availability heuristic, relying on their own experience. Another common error is to make an initial assessment of risk and then fail to revise it in the light of subsequently acquired information. For example:[76] a sailing instructor sets out on the water to give a group a sailing lesson. At that time, the risk of a gale developing is considered to be low. But if a revised weather forecast suggests that gales could occur, the instructor will probably fail to revise his original low estimate as much as he should. Also, if he originally assumed that the emergency services would assist if necessary, he is liable still to think the risk worth taking even if he is told that the lifeboat is out of action. The fact-finders who must decide whether and to what extent the actor perceived

[70] S Monsell, personal communication to the author.
[71] Monsell and Driver, above n.24.
[72] J Reason and D Lucas, 'Absent-Mindedness in Shops: Incidence, Correlates and Consequences' (1984) 23 *British Journal of Clinical Psychology* 121.
[73] *Ibid.*
[74] LJ Savage, *The Foundations of Statistics* (New York, Wiley, 1954).
[75] W Edwards, *Decision-Making* (Harmondsworth, Penguin, 1967).
[76] Example from R Wynn Owens, 'Legal and Psychological Concepts and Mental Status' in R Bull and D Carson *Psychology in Legal Contexts* (Chichester, Wiley, 1995).

the risk will base their judgment upon their own perceptions of frequency of the outcome, which also will be heavily based upon the availability heuristic, and may be affected by defensive attribution. For example, there is a common assumption that accidents are the result of conscious risk-taking. Ninety per cent of subjects in a Swedish study agreed that risk-taking is a major source of accidents,[77] a manifestation of hindsight, according to Wagenaar. He argues that commercial organisations are more likely than individuals to take conscious risks,[78] and that the differences between safe crossing and accident in the Nottingham study of drivers' behaviour[79] resides in the behaviour of the children, not in the risk considerations of drivers. Any gambler believes in the illusion of control over chance events.[80]

If behaviour is stable over time, the observer is more confident in attributing intention. If the actor's behaviour varies in the same way as someone else's, then the behaviour is attributed to the social context rather than intention.[81] Otherwise they will seek information about the actor's disposition. The defendant in *Bills*[82] was charged with wounding with intent contrary to section 18 Offences Against the Person Act 1861. He was convicted under section 20 of the same Act, which does not require intent to wound, as long as the wound is inflicted and the defendant foresaw some, albeit not serious, harm.[83] The verdict suggests that the jury was not convinced that he knew exactly how much harm he would cause. However, as the judge proceeded to sentence, Bills' criminal record for robbery and assault occasioning actual bodily harm was disclosed. One of the jurors told the usher that the foreman had delivered the wrong verdict. On being reconvened, the jury gave a unanimous verdict of guilty under section 18. This conviction was reduced on appeal to one under section 20. Was the jury's reasoning misconceived? They may have thought that the criminal record was relevant to Bills' perception of what he was doing and what the results would be. In the same way, the Theft Act 1968[84] allows evidence of previous convictions for theft and handling stolen goods to be given in evidence on the issue of whether the defendant believed the goods in question to be stolen. The assumption by the legislature is that experience should have taught the defendant something.

Clear applications of the co-variation principle may be seen in 'similar fact' cases such as *Bond*.[85] There, the accused, a medical practitioner, was charged with unlawfully procuring an abortion upon a woman named Jones. His defence was

---

[77] J Houden and TJ Larsson, 'Risk: Culture and Concept' in WT Singleton and J Houden, (eds) *Risks and Decisions* (New York, Wiley, 1987).

[78] WA Wagenaar, 'Risk-taking and accident causation' in JF Yates (ed) *Risk-Taking Behaviour* (Chichester, Wiley, 1992) 257.

[79] CI Howarth, 'The Relationship between Objective Risk, Subjective Risk, and Behaviour' (1988) 31 *Ergonomics* 527; see chapter 2.

[80] E Langer, 'The Psychology of Chance' in J Dowie and P Lefrere, (eds) *Risk and Chance: Selected Readings* (Milton Keynes, Open University Press, 1980).

[81] HH Kelley, *Attribution in Social Interaction* (Morristown NJ, General Learning Press, 1971).

[82] [1995] 2 Cr App R 643.

[83] *R v Mowatt* [1968] 1 QB 421.

[84] S. 27(3).

[85] [1906] 2 KB 389.

that he had not intended to harm the unborn child. In rebuttal, another woman, Taylor, claimed that Bond had performed the same operation on her, and that he had told her that he had 'put dozens of girls right'. Both women had been living at his house at the time and both were pregnant with his child. If someone has been performing similar acts over time with a similar outcome, the outcome will be taken to have been intended rather than accidental. An example is *Mood Music v De Wolfe*;[86] the defendants admitted publishing a melody bearing a marked resemblance to a song already published by the plaintiffs, but argued that the similarity was coincidental and not intentional. The fact that they had three times in the past published songs virtually the same as those published previously by another company was admissible to show that they had deliberately copied the plaintiff's song. In an extreme case, 'similar facts' evidence will establish not only the act and the intention, but will also rebut any defence (barring insanity) that the defendant might seek to raise. In *Smith*,[87] the 'Brides in the Bath' murder, the only evidence implicating the defendant in the murder of a woman who was found apparently drowned in her bath, was a series of coincidences. Smith had gone through a form of marriage with her, and was found to have done the same with two other women who, in the same way, had been found dead in their baths afterwards. In all three cases he had been present in the building at the time of the death. In all three, he stood to gain financially. In all three, having discovered his 'wife' under the water in her bath, he had made no effort to pull her out before calling a doctor. This evidence, although indirect, gave rise to a strong inference of deliberate killing by Smith. An identifiable pattern was the sole basis in the Australian case, *Makin v A-G for New South Wales*,[88] for the finding that the two defendants, a married couple, were guilty of murder. They were accused of the deliberate killing of a baby. The child's body had been discovered buried in the yard of their house. Three other dead babies had been buried at the same place. The bodies of seven other babies were discovered at the defendants' previous home, and two dead babies were found buried at the place they occupied before that. It transpired that a number of mothers had given the couple money to take babies off their hands. The coincidences of circumstance afforded a conclusive case of a system of deliberate baby–killing by the Makins.

In more mundane cases, there is little evidence to indicate what was in the defendant's mind at the time the harm was caused. The use of weapons makes the inference of foresight much stronger; how could someone who uses a weapon *not* anticipate causing serious harm? In the absence of a weapon, it is difficult to establish that the defendant intended really serious harm. Although juries are reluctant to convict of manslaughter in cases of vehicular homicide, it seems that they will convict of murder if there is evidence that the defendant used the vehicle as a weapon. They might infer intention, for example, if the car mounted the

[86] [1976] 1 All E.R. 463.
[87] (1915) 11 Cr App R 229.
[88] [1894] AC 57.

pavement, or where there was evidence that the defendant knew, and had quarrelled with, the victim.[89] It has been said that the importance of weapon use to findings of intention disadvantages women defendants in murder cases. A woman's relative lack of physical strength means that she is more likely than a man to use weapons to defend herself. In most cases of spousal homicide, men use body force, particularly strangulation, whereas ninety per cent of female killers use weapons. Hence women are more likely to be found guilty of murder than men.[90] Evidence of this may be seen in the cases of *Thornton*[91] and *Ahluwalia*,[92] both of whom unsuccessfully ran the defences of involuntary manslaughter (denying foresight of the risk of death or serious harm). Thornton used a knife, and Ahluwalia petrol and a lighted taper while her husband slept. Are juries right to assume that these methods of inflicting harm suggest intention whereas manual strangulation does not? As Edwards points out,[93] there is a thin line between a strangulation that appears deliberate and where the effect of vagal inhibition[94] allows the defendant to argue that the outcome was unforeseen. Both Thornton and Ahluwalia lived with persistently violent partners, yet jurors regarded their behaviour as deliberate. Their circumstances did not, apparently, affect their ability to perceive and assess risk. The bias in favour of internal attributions prevailed.

Rage and Provocation

In *Parker*,[95] the defendant had fallen asleep on a train and gone past his station. Alighting further down the line at about one o'clock in the morning, he attempted to make a telephone call and encountered a series of difficulties. Eventually he found a telephone. However, he discovered that it was not working. In exasperation he repeatedly crashed the handset down upon the dialling unit with considerable force. Broken pieces of the equipment lay around the floor. He claimed that he was not aware that he was damaging the telephone: 'I was simply reacting to the frustration which I felt.' The Court of Appeal held that Parker was fully aware that the telephone was made of Bakelite 'or some such material' and of the degree of force he was using, and that therefore he either knew of the risk that he would damage it, of if he did not, he was 'wilfully blind', in the sense of closing his mind to the obvious. This state of mind was equivalent to knowledge: 'a man certainly cannot escape the consequences of his action in this particular set of circumstances

---

[89] S Cunningham, 'The Reality of Vehicular Homicides; Convictions for Murder, Manslaughter and Causing Death by Dangerous Driving [2001] *Criminal Law Review* 679.
[90] SSM Edwards, 'Ascribing Intention; the Neglected Role of Modus Operandi — Implications for Gender' [1999/2000] *Contemporary Issues in Law* 235.
[91] [1996] 2 All ER 1023.
[92] [1992] 4 All ER 859.
[93] Edwards, above n.90.
[94] The heart stops and causes asphyxia.
[95] [1977] 2 All ER 37.

by saying "I never addressed my mind to the obvious consequence because I was in a self-induced state of temper".[96] It was stated that wilful blindness involves intentionally choosing not to ask because there is no real doubt what the answer will be,[97] or deliberately shutting one's eyes to the obvious.[98] In *Woollin*,[99] the defendant lost patience with his three-month-old son and threw him on to a hard surface. The child sustained a fractured skull and died. Woollin denied that he desired to kill or injure his son. He was tried for murder. The jury was asked whether Woollin must have realised or appreciated when he threw the child that there was a substantial risk that he would cause him serious injury. He was convicted of murder,[100] which suggests that the jury believed that he knew, despite his loss of temper, what the consequences of his action could be. Courts appear to hold that a person is aware of probable risks despite the effects of rage or frustration. There are sound pragmatic reasons for this view. Most murders and non-fatal offences of violence occur during quarrels and fights. Few killings are premeditated or for gain, taking place instead in circumstances redolent of sudden impulse, or 'hot blood'. Half the intentional killings of adult males occur in a rage or quarrel, and another fourteen per cent are motivated by jealousy or revenge.[101]

The defence of provocation is limited to murder cases, reducing the conviction to one for manslaughter,[102] not because in rage one has no *mens rea*,[103] but out of 'compassion for human infirmity'.[104] The defence depends upon a loss of control in response to provocative words or actions. In addition, the scale of the reaction, killing, must be proportionate to the provocation, a requirement that sits oddly with the insistence on a loss of control. The 'reasonable retaliation' rule also takes no account of physical changes induced by stress. Physiological research suggests that there is a 'fight or flight' reaction;[105] bodily changes include a faster pulse rate and higher blood pressure. Blood glucose levels are also increased. Breathing is faster, and the muscles of the limbs are tensed.[106] The physical reaction is not necessarily proportionate to the precipitating anger or fear.[107] Emotions may affect motor activity such as heart rate. They may not replace consciousness, but do colour it, transmitting signals at both conscious and unconscious levels.[108] At present, science cannot tell us to what extent, if at all, these reactions can be controlled. Yet to lawyers, there is no middle ground between icy detachment and

---

[96] *Ibid.*, Geoffry Lane LJ at 40.

[97] Simester and Sullivan, *Criminal Law: Theory and Doctrine*, (Oxford, Hart Publishing) 137.

[98] *Westminster City Council v Croyalgrange Ltd* [1980] 2 All ER 353.

[99] [1999] 1 AC 82.

[100] Reduced to manslaughter on appeal because of misdirection by the trial judge.

[101] E Gibson, *Homicide in England and Wales 1967-71*, Home Office Research Study 31 (HMSO, London, 1975).

[102] Homicide Act 1957.

[103] *Perera* [1953] AC 200; *Lee Chun Chen* [1963] 1 All ER 73.

[104] *Hayward* (1833) 6 C & P 157, Tindal CJ at 158.

[105] A Storr, *Human Aggression*, (London, Allen Lane, 1968).

[106] WB Cannon, *Bodily Changes in Pain, Hunger, Fear and Rage*, (New York, D Appleton, 1915).

[107] P Brett, 'The Physiology of Provocation' [1970] *Criminal Law Review* 634.

[108] Taylor, above n.18.

being completely out of control. Judges tend to equate any time lapse between the act of provocation and the killing with a recovery of self-control, rendering the defence unavailable.[109] But, in psychology, there is no reason why someone should not lose control after the event.[110]

The unfortunate Mr Parker who saw red when he found himself marooned miles from home in the middle of the night with all available telephones out of action could not have pleaded provocation. The case was not one of homicide, and no human action had provoked him. He said that he was so angry that he did not realise that the telephone would be damaged. If the jury had believed that he was unaware of the likelihood of damage he would have been acquitted; in fact he was convicted and lost his appeal. The verdict cannot be criticised on scientific grounds, since whether or not rage negates consciousness is unclear. Accounts of brain activity necessarily omit any explanation of 'naked emotional consciousness'; 'the classic philosophers always separated will, intellect, and emotion, but we cannot so easily separate them in the brain'.[111] Neither psychology nor psychiatry claim to know whether those who are 'beside themselves' with rage are aware of their actions. We do know, however, a little about learned responses. Mental processes may be driven as much by salient stimuli, such as past associations, as by intention. Where a prepotent response tendency has to be overcome, we need further input to prevent the trigger from operating.[112] The question is whether a combination of stimulus and learned response could negate awareness.

> In the case of skills like boxing (or being a commando), the aim of training is to make reactions as rapid and automatic as possible[113] when the 'task-set' of boxing or combat is engaged. Intuitively we feel that a person voluntarily elects to engage that task-set, so training him to box does not make him more likely to go round hitting people in an 'automatic' way, or excuse him if he does so.[114]

The defence of provocation depends upon the judgment that the Reasonable Man would have responded in the same way as the defendant. Yet, clearly, 'to say that the ordinary man kills for adultery is a grotesque untruth'.[115] Although no longer the most common basis of divorce proceedings in the United Kingdom, adultery is relied on in a large number of petitions, particularly in England and Wales.[116] Hence again, it seems, the Reasonable Man is not the Average Man; in this context[117] his behaviour is rather worse than that of the average person. He bears

---

[109] But see battered wife syndrome, below.
[110] Brett, above n.107.
[111] Taylor, above n.18.
[112] Monsell and Driver, above n.24.
[113] In the sense of requiring no thought or act-specific intention, as opposed to the generic permissive intention to fight effectively.
[114] S Monsell, personal communication to the author.
[115] Williams, above n.68.
[116] *Divorce: the New Law in Northern Ireland*, (Belfast, Office of Law Enforcement, 2002).
[117] As opposed to that of negligent driving; see chapter two.

no resemblance to the man of phlegm familiar to tort lawyers.[118] His individual characteristics may be taken into account.[119] In *Humphreys*[120] the jury had to decide how a female, attention-seeking hysteric would have responded to the provocation. In other cases, they have been asked to take account of obsessiveness and eccentricity,[121] and the effect of battered woman syndrome.[122] The Judicial Committee of the Privy Council doubted the wisdom of requiring jurors to think themselves into the shoes of someone suffering from such disorders,[123] and to speculate how 'the reasonable manic depressive' or 'the reasonable glue-sniffer' would react to the provocation described in a particular case. However, in *Smith*,[124] the House of Lords reiterated that the jury should take account not only of individual characteristics which affected the gravity of the provocation, but also of those that might have affected the defendant's capacity for self-control. Rather than engage in anthropomorphism, the judge should simply explain the principles of the law of provocation to the jury, and then ask them whether the circumstances, including the defendant's characteristics, but not including a mere violent temper, were such as to reduce the gravity of the offence from murder to manslaughter. They should apply what they considered to be appropriate standards of behaviour, making allowance for human nature and the power of the emotions.

Given that a person with a mental disorder could plead diminished responsibility and reduce the conviction to one for manslaughter by that route,[125] the Byzantine reasoning proposed for provocation cases appear quite unnecessary. However, it is possible that provocation takes account of less serious disorders, possibly at the risk of being too generous to defendants. Stephen Morse's example gives A killing B because he is his rival in love. A is then assessed as a dependent person who has fragile ego integration, provoked into a loss of control. Yet many who suffer that provocation do not kill. Neither do many people with that personality disorder. Suppose it is the case that other people who combine the two also do not kill, then to what extent is A's personality the reason that he did? His defence will probably argue that his stress was greater or his personality more extreme — an explanation that cannot be refuted by evidence.[126] Mullen claims that jealousy is increasingly perceived as psyco-pathological even in cases which concern ordinary, not morbid jealousy.[127] In reality, he argues, acts of

---

[118] See chapter two.
[119] *Thornton (No 2)* [1996] 2 All ER 1023.
[120] [1995] 4 All ER 1008.
[121] *Dryden* [1995] 4 All ER 987.
[122] *Thornton (No 2)* [1996] 2 All ER 1023.
[123] *Luc Thiet Thuan v R* [1996] 2 All ER 1033.
[124] [2000] 4 All ER 289.
[125] Homicide Act 1957 s. 2, below.
[126] SJ Morse, 'Failed Explanations and Criminal Responsibility; Experts and the Unconscious' (1982) 68 *University of Virginia Law Review* 971, 1031.
[127] PE Mullen, 'The Crime of Passion and the Changing Cultural Construction of Jealousy' (1993) 3 *Criminal Behavior and Mental Health* 1.

jealous violence are simple cries of anger. Jealousy is in the main an everyday experience:

> Courts do not require, and should not be provided with, expert testimony from mental health professionals to legitimise how they choose to deal with those in whom it has produced criminal violence.[128]

In the United States, sexual jealousy is responsible for most spousal killing. In most cases it is the husband whose jealousy leads him to kill his wife. A psychobiological explanation of this might be man's struggle to control the reproductive capacity of the woman. Whether lethal or not, violence is quite a successful way of doing this.[129]

Meanwhile, female defendants suffer from judicial hostility to a 'cooling-off' period between the provocation and the killing. A comparative lack of strength means that few women provoked by men are in a position to kill in the heat of the moment.[130] It has been argued that, inevitably, women retaliate some time after the event, probably using a weapon, and so may be unable to plead provocation. Some feminists argue that, to the law, 'male patterns of violence are acceptable but female patterns are not'.[131] Judges have struggled with the notion of the 'slow burn', a rage that builds up until it causes homicidal violence. In *Ahluwalia*,[132] the Court of Appeal was anxious not to blur the distinction between that state and deliberate retribution. Although a slow burn is possible, there must be a sudden loss of control afterwards. Judges have pounced upon battered woman syndrome as a quasi-medical solution to this problem.[133] While some feminists protest that medicalisation of the killing by a woman of her male partner is offensive insofar as it suggests that it is not a rational response to the man's violence, battered woman syndrome has proved a valuable tool in the defence of such women. The syndrome is said to be a subset of post-traumatic stress disorder,[134] and has been used by female defendants in murder cases not only as part of the defence of provocation, but also to establish diminished responsibility. The tendency to medicalise violent behaviour in women is a long-established legal tradition, and is discussed later in this chapter.

MENTAL DISORDER AND CRIMINAL RESPONSIBILITY

To impute insanity depersonalises a crime. From a lay point of view, the mental illness of the perpetrator can provide a satisfactory explanation of a traumatic

---

[128] *Ibid.*, 10.

[129] M Daly and M Wilson, *Homicide* (New York, De Gruyter, 1988).

[130] From *Duffy* [1949] 1 All ER 932, there should be a sudden and temporary loss of self-control.

[131] D Nicolson, 'Truth, Reason and Justice: Epistemolology and Politics in Evidence Discourse' (1994) 57 *Modern Law Review* 726.

[132] [1992] 4 All ER 889.

[133] M Redmayne, *Expert Evidence and Criminal Justice* (Oxford, Oxford University Press, 2001).

[134] AA Stone, 'Post-Traumatic Stress Disorder and the Law: Critical Response to the New Frontier' (1993) 21 *Bulletin of the American Academy of Psychiatry and the Law* 23.

event. Psychiatrists become mediators between the 'human and non-human realm'.[135] To lawyers, mental illness is incompatible with moral responsibility. Experts are required to protect the morally incompetent from the otherwise inevitable punitive response to causing harm. They must demonstrate the lack of the rationality that underpins the 'guilty mind'. For the expert, the problem is that people who are mentally ill do not necessarily lack rationality. The law might do better to treat them in the same way as it does children, who when young are not regarded as moral agents.[136] Psychiatrists are rarely able to testify that an illness excludes awareness, and therefore, if a non-punitive outcome is preferred, must effect a pragmatic compromise with the legal system, and pretend that it does. Their willingness to do so is particularly visible in homicide cases, where the issues of diminished responsibility and infanticide come into play. The explanation for their compliance probably lies in the seriousness of the sanction for murder:

> That doctors routinely testify to matters that are not within their professional competence and that judges accept and act upon that testimony, bears witness to the necessity, while the mandatory sentence for murder exists, of making the diminished responsibility defence work.[137]

Unlike the law, psychiatry sees a medical condition as definitive of the person in all his or her actions,[138] although psychologists might disagree. In psychology, violent behaviour might be separated from the condition, for example, if it has a 'pay-off', as where force is used in order to steal.[139]

Legal Perceptions of Mental Responsibility

A pragmatic approach to diagnosis and recommendation may be observed in the psychiatric response to the pre-trial issue of the defendant's fitness to plead. Since the criminal justice system is founded upon a perception of individual responsibility that depends upon moral competence, it baulks at the prospect of allowing a trial to proceed if the defendant is unable, by reason of disability, to instruct or conduct his own defence. Thus, to be fit to plead, the accused must be of sufficient intellect to comprehend the course of proceedings in the trial so as to make a proper defence, to challenge a juror to whom he might wish to object and to comprehend the details of the evidence.[140] An accused who suffers from delusions

---

[135] R Smith, 'Expertise and Causal Attribution in Deciding between Crime and Mental Disorder' (1985) 15 *Social Studies of Science* 67.
[136] M Moore, 'Causation and Excuses' (1985) 73 *California Law Review* 1091.
[137] S Dell, 'Diminished Responsibility Reconsidered' [1982] *Criminal Law Review* 810, 817.
[138] Norrie, above n.44, 185.
[139] Sometimes violence produces apparently no practical advantage for the perpetrator, and may be seen as a response to stress: RG Owns and JB Ashcroft, *Violence: a Guide for the Caring Professions*, (Beckenham, Croom Helm, 1985).
[140] *Pritchard* (1836) 7 C & P 303.

may yet be fit to be tried. In *Robertson*,[141] a paranoid defendant in a murder trial was thought by the Crown to be unable properly to defend himself. The Court of Appeal held that the 'mere fact that the appellant was not capable of doing things which were in his own best interests' was insufficient ground for a verdict of unfit to plead.[142] The difficulty of measuring the defendant's capacity to comprehend is indicated by evidence that the majority of those defendants found unfit to plead are little different from the majority of mentally disturbed or mentally handicapped defendants who come before the court on a regular basis. Two-thirds of those found unfit to plead had on previous occasions been dealt with by courts in a normal manner, and some went on to be convicted of further offences while still technically unfit to plead on a previous charge.[143] Grubin concludes that the test is a confusing muddle between intellectual ability and mental state. This may explain why, in cases where fitness to plead was raised, only twenty-one out of a hundred and ninety-seven reports studied addressed all the *Pritchard* criteria. Twenty-eight reports declared the defendant unfit without addressing any trial-specific criteria at all.[144]

Usually, the jury role is only a formality as disputes are rare.[145] If there is one, the finders of fact must decide whether the accused is unable or merely unwilling to participate.[146] Decisions appear haphazard. Some defendants have been deemed to have recovered sufficiently to plead without any apparent change to their mental state. Most have been dealt with in earlier prosecutions without their fitness being challenged.[147] It may be argued that psychiatrists dislike the prospect of indefinite detention before trial. To find a defendant with an untreatable disorder unfit to be tried can present the health services with practical and therapeutic problems. The treatment received is unlikely to be directed at rendering the patient fit to plead.[148] Doctors are therefore more likely to recommend that the trial go ahead with a plea of insanity entered.[149] However, once legislation ensured that a finding of unfitness to plead would not necessarily lead to indefinite detention,[150] the number of pleas increased.[151] Mackay found the procedure being employed where destitute or mentally ill defendants unable to pay for meals

---

[141] [1968] 3 All ER 557.

[142] 557.

[143] D Grubin, 'What Constitutes Fitness to Plead?' [1993] *Criminal Law Review* 748.

[144] RD Mackay and G Kearns, 'An Upturn in Unfitness to Plead? Disability in Relation to the Trial under the 1991 Act' (2000) *Criminal Law Review* 532.

[145] *Ibid.*

[146] According to *Pritchard*, n.140, the question is whether the defendant is 'mute of malice or mute by visitation of God'. Up until the early eighteenth century starvation and crushing were employed against defendants who would not enter a plea.

[147] Grubin, above n.143.

[148] DB Wexler and BJ Winick, *Therapeutic Jurisprudence* (Carolina Academic Press, Durham, North Carolina, 1991) 314.

[149] Grubin, above n.143.

[150] Criminal Procedure (Insanity and Unfitness to Plead) Act 1991

[151] Mackay and Kearns, n.144.

or services had committed minor theft-related offences. Quite often, psychiatrists were not involved:

> The key to this escape route for the insane offender has been in the hands of the prison doctor ever since such an official came into existence.[152]

For those defendants who slip through this filtering process, the only mental disorder defence which applies generally to all crimes is insanity. The definition of insanity in law is archaic and incoherent. It embodies the idea of a diseased will, of involuntariness, a legal rather than medical construct — an 'obscure and pseudo-medical reference to irrationality'.[153] A defendant insane at the time of the criminal act is thought to have had no subjective awareness of its likely consequences. Judges often express this as the overthrow of the will, suggesting a dichotomy between a false will and a true one. Whether or not this condition is known to psychiatric medicine, lawyers look to expert witness to identify cases where it exists. Originating in the thirteenth and fourteenth centuries as a matter of pardon rather than defence, insanity became a recognised defence supported by medical evidence by the end of the eighteenth century.[154] But the legal conception of insanity remained vague until Daniel M'Naghten, a Scottish woodcutter, assassinated Edward Drummond in mistake for Sir Robert Peel, the Prime Minister.[155] Nine medical witnesses described M'Naghten as an extreme paranoiac entangled in an elaborate system of delusion.[156] At that time defendants found to be insane were simply acquitted. So that the process could be formalised to allow M'Naghten's detention, fifteen judges were summoned to the House of Lords to explain the nature of the defence. The test they formulated was out of step with medical knowledge even as it was then, for in the past there had been cases allowing a defence of irresistible impulse.[157] The Rules provide that a defendant was insane if, at the time of the act, he was:

> labouring under such a defect of reason, from disease of the mind, as not to know the nature and quality of the act he was doing, or, if he did know it, that he did not know he was doing what was wrong.

Even on the facts of the case, the test was clearly inappropriate: M'Naghten knew what he was doing and that his actions were against the law. Judges were required to instruct juries in a test that did not serve their own purpose, and promptly handed over the responsibility for making it work to medical experts.[158]

---

[152] N Walker, *Crime and Insanity in England* vol 1, (Edinburgh, Edinburgh University Press, 1968) 226.
[153] H Fingarette and AF Hasse, *Mental Disabilities and Criminal Responsibility* (University of California Press, Berkeley, 1979) 60 n.30.
[154] Walker, above n.152.
[155] *M'Naghten* (1843) 10 Cl & F 200.
[156] RJ Simon, *The Jury and the Defense of Insanity* (Boston, Little Brown, 1967).
[157] RJ Simon and DE Aaronson, *The Insanity Defense* (New York, Praeger, 1988).
[158] DN Robinson, *Wild Beasts and Idle Humors* (Cambridge MA, Harvard University Press, 1996).

The second limb of *M'Naghten*, the wrongness test, is a curiosity. Neither lack of moral perception nor ignorance of the law is generally an excuse. 'Unless very benevolently interpreted, it adds almost nothing to the other questions'.[159] It also seems inconsistent with the underlying principle of the insanity defence, which amounts to a denial of *mens rea*. Little attempt has been made by judges in this context to define moral and legal wrong. This greatly assists expert witnesses, who seem to prefer using that limb, rather than the 'nature and quality' of the act.[160] Most commonly, medical evidence in insanity cases comprises bare statements, with no elaboration, to the effect that the defendant did not think that what he or she was doing was wrong. Courts seem to accept this.[161] There are indeed some defendants, clearly mentally ill, who believed themselves justified in what they did, for example, because they heard voices telling them to do it. But many of even these defendants fall outside the M'Naghten criteria because they know that society disapproves. Thus the collusion between courts and experts in the *M'Naghten* fiction has not managed to produce more than half a dozen or so insanity verdicts in any year.[162]

The M'Naghten test is based on the belief, now obsolete in medical circles, in the pre-eminent role of reason in controlling social behaviour. A deterministic legal system wants to excuse people morally if they have not acted out of choice. But psychiatrists cannot testify as to who is blameworthy and who is not. Contemporary psychiatry and psychology emphasise that man's social behaviour is determined more by how he has learned to behave than by what he knows or understands. Many mentally ill persons may lack the capacity to control their actions, while not apparently suffering from major cognitive disruption,[163] and while knowing the act is wrong. The Rules classify as them as sane and culpable. The first limb of *M'Naghten* requires that the defendant did not know what he or she was doing. In the United States, post-traumatic stress disorder has been successfully argued to fall under this definition, if defendants were experiencing 'flashback' at the time of the offence, making them believe they are actually back within the traumatic event.[164] But 'the madman who believes that he is squeezing lemons when he chokes his wife'[165] is a rare bird indeed.

> There is a class of psychotic patients whose illness is clearest in symptomology, most likely biological in origin, most eminently treatable and potentially most disruptive in penal detention.

---

[159] G Williams, above n.68, 645.

[160] RD Mackay, *Mental Condition Defences in the Criminal Law* (Oxford, Clarendon, 1995) 102–3.

[161] RD Mackay and G Kearns, 'More Facts about the Insanity Defence' (1999) *Criminal Law Review* 714.

[162] *Ibid.*

[163] For a special verdict there has to be a defect of reason, not just absent-mindedness, even if exacerbated by depression *Clarke* [1972] 1 All ER 219.

[164] AA Stone, 'Post-Traumatic Stress Disorder and the Law: Critical Response to the New Frontier' (1993) 21 *Bulletin of the American Academy of Psychiatry and the Law* 23.

[165] American Law Institute, *Model Penal Code*, 4.01.

who fall outside the *M'Naghten* definition.[166] The Rules express a form of insanity based on the exclusion of all rational elements.[167] Ironically this is easier to find in defendants who are not in the least mentally ill, but who were at the time of the offence in a state of automatism. The *M'Naghten* version of insanity therefore applies more conveniently to physiological than to mental disorders.[168] In Mackay's study of insanity verdicts between 1975 and 1989, three of the six cases in which 'nature and quality' was relied on concerned epilepsy.[169]

Legal insanity insists that the mental condition removed all vestiges of awareness. The defence of diminished responsibility is more flexible, applies to 'irresistible impulse', and is preferred by defendants.[170] Unfortunately, it is available only in murder cases. A defendant may be convicted of manslaughter rather than murder, if he was:

> suffering from such abnormality of mind (whether arising from a condition of arrested or retarded development of mind or any inherent cause or induced by disease or injury) as substantially impaired his mental responsibility... for the killing.[171]

It envisages a diminution rather than a negation of criminal responsibility. Even so, the law may be assuming too much of medicine here. There is little information available to science of the extent, if any, to which people, including the disordered, are incapable of forming *mens rea* or acting without reasonable rationality and self-control.[172] And there is no logical way of inferring substantial impairment of responsibility (which is not a psychiatric concept) from abnormality of mind (which requires psychiatric testimony).[173] The dilemma for expert witnesses is that they are required to provide expert assistance on the non-medical concept of responsibility:

> Within the scientific discourse of the psychiatrist, mental condition can be studied to reveal the relationship between abnormality of mind and the propensity to crime as a matter of cause and effect, but the question of the mental responsibility of the accused raises a metaphysical question of the freedom of the will which scientific discourse does not recognise and cannot answer.[174]

---

[166] Governor's Task Force to Review the Defense of Insanity, Executive Department, State of Maryland, *Report to the Governor* 1984.
[167] A Norrie, above n.44, 180.
[168] See automatism cases above.
[169] Of the mentally ill defendants, the most common diagnosis was schizophrenia; Mackay, above n.160, 103.
[170] Walker, above n.152, 158.
[171] Homicide Act 1957 s. 2.
[172] SJ Morse, 'Crazy Behavior, Morals and Science: an Analysis of Mental Health Law' (1978) 51 *Southern California Law Review* 527.
[173] Norrie, above n.44, 182.
[174] *Ibid.*

Like insanity, the defence of diminished responsibility requires a causal link between the abnormality and the outcome. The causal issue appeared to be central at the trial of Peter Sutcliffe, the 'Yorkshire Ripper' in 1981. His defence was undermined by the apparent inconsistency between his alleged paranoid delusions that God instructed him to kill prostitutes and the fact that he killed women whom he knew not to be prostitutes. In fact, some of the expert witnesses conceded under cross-examination that this undermined their diagnoses,[175] thus apparently accepting that the mental condition was not sufficiently exculpatory by itself.

The Butler Committee sought to break with the assumption that someone can retain some element of responsibility while suffering from a severe mental illness. Rather than search for illusory causal links, their Report proposed replacing *M'Naghten* with a new special verdict of 'not guilty on evidence of mental disorder'.[176] This recommendation has been completely shelved. The United States attempted to find a more appropriate definition of insanity, but this has backfired violently. The new test, laid down in *Durham v US*,[177] provides that an accused is not criminally responsible if his unlawful act was the product of mental disease or mental defect. The increased psychiatric control over the ultimate issue, guilt, incensed conservatives who felt that the jury should render the ultimate moral judgment about blameworthiness.[178] Controversy became furore once William Hinckley was acquitted in 1981 on grounds of insanity of all charges arising from his attempted assassination of President Reagan.[179] Some states abolished the insanity defence altogether, and many others reversed the burden of proof from prosecution to defence.[180] Judge Bazelon, the author of the Durham formula, regretted that it had failed to remove the vital issue of criminal responsibility from the psychiatric domain.[181]

Norrie suggests that the resistance to psychiatric power in this context arises from fear in legal circles that socio-economic factors could begin to play a role in the denial of responsibility. Although to date, psychiatry has effectively colluded with law to deny any link between social context and criminal behaviour,[182] the American Medical Association has argued that, since poverty is a 'stronger' cause of crime than mental disorder, the insanity defence should be abolished altogether.[183]

---

[175] J Bennett-Levy, 'Psychiatric Diagnosis in the Witness Box: a Postscript on the "Yorkshire Ripper" Trial' (1981) 34 *Bulletin of the British Psychological Society* 305.

[176] Meaning severe mental illness or severe subnormality; *Report of the Committee on Mentally Abnormal Offenders* (Butler Report) Cmnd 6244 (1975) 18.36.

[177] (1954) 214 F 2d 847 (DC Court) Jersey has similarly rejected *M'Naghten: A-G v Prior* (2001) Royal Court of Jersey http://www/jerseyinfo.co.uk/judgments.

[178] DL Bazelon, 'Psychiatrists and the Adversary Process' (1974) *Scientific American* 23.

[179] (1982) 672 F 2d 115.

[180] SL Golding, 'The Adjudication of Criminal Responsibility' in DK Kaegehiro and WS Laufer, (eds) *Handbook of Psychology and Law* (New York, Springer-Verlag, 1991); RJ Simon and DE Aaronson, *The Insanity Defense* (New York, Praeger, 1988).

[181] Above n.178.

[182] Norrie, above n.44, 184.

[183] SJ Morse, 'The Guilty Mind: Mens Rea' in DK Kaegehiro and WS Laufer, (eds) *Handbook of Psychology and Law* (New York, Springer-Verlag, 1991) 207.

It has been argued that exculpatory reasoning should be extended beyond insanity to include poverty or lack of education.[184] In the same vein, there are psychologists who criticise the criminal law's dichotomy between those who have moral responsibility, being aware, and those who have none. Since situational causation and personal responsibility are inversely related on a continuum, strong situational factors do not negate *mens rea* but diminish it. The law therefore should recognise diminishing degrees of responsibility, which can accommodate environmental as well as medical issues.

According to Professor Morse,[185] this argument drags the debate into the battleground, already established in psychology, between situational and personality-trait explanations of behaviour. He believes that there is currently insufficient data on that issue to justify a change in the law, which rightly emphasises mental state and the capacity for control. The belief that there is a large number of persons who are not responsible for their conduct, and that there are experts who somehow can 'simplify the extraordinarily complex and difficult question of criminal responsibility' should be resisted. Insanity has in all cultures to be accommodated within the prevailing moral philosophy and view of society and man's obligations to it. What matters is to compare mental incapacity with the legal outcome.[186] But psychiatrists, when asked by lawyers to assess a suspect in a criminal case, are not asked for, and would not claim to be competent to make, a moral assessment. They are asked to make a judgment on the applicability of a conception of mental disorder that is meaningless in their terms. Yet they are aware of the consequence for the suspect if the legal definitions are found not to fit.

Tribunal of Fact and Mental Responsibility

We have seen above how moral, medical and social issues can lie behind a defence based on mental condition. The confusion of purposes is not overt. At trial, the issue is likely to be presented to finders of fact as a matter of science. And although in these cases, unusually, experts may testify on the ultimate issue,[187] the final decision is for the tribunal of fact alone. For example, a jury may reject even unanimous psychiatric evidence of diminished responsibility in the light of 'other circumstances'.[188] So the final decision is not a matter of pure scientific judgment, while the fact that medical experts must be present[189] provides it with some kind of scientific legitimacy. Jurors and magistrates meanwhile are confronted with a plurality of unarticulated objectives. These they must resolve with the help of expert testimony from witnesses who themselves are at a loss to explain how the facts

---

[184] R Smith, above n.135.
[185] Morse, above n.126.
[186] Robinson, above n.158.
[187] See chapter 7.
[188] *Walton v R* [1978] 1 All ER 542.
[189] Criminal Procedure (Insanity and Unfitness to Plead) Act 1991.

relate to legal concepts which mean nothing to them. To add to the predicament of the fact-finder, expert witnesses may present them with conflicting opinions; they may belong to different schools of thought within the field of psychiatry, they may resolve in different ways the lack of fit between legal and medical conceptions of mental responsibility, and their experiences of the defendant may not have been similar. Psychiatric assessments can take place long after the event in question, and will normally be carried out by both defence and prosecution experts. The defendant may go through a number of interviews. It is unlikely that the psychiatrists involved will have identical encounters with any individual being assessed. In fact the subject may react differently according to the effect of the personality of the person doing the assessment: 'The measuring tool changes from examiner to examiner'.[190]

Juries receive little guidance from the law in the resolution of these contradictions. For example, in diminished responsibility 'abnormality of mind' has been said to mean 'a state of mind so different from that of an ordinary human being that the reasonable man would term it abnormal'. It is wide enough to cover 'the mind's activities in all its aspects',[191] and appears to include not only the ability to exercise will power, but a whole range of mental conditions. The verdict depends upon an equation in which the degree of abnormality is balanced against the amount of responsibility.[192] This may become even more complicated where there are other factors at work. In *Dietschmann*,[193] the defendant was said by the defence psychiatrist to be suffering from an adjustment disorder in the form of a depressed grief reaction following the death of his aunt. He had been having a sexual relationship with her. Having consumed a number of sleeping tablets and a quantity of alcohol, he killed a man who accidentally broke the watch his aunt had given him. The jury was told to dismiss the effect of the alcohol and ask whether he would have killed as he did without it, and whether his responsibility at that time was diminished. Hence, they had to decide whether the abnormality would have led the defendant to commit the act irrespective of the effect of the sleeping tablets combined with his drinking.

If the object of the trial is to arrive at the verdict and disposal most consistent with scientific principles, jury decision would not appear to be the most obvious way of achieving it. Fingarette and Hasse therefore advocate a defence of 'disability of mind', which could be broadly defined. In their scheme, once the disability has been proven, all questions of exact diagnosis, disposal and so on would be explored after the verdict in a non-adversarial context.[194] But their argument disregards the emotional or symbolic function of insanity which may be observed in the public furore that followed the insanity verdict in the Hinckley case, although

---

[190] Morse, above n.126, 1027.
[191] *Ibid.*
[192] Means both legal and moral responsibility, *Butler Report*, n.176, 19.5.
[193] [2002] Crim LR 133.
[194] Fingarette and Hasse, above n.153.

no one at the trial seriously suggested that Hinckley was faking mental illness.[195] In the case of Sirhan Sirhan, who shot and killed Senator Robert Kennedy, there was powerful medical evidence of disorder, but no outcry when the jury rejected it. He received a death sentence. There have been several similar cases in the United States, where notorious gunmen shot, and in some cases killed, notable public figures; no criticism was made of jurors who overruled medical opinion on the insanity issue.[196]

In England, the judge who presided over the trial of Peter Sutcliffe, the 'Yorkshire Ripper', appeared conscious of the symbolic importance of a finding of diminished responsibility. Sutcliffe was tried for the murder of thirteen women. Prosecution lawyers consulted psychiatrists and agreed that he suffered from severe mental illness, but the judge refused to allow them to accept a plea of guilty to manslaughter. The psychiatric evidence was unanimous, yet the jury rejected it and convicted Sutcliffe of murder. The prosecutor, forced to argue against diminished responsibility with no expert evidence to help him, had relied on Sutcliffe's calm demeanour in court and apparent rationality in the witness box. This persuaded jurors that he had been faking the delusions and other symptoms of paranoid schizophrenia the experts had observed.[197] Similarly, in *Sanders*,[198] the defendant suffered from a severe form of diabetes. He discovered that his wife was having an affair. He hit her over the head with a hammer and cut her wrists, then tried to kill himself. Two defence psychiatrists said that his responsibility was impaired, although they disagreed as to the causes. The prosecution accepted that he had an abnormality of mind, but argued that it had not diminished his responsibility. They relied on the amount of planning. The jury agreed, and convicted Sanders of murder. The Court of Appeal upheld the jury decision, although it involved rejection of the medical evidence and substitution of their own judgment. These verdicts are consistent with the findings of the Chicago Jury Project,[199] that although jurors appeared to understand the role of expert witnesses, they weighed against their evidence any indicators of rationality, such as the defendant gaining from the crime, or signs of planning. They were aware that the decision ultimately was a matter for them.

It may be that scientific analysis of cause and effect is out of place in a criminal trial, which, arguably, functions as a ritualistic allocation of responsibility. Smith argues that where an issue such as insanity is raised, the trial can become 'quite overburdened with meaning'. It develops into the symbolic enactment of the community perception of responsibility in general, not just a judgment of the specific case. Hence, expert evidence in relation to a particular defendant is of marginal significance.[200] Certainly, courts have appeared, from time to time, anxious to

---

[195] Simon and Aaronson, above n.157; Fingarette and Hasse, n.153.
[196] Simon and Aaronson, above n.157.
[197] Bennett-Levy, above n.175.
[198] (1981) 93 Cr App R 245.
[199] Simon, above n.156.
[200] *Ibid.*, 87.

assuage public anxiety, even if it is based upon a misconception. Although a manslaughter verdict would not have dictated Peter Sutcliffe's immediate or early release into the community, the trial judge was praised by the popular Press for insisting that the jury should be allowed to decide whether it was appropriate.

> Mr Justice Boreham must have known well that the psychiatrists and do-gooders who sit on the paroles of the supposedly mad are all too fallible.[201]

People tend[202] severely to overestimate the use and success of the plea of insanity, to underestimate the level of agreement between experts and therefore between the two sides, and to misunderstand the effect of an insanity verdict. It would appear that the medical opinion in this case 'got in the way of the public need to exact the maximum revenge on a hated figure'.[203] Nevertheless, immediately after the verdict, defence psychiatrists were summoned back to court, suddenly rehabilitated, to assist the judge to arrive at a recommendation for a minimum term of imprisonment. Sutcliffe was considered so dangerous that a term of thirty years was recommended; in fact, his mental condition was so serious that he had to be transferred from prison to secure hospital two years later. This case is one of the many that clearly demonstrate that the power apparently afforded by the legal system to the medical profession is merely on loan and can be withdrawn at any time.[204] In Sutcliffe's case,

> the opinion of twelve men and women on the Clapham omnibus was preferred to the unanimous opinion of no fewer than four experienced psychiatrists. Forensic psychiatry was itself on trial and, rightly or wrongly, was found sadly wanting.[205]

The fact that hostility to medical evidence is greatest where serious harm is caused suggests a reaction based on defensive attribution, possibly in terms of the desire for a safe world. Peter Sutcliffe preyed upon women whom he found alone, at night, in public places. He began his homicidal career murdering and mutilating prostitutes, but, later, killed other women. He created such fear that, all over the North of England, women were advised to make sure they did not go home alone in the dark. The jury rejected evidence of his paranoid psychosis. In contrast, pleas of diminished responsibility have been accepted following evidence of much less serious mental disorder. Reactive depression, for example was accepted as the basis of manslaughter verdict in a case of mercy killing.[206] It is said that 'on the

---

[201] *News of the World* 24 May 1981.
[202] VP Hans, 'An Analysis of Public Attitude to the Insanity Defense', (1986) 24 *Criminology* 393; RA Pasewark, 'A Review of Research on the Insanity Defense' in SA Shah (ed) *The Law and Mental Health Annals of the American Academy of Political and Social Science* (Beverley Hills, Sage, 1986) 100.
[203] J Gunn, A Maden and M Swinton, 'Treatment Needs of Prisoners with Psychiatric Disorders' (1991) 303 *British Medical Journal* 54.
[204] *Ibid.*, 55.
[205] H Rollin, 'Nineteenth Century Doctors in the Dock' (1981) 283 *British Medical Journal* 171.
[206] *Pachy* (1961) *The Guardian* 14 November.

flimsiest of evidence' juries will avoid murder convictions in sympathetic cases.[207] Judges are just as compassionate. A father who was found guilty of manslaughter by way of diminished responsibility having drowned his severely handicapped son in a river, was told by the trial judge, 'I hope that in the passage of time you will be able to forget about this matter'.[208] In cases like this, members of the medical profession are required to join lawyers and jurors in manipulation of the system to achieve the desired result. Diminished responsibility has accordingly been diagnosed in the case of the mildest of personality disorders, such as morbid jealousy[209] and pre-menstrual tension,[210] in 'cases which would hardly have attracted the label had it not been for the offence'.[211] Dell notes the success of the defence in cases where elderly men have killed their physically or mentally ill wives. If the defendant exhibits no signs of mental illness, doctors nevertheless may argue that it can be inferred from the circumstances that anxiety had caused abnormality of mind at the time of the killing.[212] Diminished responsibility, like infanticide, relies heavily upon the compliance of psychiatrists. Indeed, 'the role of psychiatrists in providing the means to the end is often unacceptable and may stretch conscience to the limit'.[213]

These defendants represent no threat to the citizen's perception of the world as a safe place, any more than does the mother who kills her baby. The tribunal of fact can afford to be compassionate. Magistrates and jurors are not at risk of infanticide, and they are unlikely to be subject to an unwanted mercy killing. The random attacks of a delusional psychopath are a very different matter. And the extreme reaction to the assassination or attempted assassination of famous persons described above may derive not so much from affection for the victim but from the perception that if such a powerful figure can be attacked by a stranger, so might we all. Suddenly the community is aware of an alarming shift of power to someone who is unpredictable. Chapter seven examines the way expert evidence is treated in courts of law, and its effect on fact-finders. It will be observed that lawyers are far more hostile to medical evidence about states of mind than they are to any other kind of expert testimony. Psychiatry and psychology are entirely acceptable when they co-operate in the marrying together of determinist theories of responsibility and the creation of a safe world. But if any attempt is made to

---

[207] Williams, above n.68, 693.

[208] *Ibid.*, 694.

[209] *Ibid.*, 692–3.

[210] *Smith (Sandie)* [1982] Crim LR 531.

[211] S Dell, '*Murder into Manslaughter: the Diminished Responsibility Defence in Practice*' (Oxford, OUP, 1984) 35.

[212] In general such cases are dealt with by way of non-custodial sentences. *Taylor* [1980] CLY 510. Father of autistic boy with a maximum potential mental age of three battered him to death with an axe and cut his throat. He was sentenced to 12 months' probation. Heilbron J said that he had suffered enough. *Jones* (1979) *The Guardian* 4 December: 29-year-old man, whose father had died of cancer, suffocated his terminally ill mother — conditional discharge.

[213] R Bluglass, *Psychiatry, the Law, and the Offender: Present Dilemmas and Future Prospects* (London, Institute for the Study and Treatment of Delinquency, 1980) 9.

shift the legal system's emphasis on internal as opposed to external explanations of behaviour, war will instantly be declared on them.

'NO PLACE FOR A WOMAN'[214]

Women historically have been seen to be closer to nature than men, strongly connected with family, but liable to be swept away by emotion. Both lay and medical discourse tended to represent women — especially in activities connected with reproduction — as lacking in responsibility.[215] There is a wealth of research on the link if any between criminality in women and the menstrual cycle. Pre-menstrual syndrome was run successfully as diminished responsibility in three murder trials at which the expert witness for the defence was Dr Dalton, a proponent of the progesterone deficiency theory.[216] Males who kill are much more likely to be regarded as the instigators of action, killing out of free choice. Stephenson suggests that this may explain the high proportion of mentally ill male offenders to be found in the prison system.[217] In the case of women who kill, a link between mind and action seems to be ruled out. They are thought to find themselves in situations rather than to create them. Court decisions tend to amount to:

> reinforcement of popular notions about women: that they are not fully responsible for what they do, that their problems are not social but individual and so require attention from helping agencies, and that when they do take deliberate action (commit crimes) such behaviour is an irrational manifestation of 'crime disturbance'.[218]

The continued survival of the Infanticide Act 1938, the provisions of which are no longer considered to have any basis in medical science, is probably a testament to the widely-held belief that any mother who kills her baby cannot be mentally well.[219] Even in the case of more mundane female criminality, psychological reports may be requested in cases where there is no particular reason to suspect mental disturbance.[220] Women are more likely to be dealt with by psychiatrists

---

[214] 'Judges told: Think Twice Before Jailing Women' was a headline in 2002. Lord Woolf CJ was apparently anxious about the increase in the population of women prisoners in England and Wales: *The Times* 25 February 2002.

[215] R Smith, *Trial by Medicine* (Edinburgh, Edinburgh University Press, 1981) 144.

[216] J Gunn and PJ Taylor, *Forensic Psychiatry: Clinical, Legal and Ethical Issues*, (Butterworth, London, 1993) 606. The authors observe that the theory is by no means universally accepted within the medical profession.

[217] GM Stephenson, *The Psychology of Criminal Justice* (Oxford, Blackwell, 1992) 216.

[218] R Pearson, 'Women Defendants in Magistrates' Courts' (1976) 3 *British Journal of Law and Society* 265.

[219] K O'Donovan, 'The Medicalisation of Infanticide' (1984) *Criminal Law Review* 259: RD Mackay, 'The Consequences of Killing Young Children' (1993) *Criminal Law Review* 21.

[220] Pearson, above n.218.

than by penal means; 'We are sorry to see you here' is a phrase men rarely hear from the court.[221]

Heuristical assumptions about women and criminality appear to be shared by courts, social workers and the probation officers who compose social enquiry reports for the sentencer. One of these appears to be that women rarely 'intend' criminality.[222] Another explanation for their behaviour must be found, and a medical one is the most obvious and convenient. Sentences under the Mental Health Act are twice as likely for women as men.[223] Although the rates of psychiatric abnormality amongst the population of women prisoners as a whole are very high in the United Kingdom[224] and the United States,[225] there is also a high incidence of psychiatric disturbance amongst the men. It has been suggested that even so, the figure for male prisoners has been underestimated.[226] Of offenders found not guilty by reason of insanity, women are less likely to have previous convictions than men, suggesting that they are more likely to be perceived to be abnormal early on in their criminal history. Male offenders in this group are more likely to have had psychiatric treatment in the past irrespective of any crime having been committed. Women then, are perceived as psychiatric cases by dint of having committed a crime.[227] Susan Edwards argues that any woman who clearly does not suffer from mental disorder may suffer from the contrast. A 'normal' woman who resorts to violence can expect to be dealt with harshly by the sentencer because her behaviour has deviated from the norm of appropriate female conduct.[228] But in general, the perception is that women commit crimes only when they are unwell. The stereotype of women as loving and nurturing is nowhere more powerful in the legal context than it is in relation to the offence of infanticide, for there the issue is motherhood itself.

Infanticide

It is clear that law has difficulty reconciling its Madonna-like vision of a woman with a child with its own conception of free will and responsibility. Historically, there has been a marked reluctance to hang mothers who killed their children. Early infanticide cases were frequently dealt with as instances of insanity, although the commonest reason for mothers killing babies was the abject poverty with which they were struggling. In such cases, judges often did not bother with medical evidence.[229]

---

[221] H Allen, 'One Law for all Reasonable Persons?' (1988) 16 *International Journal of the Sociology of Law* 419.
[222] *Ibid.*, Stephenson, above n.217.
[223] H Allen, *Justice Unbalanced: Gender, Psychiatry and Judicial Decisions* (Milton Keynes, OU, 1987).
[224] J Gunn, A Maden and M Swinton, 'Treatment Needs of Prisoners with Psychiatric Disorders' (1991) *British Medical Journal* 303.
[225] SB Guze, *Criminality and Psychiatric Disorders* (NY, OUP, 1976).
[226] Allen, above n.225.
[227] RD Mackay, *Mental Condition Defences in the Criminal Law* (Oxford, Clarendon Press, 1995) 101.
[228] S Edwards, *Women on Trial*, (Manchester, Manchester University Press, 1984).
[229] R Smith, n.135, 148.

In the mid nineteenth century, the growth in the number of babies killed by women failed to change the general reluctance to punish infanticidal mothers.[230] In 1854, it was said of Mrs Brough, who killed her six children 'The act itself bears insanity stamped on its very face'.[231] In modern times, an annual average of seven women a year are convicted of infanticide, of whom most are put on probation. Few, if any, are imprisoned. This allows the law, says Norrie, to maintain a general punitive stance together with an 'unthreatening show of compassion'.[232] In 2002 Dame Heather Hallett displayed great reluctance to impose the mandatory sentence of life imprisonment when Angela Cannings was convicted of the murder, on separate occasions, of her two sons, both babies at the time. The judge said;

> There is no medical evidence to suggest there was anything wrong with you at the time of the death of your children. But I have no doubt that for a woman like you to have committed these terrible acts of suffocating your own babies there must have been something seriously wrong with you. It is no coincidence that these events took place within weeks of you giving birth.[233]

The Infanticide Act 1938 provides that it is infanticide, rather than murder:

> Where a woman by any wilful act or omission causes the death of her child being a child under the age of twelve months, but at the time of the act or omission the balance of her mind was disturbed by reason of her not having fully recovered from the effect of giving birth to the child or by reason of the effect of lactation consequent upon the birth of the child.[234]

The language of the statute is linked to a spurious psycho/physiological view of the effects of childbirth. There is little or no evidence to support a specific relationship between lactation and mental disorder (referred to as 'lactational insanity' in the early part of the twentieth century). Indeed, there is no unambiguous biological factor associated with puerperal psychosis or any postpartum mental disorder.[235] Post-puerperal psychosis has been thought to be associated with hormonal imbalance following pregnancy, but there is little firm evidence.[236] Postpartum depression may just as possibly be a consequence of intrinsic psychological vulnerability and stress as of hormonal or other physiological

---

[230] There is no crime that meets with so much sympathy, even of the most ill-judged kind, WB Ryan, *Infanticide, the Law, Prevalence and History* (London, Churchill, 1862).

[231] F Winslow, 'Recent Trials in Lunacy' (1854) 7 *Journal of Psychological Medicine and Mental Pathology* 572.

[232] Norrie, above n.44 189.

[233] *The Times* 16 April 2002.

[234] S. 1.

[235] I Brockington, *Motherhood and Mental Health* (Oxford, Oxford University Press, 1996).

[236] PT d'Orbán, 'Women Who Kill their Children' (1979) *British Journal of Psychiatry* 134.

changes linked with pregnancy and childbirth.[237] Puerperal psychosis is rare,[238] but the puerperal period is associated with an increased risk of mental illness.[239] However, the legal assumption that mental or emotional instability during this period explains why a mother kills her baby is somewhat confounded by the fact that rarely does mental illness of any kind accompany the event.[240] Although the majority of children aged less than a year who are killed are indeed killed by their mothers,[241] the majority of children killed by their mothers are older than that.[242] Frequently, the death of a young child at the hands of its mother follows a period of consistent violence and is related to a sudden loss of temper.[243] Otherwise, the most frequent kind of case is the killing of a newborn in the context of an unwanted and concealed pregnancy.

The 1938 definition therefore presents a dilemma for those psychiatrists anxious to prevent a conviction for murder. They have little choice but to go along with the bogus biology espoused in the Act.[244] In psychiatric reports claiming that the defendant's mental condition fulfilled the requirements for infanticide, the favoured explanation is the effect of giving birth, rather than the effects of lactation.[245] About half of the women who plead guilty to or are convicted of infanticide are not suffering from any identifiable mental disorder at all.[246] Meanwhile, it seems that courts will accept a lesser degree of mental abnormality in infanticide cases than they require for diminished responsibility.[247] Most prosecutors would far rather charge infanticide than murder. In fact, the Act is nearly always invoked where a child is killed by its mother within twelve months of its birth.[248] To many lawyers, the fact that a mother killed her baby is evidence enough that she is not well.[249] It is the practice of the Crown Prosecution Service obtain medical evidence in every case where a woman kills her child, irrespective of its age. The vast majority (ninety-two per cent) of women initially suspected of murder are convicted on a lesser charge. The majority are given probation with or without a condition to undergo psychiatric treatment.[250] In almost all the infanticide

---

[237] Brockington, n.235.

[238] d'Orbán, above n.236, 560.

[239] RE Kendell, S Wainwright, A Hailey and B Shannon, 'The Influence of Childbirth on Psychiatric Morbidity' (1976) 6 *Psychological Medicine* 297.

[240] Gunn and Taylor, above n.216, 606.

[241] E Gibson, above n.101, 611.

[242] DJ West, *Murder followed by Suicide* (Cambridge, Cambridge Institute of Criminology, 1965).

[243] d'Orbán, above n.236, 560.

[244] At least, unlike the defences of insanity and diminished responsibility, infanticide does not require them to find a causal link between the disorder and the crime itself.

[245] RD Mackay, 'The Consequences of Killing Very Young Children' (1993) *Criminal Law Review* 21.

[246] PT d'Orbán and P Cheung 'Maternal Filicide in Hong Kong' (1986) *Journal of Medicine, Science and the Law* 185–192.

[247] d'Orbán, above n.236, 560: cf Mackay, above n.245.

[248] Butler Report, above n.176, 21.9.

[249] d'Orbán, above n.236, 560.

[250] Mackay, above n.245.

cases where there are proceedings the sentence is probation, but, frequently, proceedings are not brought.[251]

The lawyer-doctor conspiracy to confer medical legitimacy on the Infanticide Act allows courts to use socio-economic conditions to mitigate murder to manslaughter. It has been suggested that it would be more honest and coherent to allow a woman to resist a murder charge if the balance of her mind was disturbed by all factors related to child-bearing, including socio-economic problems.[252]

> Puerperal psychoses are now regarded as no different from others, childbirth being only a precipating factor.[253]

D'Orbán found that multiple killings of children by their mothers are not uncommon. The deaths of the older children fall outside the terms of the 1938 Act, so the most likely defence is diminished responsibility manslaughter. This does not depend upon any particular cause being established, and therefore could include socio-economic factors. Sentences for diminished responsibility manslaughter are higher than those for infanticide, which has a much lower proportion of hospital orders.[254] But if socio-economic factors are relevant, then they must apply also to fathers who kill their children, and to any killing of a child aged more than twelve months.[255] A father who successfully pleads diminished responsibility, having killed his child, will be treated more harshly than a mother. Men in this category are more frequently sent to prison, and for longer, than women convicted of the manslaughter of their children.[256] Women are more likely to get probation and psychiatric dispositions, not only in infanticide cases, but for all homicides of children.[257] Although women kill less often than men — even in spouse killing only twenty per cent of offenders are women — diminished responsibility manslaughter is the only category of homicide where women and men are equal in number. Yet, Mackay concludes, women are:

> viewed overwhelmingly as tragic cases which the prosecution was prepared to deal with leniently while the males, although avoiding murder convictions, were considered much more culpable.[258]

Therefore it seems that not only do socio-economic conditions frequently form the real basis of the case, but many young, single mothers who cannot cope with

[251] d'Orbán and Cheung, above n.246.

[252] Working Party, Royal College of Psychiatry, *Evidence to Criminal Law Revision Committee*, 1978.

[253] See Butler Report, above n.176 para.19.23.

[254] Mackay [1993] *Criminal Law Review*.

[255] d'Orbán, above n.236, 560: Mackay, above n.245.

[256] MN Marks and R Kumar, 'Infanticide in England and Wales' (1993) 33 *Journal of Medicine, Science and the Law* 329; Mackay [1993] *Criminal Law Review*.

[257] A Wilczynski and A Morris, 'Parents who Kill their Children' (1993) *Criminal Law Review* 31.

[258] Mackay, above n.227, 211.

their young children may actually benefit in the end from killing them.[259] They may expect a psychiatric disposal, but these tend not to involve deprivation of liberty. A man who kills a child while suffering from diminished responsibility may be perceived to be dangerous. A mother who does the same is seen as a victim herself.

---

[259] Allen, above n.223.

4

Finders of Fact

MAKING JUDGEMENTS OF FACT

W E HAVE SEEN in chapter three how blithely lawyers leave complicated problems to be solved by the jury as the finder of fact in a criminal trial. This can be to some extent justified by their role as the representatives of the moral conscience of their communities. Occasionally, this role is made explicit, as in the case of *Feely*,[1] where the Court of Appeal decided that jurors and magistrates do not require 'dishonesty' to be defined for them:

> Jurors, when deciding whether an appropriation was dishonest can be reasonably expected to, and should, apply the current standards of ordinary decent people. In their own lives they have to decide what is and what is not dishonest. We can see no reason why when in a jury box, they should require the help of a judge to tell them what amounts to dishonesty.[2]

On the other hand, the law of evidence represents an uneasy compromise between the insistence that fact-finders apply their own common sense to questions of fact and the nagging doubt harboured by lawyers that many questions of fact are beyond them. Hence a plethora of exclusionary rules contrive to shield fact-finders from matters that may be prejudicial or unreliable in ways they may not realise.

Magistrates and juries are routinely expected to make difficult adjudications on the facts and to understand and apply the law. In a magistrates' court advice on the law is provided at the end of the trial by the clerk, and, in a trial by jury, by the trial judge in his summing-up. In the Birmingham juries studied by Baldwin and McConville[3] there was significant under-representation of women and ethnic minorities. The relative ease with which those summoned for jury duty can get themselves excused[4] is thought to mean that the unemployed and poorly educated are over-represented. Thirty-eight per cent of those summoned for jury service in

---

[1] [1973] 1 All ER 341.
[2] Lawton LJ at 345.
[3] J Baldwin and M McConville, *Jury Trials* (Oxford, Clarendon, 1979) 18.
[4] Although see Sir Robin Auld, *Criminal Courts Review* (London, HMSO, 2001) www.criminal-courts-review.org.uk. Paras 5.25–5.40.

England and Wales in June and July 1999 were excused.[5] There is little incentive for those with pressing commitments at work to take time off to serve on a jury, particularly in view of the courts' apparent lack of concern for their convenience or comfort.[6] The Law Commission of New Zealand observed that jurors should be given more information on housekeeping matters like car parking and making telephone calls, as well as the procedural issues such as note-taking, asking questions, and selection of foreman.[7]

> Any experienced court observer has only to note the exhaustion, and sometimes distress, of jurors as a case of some length and complexity moves towards its end and the enormity and complications of the decision-making task is belatedly brought home to them.[8]

There is reassuring evidence of the energy and commitment of jurors, however. It comes from research conducted on behalf of the New Zealand Government and published by the New Zealand Law Commission.[9] It investigated a whole range of issues, taking account of the experiences of real jurors. Jurors from forty-eight trials completed a pre-trial questionnaire and were interviewed after the trial. Researchers also interviewed trial judges, read transcripts and observed parts of the trial. On the whole, jurors proved conscientious and responsible, although there were some difficulties of understanding, which are discussed below and in chapter five.

Getting the Right Answer

All trial lawyers have a supply of anecdotes in which jurors have manifestly and alarmingly failed to grasp the issues at trial. Juries are currently under attack for acquitting too many defendants. Whereas the overall acquittal rate for contested trials was about twelve per cent[10] in 2000, the rate for jury trials was forty-six per cent.[11] The explanation may in part be that defendants who suspect weakness in the prosecution case will opt for trial by jury — a factor in the current debate on whether defendant choice should be restricted.[12] But there is some empirical evidence to suggest that juries may be over-inclined to acquit. Kalven and Zeisel's study compared jury verdicts in real cases with the opinion of the trial judge, and

---

[5] J Airs and A Shaw, *Jury Excusal and Deferral*, RDSD Report No 102 (London Home Office 1999).

[6] P Darbyshire, A Maugham and A Stewart, *What Can the English Legal System Learn from Jury Research Published up to 2001* Criminal Courts Review, www.criminal-courts-review.org.uk.

[7] W Young, N Cameron and Y Tinsley, *Juries in Criminal Trials*, Law Commission of New Zealand Preliminary Paper 37, Vol 2, (Wellington, New Zealand, 1999).

[8] Auld, n.4, para.8.18.

[9] Young, Cameron and Tinsley, n.7.

[10] Only 9.6% in 1995–6.

[11] *The Times* 15 March 2002.

[12] White Paper, *Justice for All*, CM 5563 (London, The Stationery Office, 2002).

found no significant difference of opinion as to findings of guilt,[13] although they found less unanimity on acquittals. In an English study conducted by Baldwin and McConville,[14] real verdicts were similarly compared with the opinions of professionals involved in the case. A high level of what were deemed perverse acquittals was discovered.[15] There were also some perverse convictions, which amazed even the police. Sometimes the jury ignored a virtual direction to acquit; they were more likely to do this where the defendant was black.

The criminal justice system is strikingly reluctant to inform itself of the basis of jury decisions. For example, a judge sentencing in the wake of a verdict of manslaughter may not know whether the jury accepted a plea of provocation, or in fact rejected that evidence but found insufficient mens rea for murder. It is thought undesirable in manslaughter cases that jury should be asked to explain their verdict[16] although there is a discretion for the trial judge in a case where diminished responsibility or provocation has been raised. The jury should be warned in advance that they will be asked. But the Court of Appeal seem to think it perfectly possible for a judge to proceed to sentence without knowing whether the jury thought the defendant was suffering diminished responsibility, was provoked, or committed an act of gross negligence;

> if the jury agree that he is guilty of manslaughter in the sense that they are sure that he perpetrated an unlawful act which caused the death of the accused, it is unnecessary that there be any unanimity by the jury as to the route by which that verdict is achieved.[17]

This statement acknowledges the risk that there may have been disagreement within the jury as to precisely which kind of manslaughter verdict was appropriate in the particular case.

Judges seem to fear that once an explanation for a jury verdict is articulated in public, it will become apparent that the case has been misunderstood and that the verdict is unsound. Some academics agree. Professor Smith argues that ignorance of the manner of jury deliberations might be preferable to revealing what is actually going on.[18] This reluctance to lay bare jury reasoning processes applies even to the question of profound error. Courts do not want to know what happened in the jury room. In *Vaise v Delaval*,[19] two jurors swore an affidavit that the verdict had been arrived at by tossing a coin. Though 'a very high misdemeanour', the court refused to allow the jurors to be questioned about this. The defendant

---

[13] H Kalven and H Zeisel, *The American Jury* (Boston, Little Brown, 1966).

[14] Baldwin, and McConville, above n.3.

[15] Doubted by at least two professionals.

[16] *Larkin* [1943] KB 174.

[17] *Jones* (1999) *The Times* 17 February.

[18] J Smith, 'Is Ignorance Bliss? Could Jury Trial Survive Investigation?' (1988) 38 *Journal of Medicine, Science and Law* 98.

[19] (1785) 1 Term Report 11.

in *Qureshi*[20] had been convicted of arson, following which his solicitor received a communication from a member of the jury. This made some startling allegations, namely, that some members of the jury had made disparaging remarks throughout the trial about the defendant's appearance, accent, poor English, mannerisms and business integrity. Further, it was alleged that some of the jurors reached a decision at the outset of the trial and did not change their minds; that newspapers dealing with the trial were brought into the jury retiring room and shown around; that at least three jurors were contacting people outside the courtroom during the course of the trial and discussing its progress; that one juror fell asleep during the evidence; that one was deaf and could not hear the evidence; and that other members of the jury behaved in a bullying manner. Leave to appeal was refused, as the court could not inquire into what happened in the jury room.

In *Stephen Young*,[21] a conviction for murder delivered by a British jury had to be set aside when it was discovered that four jury members had been influenced by a séance they had conducted in order to receive a posthumous message from the victim. If the irregularity had taken place within the jury room rather than a hotel room, the Court of Appeal would have refused to hear evidence of it.[22] Strangers are not allowed in the jury room. A deaf man was rejected as a potential juror by Woolwich Crown Court because it would mean having a thirteenth person in the jury room as a sign-language interpreter for him.[23] This delicacy means that in cases where the defence allege that widespread Press coverage of the trial might have influenced the jury, the Court of Appeal can only speculate as to the effects of the publicity.[24] British courts have refused to follow the American practice of asking potential jurors whether they have been reading about the case in the Press. The Court of Appeal upheld a conviction for murder in a case where judge refused to allow a defence lawyer to use a questionnaire designed to test the effect of Press reporting on jurors. It was suggested that this might have had the effect only of bringing to their attention matters which would be better disregarded.[25] It seems to make no difference if jurors got things badly wrong. In *Nanan v The State*,[26] the defendant was convicted of murder and sentenced to death. The day afterwards, the foreman of the jury went with another jury member to the Registrar of the Supreme Court of Trinidad and Tobago to say he was confused when asked whether the jury had reached a unanimous verdict. Although he had confirmed that they had, the verdict in fact was reached by majority of 8:4. The case reached the Privy Council by way of appeal nine years later, and the Court refused to admit the foreman's evidence. If any member of

[20] [2002] *Criminal Law Review* 62.
[21] [1988] 2 WLR 430.
[22] Young was convicted at retrial.
[23] *The Times* 10 November 1999.
[24] [1996] 2 Cr App R 574.
[25] *Andrews, The Times* 15 October 1998.
[26] (1986) 35 WILR 358.

the jury disagrees with the verdict, he or she must express this at the time. The Contempt of Court Act 1981 makes it an offence

> to obtain, disclose or solicit any particulars of statements made, opinions expressed, arguments advanced or votes cast by members of a jury in the course of their deliberations.[27]

This makes it impossible to conduct the kind of research into actual jury decision-making that was carried out in New Zealand. In England there has been some judicial support for allowing research into jury decision-making,[28] but unless and until the law is reformed to allow it, legal debate as to the ability of jurors to cope with complex trials will remain desperately uninformed.

In criminal jury trials, the judge is the arbiter of law and decides on sentence while the jury is the arbiter of fact. In civil cases judgments of fact are usually made a judge sitting alone.[29] The dual role of deciding on facts as well as law is shared by magistrates in summary criminal trials, and also by judges sitting in the 'Diplock Courts' of Northern Ireland, where there is no jury. It has been observed that in those cases where a judge must resolve disputed facts, the level of activity and intervention bears no resemblance to the muted role of the jury when it fulfils such a role:

> The ideal juror is characterised as a relatively passive record keeper who encodes the events of the trial verbatim.[30]

Judges are far more active during the course of a trial. The relationship between judge and advocate which develops as a consequence may colour the final outcome.[31] Jurors are excluded from the interaction between the participants in the trial, although they observe the relationships between advocates and judges and may be influenced by their behaviour.[32] Another striking difference between a verdict arrived at by a single judge and one reached by a jury is that the latter is the product of group discussion, and may be influenced by group dynamics. There is a substantial body of research into group deliberation, the effect of a strong personality and of physical conditions.[33] Probably the most interesting

---

[27] S.8(1).

[28] Auld, n.4, 5.87.

[29] In England and Wales, juries are used nowadays in only about twelve to fourteen civil trials a year: S Lloyd-Bostock, 'Juries and Jury Research in Context' in G Davies, S Lloyd-Bostock, K MacMurran, and C Wilson, (eds) *Psychology Law and Criminal Justice* (Berlin, de Gruyter, 1996).

[30] R Hastie, S Penrod, and N Pennington, *Inside the Jury* (Cambridge, Mass., Harvard University Press, 1983) 18.

[31] J Jackson, and S Doran, *Judge Without Jury: Diplock Trials and the Adversary System* (Oxford, Clarendon, 1995).

[32] NL Kerr, 'Trial Participants' Behaviors and Jury Verdicts: an Exploratory Field Study' in VJ Konecki and EB Ebbeson, (eds) *The Criminal Justice System: a Socio-Psychological Analysis* (San Francisco, WH Freeman, 1982). Curiously, a cold, relentless prosecutor achieved better results than one who displayed any warmth towards the defence.

[33] Hastie, Penrod, and Pennington, n.30.

finding in this context is that an individual reaction to evidence prior to discussion is quite a good predictor of verdict. Opinions do change, however. The most common shift of opinion after group deliberation is from a preference for a conviction to a verdict of 'Not Guilty', although it may be that the individual juror who changes vote to satisfy colleagues retains his or her original opinion.[34] But views tend to polarise less if the prosecution case is strong; the few jurors who initially would have acquitted are likely to be won over.

In courts in England and Wales, jury trial is statistically infrequent. Most crimes are dealt summarily in the magistrates' courts. Proposed reforms will make summary trial even more dominant.[35] Lay magistrates generally sit over a number of years, in panels of three. Although they are not lawyers, they are trained, and accumulate experience both of criminal procedure and of the patterns of crime in their neighbourhood. It would be simplistic to assume that judges, magistrates and jurors (mock or actual), reason in the same way. Apart from the obvious differences in levels of familiarity with court proceedings, their roles differ significantly during a trial.

RECOGNISING LIARS

Even lawyers do not pretend that it is an easy matter to decide which witness to believe when stories conflict. The burden of proof is a useful tool to resolve cases where doubt remains, but judges appear confident that in any event accurate assessment of the facts is possible:

> By the time both parties have explored every point which they think may help them or damage their adversary, not much remains obscure.[36]

Lord Bingham believes that few substantial civil cases turn on the burden of proof. In his book he sets out the tests that judges apply in order to determine whether a witness is telling the truth. These are[37]:

1 — the consistency of the witness's evidence with what is agreed, or is clearly shown by other evidence, to have occurred;
2 — the internal consistency of the witness's evidence;
3 — the consistency of the testimony with what the witness has said or deposed on other occasions;

---

[34] R Arce, F Fariña, and J Sabral, J, 'From Juror to Jury Decision Making: a Non-Model Approach' in G Davies, S Lloyd-Bostock, K MacMurran, and C Wilson, (eds) *Psychology Law and Criminal Justice* (Berlin, de Gruyter, 1996).
[35] Auld, n.4. Criminal Justice Bill 2003.
[36] *Air Canada v Secretary of State for Trade* [1983] 2 AC 394, Lord Denning, MR at 411.
[37] T Bingham, *The Business of Judging: Selected Essays and Speeches* (Oxford, Oxford University Press, 2000) 6.

4 — the credit of the witness in relation to matters not germane to the litigation;

5 — the demeanour of the witness.

There is some scientific approval for the first three of these criteria which, with many others, form part of the checklist of reliability employed in Statement Validity Analysis. This technique was developed in Germany to test the statements of child witnesses in sexual abuse cases. Such assessment is employed in Canada,[38] the United States and Germany, where there are court psychologists to carry it out. The method, which is not standardised, involves a comparison of the statement against a checklist of factors thought to indicate reliability. Consistency is an element, and for external consistency the expert will check the statement for contextual details such as references to the weather, or what the witness was doing at the time. The list of factors is long, and techniques are not uniform. As well as the objective criteria already mentioned, the technique includes more controversial motivational-related content, such as the witness's interest in the proceedings. Some psychologists include such factors as any spontaneous corrections the witness might make, any admitted failure of memory, self-deprecation and expressed doubts as to accuracy.[39] The usefulness of Statement Validity Analysis is open to debate. Its overall accuracy appears to be only slightly better than chance. Vrij concludes that therefore evidence of this kind should not be admitted in court, particularly as so little is known of the possible effects of interviewing style upon the nature of the statement obtained.[40]

Witness Consistency

Cross-examination to uncover inconsistency is a favourite tool of cross-examiners. They claim success where cross-examination elicits or exposes either internal inconsistency or inconsistency with other evidence, but this may have little relevance to reliability, particularly in the case of children. Children are less likely than adults to be able to describe a traumatic event in a chronological sequence. They are also more prone to include fantasy in a true account, probably to protect themselves from excessive trauma.[41] In *Parnell*[42] a ten-year-old described a sexual assault, but mistook the relevant date. The trial judge directed the jury that this

---

[38] Eg. JC Yuille, 'The Systematic Assessment of Children's Testimony' (1988) 29 *Canadian Psychology* 247.

[39] See generally, A Vrij, *Detecting Lies and Deceit* (Chichester, Wiley, 2000) 113–56 for an account and a critique.

[40] *Ibid.*, 145.

[41] RS Pynoos and K Nader, 'Children who Witness the Sexual Assaults of their Mothers' (1988) 27 *Journal of the American Academy of Child and Adolescent Psychiatry* 567; RS Pynoos and K Nader, 'Children's Memory and Proximity to Violence' (1989) 28 *Journal of the American Academy of Child and Adolescent Psychiatry* 236.

[42] (1985) 98 CCC (3d) 83 (Ontario CA).

did not adversely affect her credibility, given her age, observing that there was a good deal of literature showing that children are poor at recalling precise dates. Nevertheless, cross-examination by defence lawyers in child abuse cases is preoccupied with questions about peripheral detail, for example, 'What colour was the duvet?'[43] Even in the case of adults, it is well established that memory for detail fades over time.[44] But cross-examiners take the simplistic approach that failures in recall of some details mean that the entire account is unreliable.[45] Lord Bingham himself notes that asking witnesses to recall every detail is unrealistic; if people who are watching a football match are asked about a goal that has been scored, they could probably name the player, but not give an accurate description of all the moves and passes that led up to it. Although Lord Bingham cites the work of Elizabeth Loftus on memory[46] he observes, apparently without dismay, that witnesses are routinely expected to answer questions such as the following, in cases of motor car accident: Counsel (showing the witness a photograph of the road), 'Had you reached the second telegraph pole on the left in photograph no. 3 when you saw the oncoming vehicle?[47] The legal obsession with consistency means that a witness should have provided, across a series of interviews, an account that does not vary. But it not clear that changes of detail are associated with unreliable accounts.[48]

Cross-examination plays upon the suggestibility of witnesses — their readiness to accept and adopt information 'planted' by a leading question.[49] A primary aim of cross-examination is to lure witnesses into inconsistency, thus undermining their credibility. The famous study on leading questions by Loftus and Palmer showed that witnesses were influenced by the language used by the questioner. So if asked, 'About how fast were the cars going when they smashed into each other?' the reply gave a higher estimated speed than if a witness is asked, 'About how fast were the cars going when they collided with each other?'[50] The power of suggestion is such that it can have a permanent effect on memory.[51] Against this, it seems that the personalities of some people make them more difficult to mislead

---

[43] G Davies, C Wilson, R Mitchell and J Milsom, *Videotaping Children's Evidence: an Evaluation* (London, Home Office, 1995) p 33.

[44] IML Hunter, *Memory* (Harmondsworth, Penguin, 1957); PN Shapiro and S Penrod 'Meta-Analysis of Facial Identification Studies' (1986) 100 *Psychological Bulletin* 139; A Kapardis, *Psychology and the Law* (Cambridge, Cambridge University Press, 1997). Yet quantity of detail is part of the test in Statement Validity Analysis.

[45] GL Wells, 'Applied Eyewitness Testimony' in LS Wrightsman, SM Kassin and CE Willis, *In the Jury-Box: Controversies in the Courtroom* (Newbury Park, Sage, 1987).

[46] Bingham, above n.37, 17–18.

[47] *Ibid.*, 16.

[48] T Jaskiewicz-Obydzinska and A Czerederecka, 'Psychological Evaluation of Changes in Testimony given by Sexually Abused Juveniles' in G Davies, S Lloyd-Bostock, K MacMurran, and C Wilson, *Psychology Law and Criminal Justice* (Berlin, de Gruyter, 1996).

[49] EF Loftus, 'Leading Questions and the Eyewitness Report' (1975) 7 *Cognitive Psychology* 560.

[50] EF Loftus and JC Palmer, 'Reconstruction of Automobile Destruction: an Example of the Interaction Between Language and Memory' (1974) 17 *Journal of Verbal Learning and Verbal Behaviour*, 585.

[51] *Ibid.* EF Loftus and JC Palmer, 'The Malleability of Eyewitness Accounts' in S Lloyd-Bostock and BR Clifford, (eds) *Evaluating Witness Evidence* (Chichester, Wiley, 1983).

than others.[52] It is also more difficult to mislead a witness in relation to a fact of central importance, and where the witness was heavily involved with the event.[53] But if the questioner demonstrates an apparent level of knowledge, the suggestibility of the witness increases. Suggestibility may derive from people's reluctance to admit that they are not sure. They may believe that they must provide an answer, or that it is expected that they know the answer and are capable of giving it.[54] Courts of law, by accident or design, tend to demand answers as if the witness must know them. Cross-examination is not the only source of possible contamination of the memory of witnesses. Witness statements are based upon answers supplied to police officers at interview. Any number of leading questions may have been asked during the questioning process, and may have been subsequently adopted as part of the memory. Before going into court, witnesses are allowed to read through their statements,[55] so the contents are likely to become incorporated into the evidence-in-chief. Although this possibility appears not to have caused particular alarm, a very different atmosphere may be detected in the controversy surrounding techniques used in 'disclosure' interviews with children suspected of having suffered abuse.[56]

It is not clear that children are particularly susceptible to suggestion, although there is some evidence that they are.[57] Cohen and Harnick[58] found twelve-year olds more suggestible than adults, with nine-year-olds more suggestible still. Learning disability similarly is associated with a higher than average degree of suggestibility.[59] But a child's suggestibility depends also on the interaction of age with other social and cognitive factors.[60] Anxiety to please may explain why young children appear more suggestible than older children. In the same vein, an eight-year-old is more likely than an older child to select a face from a series of photographs when that of the real subject is not there.[61] Younger children may assume

---

[52] GH Gudjonnson and AK Clark, 'Suggestibility in Police Interrogation; a Social Psychological Model' (1986) 1 *Social Behaviour* 83; see chapter six.

[53] JC Yuille, 'A Critical Examination of the Psychology and Practical Implications of Eyewitness Research' (1980) 4 *Law and Human Behaviour* 335.

[54] VL Smith and PC Ellsworth, 'The Social Psychology of Eyewitness Accuracy: Misleading Questions and Communicator Expertise' (1987) 72 *Journal of Applied Psychology* 294.

[55] *Richardson* [1971] 2 QB 484.

[56] See chapter eight.

[57] B Marin, D Holmes, M Guth and P Kovac, 'The Potential of Children as Eyewitnesses' (1979) 3 *Law and Human Behavior* 295.

[58] RC Cohen and MA Harnick, 'The Susceptibility of Child Witnesses to Suggestion' (1980) 4 *Law and Human Behavior* 295; Cf. GS Goodman and RS Reed, 'Age Differences in Eyewitness Testimony' (1986) 10 *Law and Human Behavior* 317.

[59] GH Gudjonnson and AK Clark, 'Suggestibility in Police Interrogation; a Social Psychological Model' (1986) 1 *Social Behaviour* 83.

[60] C Goodman and B Schwartz-Kennedy, 'Why Knowing a Child's Age is not Enough; Influence of Cognitive, Social and Emotional Factors on Children's Testimony' in H Dent and R Flin, (eds) *Children as Witnesses* (Chichester, Wiley, 1992).

[61] JC Yuille, JL Cutshall and MA King, 'Age-Related Changes in Eyewitness Accounts and Photo-Identification' (Unpublished; quoted, C Hedderman, *Children's Evidence; the Need for Corroboration*, Home Office Research and Planning Unit Paper 41 (London Home Office) 13–14.

they are being tested in some way.[62] But where an event made a strong impression, the child's age seems to matter less.[63] It is much harder to get a child to accept 'planted' information where he or she had central, as opposed to peripheral, involvement in it. Professor Davies concludes that the preponderance of evidence shows suggestibility in children to be more a function of setting and task than state of mind.[64] Most of the experiments dealing with suggestibility in children focus on morally neutral matters. It has been suggested that results are different if children perceive the questioner to have a view as to the guilt or innocence of the person under discussion.[65] However, even three-year-old children appear to resist questions that imply impropriety after a conventional non-abusive intimate medical examination.[66] It may be that aggressive cross-examination would lead a child into contradiction, but advocates tend to use friendliness and persuasion, rather than risk alienating the jury.[67] Learning disabled witnesses may be treated less gently. People suffering from Down's Syndrome in particular tend to be sensitive to negative emotion. Sometimes they respond to what they perceive as aggression ('tough' questioning) by attempting to appease the questioner, so that suggestibility and contradiction result. Professor Sanders observed a case in which a Downs' witness was subjected to hostile questioning from the defence for two days. This resulted in a mass of contradictions, and one juror burst into tears.[68]

Apart from the use of suggestion in leading questions, there may be other problems confronting truthful witnesses who wish to tell their story in court. One is the highly stylised fashion in which they are expected to give oral testimony. Counsel has close control and tends to disrupt the narrative flow. Penman argues[69] that the conversational rules enforced by the court are merely the social rules that govern coherence in ordinary conversation. These include having to answer the question, not indulging in irrelevance, not giving more information than is asked for, and not interrupting. Since we find it difficult to comply with these rules in everyday life, courts are forced to coerce witnesses into co-operation. Indeed, even the conversation of suspects tape-recorded by undercover police officers may be subtly controlled by the agent attempting to achieve the desired result.[70] In court,

[62] S Moston, 'The Suggestibility of Children in Interview Studies' (1987) 7 *First Language* 67.

[63] GS Goodman, C Aman and J Hirschman, in SJ Ceci, MP Toglia and DF Ross, (eds) *Children's Eyewitness Memory* (New York, Springer-Verlag, 1987).

[64] G Davies 'Research on Children's Testimony: Implications for Interviewing Practice' in C Hollins and K Howells, (eds) *Clinical Approaches to Sex Offenders and their Victims* (Chichester, Wiley, 1991).

[65] A Clarke-Stewart, W Thompson and S Lepore, '*Manipulating Children's Interpretations through Interrogation*', paper presented at Society for Research on Child Development, Kansas City USA, 1989. See Davies, n. 64.

[66] K Saywitz, GS Goodman, E Nichols and S Moan, '*Children's Memory for a Genital Examination*' (1989), paper presented to the Society for Research on Child Development, Kansas City, USA.

[67] Davies, above n.64.

[68] A Sanders, J Creaton S Bird and L Weber, *Victims with Learning Disabilities:Home Office Research Findings* 44 (London, HMSO, 1996).

[69] R Penman, 'Regulation of Discourse in the Adversary Trial' (1987) 7 *Windsor Yearbook of Access to Justice* 3.

[70] RW Shuy, 'Conversational Power in FBI Covert Taperecording' in L Kedar, (ed) *Power Through Discourse* (Norwood, New Jersey, Ablex, 1987).

the combination of direct admonitions and orders from the judge with the use of closed questions from the advocate in cross-examination denies the witness the general pattern of discourse. Normally, this includes the freedom to negotiate the right to speak, to demand respect and to distance or withdraw, if necessary, to save face. Is this conducive to arriving at the facts in a more effective and orderly way? Penman suggests that the answer depends on whether barristers ask the right questions. This may be difficult, and, indeed, advocates themselves have trouble complying with the discourse model employed by the courts. Stress caused by the fact that witnesses cannot control the way they tell their story nor withdraw from a humiliating situation may add to the apparent contradictions or incoherence of their testimony. It has been said that in adversarial proceedings, questions can be used as symbolic punishment. This tendency was found at its most extreme in American trials, suggesting that British trials are more polite, and British lawyers less combative.[71]

Witnesses will find even polite questioning impossible to deal with if they do not understand what they are being asked. Witnesses lose confidence if they become confused,[72] and legal language differs substantially from the way most people express themselves. It characteristically employs a large number of double negatives and advanced vocabulary. Questions are multi-part, or may jump from topic to topic. Lawyers have been heavily criticised for failing to adjust their questions to accommodate any comprehension problems a witness might have. There has been pressure for improvement in Australia[73] and the United States.[74] Scottish lawyers appear to have been particularly slow to adjust their use of language for children.[75] In a sample of Scottish child witnesses,[76] sixty-three per cent found the questions, particularly those asked in cross-examination, difficult to understand. The children reported difficulties to a greater degree even than the research team had observed themselves; it may be that the problem is difficult to detect through the live link. Words such as 'imaginary', 'narrate' 'involve', and 'incident' confused the children, as did the use of double negatives, and phrases such as 'Where was the bed in relation to the television?' Prosecutors were significantly more ready to adapt their language and grammar to that of the child where the live link was used. This might have been an effect of the screen, or a function of

---

[71] P Danet and P Bogosch, 'Fixed Fight or Free-For-All: an Empirical Study of Combativeness in the Adversary System of Justice' (1980) 7 *British Journal of Law and Society*. But see, R Dunstan, 'Context for Coercion: Analyzing Properties of Courtroom Questions' (1980) 7 *British Journal of Law and Society* 61.
[72] M Kebbell and D Johnson, 'Lawyers' Questioning: the Effect of Confusing Questions on Witness Confidence and Accuracy' (2000) 24 *Law and Human Behavior* 629.
[73] M Brennan and RE Brennan, *Strange Language: Child Witnesses Under Cross-Examination* (Wagga Wagga, New South Wales, Riverina Murray Institute of Higher Education, 1988); M Brennan, 'The Discourse of Denial: Cross-Examining Child Witnesses' (1999) 23 *Journal of Pragmatics* 71.
[74] AG Walker, *Handbook on Questioning Children: a Linguistic Perspective* (Washington Bar Association, 1994); AG Walker, 'Questioning Young Children in Court: a Linguistic Case Study' (1993) 17 *Law and Human Behavior* 39.
[75] GM Davies and E Noon, *An Evaluation of the Live Link for Child Witnesses*, (London, HMSO, 1991).
[76] K Murray, *Live Television Link: an Evaluation of its use in Scottish Criminal Trials* (Edinburgh, HMSO, 1995).

the children's age. Over England and Wales there has been gradual improvement in the way lawyers speak to child witnesses. Given that prosecutors tend to be more adaptable than defence lawyers, since most child witnesses are called by the prosecution, it is encouraging that Davies found decreased use of age-inappropriate language by the defence.[77] An earlier study by Davies and Noon[78] indicated that age-appropriate questioning enhances both the consistency of the testimony and the witness's resistance to suggestion. But whatever language they employ, defence lawyers will still be tempted to exploit the immaturity of a child. A common tactic was to imply that the witness has been coached by an adult. In one case it was suggested to a ten-year-old boy that Mummy had told him what to say. He admitted that this so, 'then after a short pause informed the court that she had told him to speak up, tell the truth and do his best'.[79] Another strategy is to suggest the child has devious motives for lying. Training for advocates may help prevent the ambush of vulnerable witnesses. The Crown Prosecution Service now insists that any barrister engaged to prosecute a case involving a child witness must watch a video it has issued jointly the National Society for the Prevention of Cruelty to Children. However no such control is currently possible for defence advocates; it is for the trial judges to ensure that questioning is appropriate.

Learning-disabled witnesses appear to fare no better. A Government Working Group Report describes how witnesses with learning difficulties tend to become confused about the difference between 'your memory of the event' and 'your memory of what you said to the police'.[80] In Sanders' study, one witness reported:

> Every time he [the defence barrister] said something to me I had to agree. He got me where he wanted me. The reason I agreed with everything he said was because I didn't understand what he was saying, which was all making me worse.[81]

The speaker was twenty-two and had been cross-examined in relation to his allegation that his father had indecently assaulted him. He suffered from a mild learning disability and had got very confused. He contradicted himself to such an extent that the judge directed an acquittal. Sanders reports that many other learning disabled witnesses were questioned with no apparent concession to their individual difficulties. Judges also appeared unable to communicate with such witnesses in a way they were likely to understand. Testing the competence to give evidence of a

---

[77] Davies, Wilson, Mitchell and Milsom, above n.43.

[78] Davies and Noon, above n.75.

[79] *Ibid.*, 93–4.

[80] *Report of the Interdepartmental Working Group on the Treatment of Vulnerable or Intimidated Witnesses in the Criminal Justice System* (London, Home Office, 1998) 8.70.

[81] A Sanders, J Creaton S Bird and L Weber, above n.68; A Sanders, J Creaton S Bird and L Weber, *Victims with Learning Disabilities: Negotiating the Criminal Justice System*, Oxford, Oxford Centre for Criminological Research, Occasional Paper No 17 1997 p 75; H Dent, 'An Experimental Study of the Effectiveness of Different Techniques of Questioning Mentally Handicapped Witnesses' (1995) 25 *British Journal of Clinical Psychology* 13.

nineteen- year-old rape complainant with a learning disability,[82] the judge wanted to see if she could recognise truthful statements: 'Suppose I said I was wearing an emerald green cloak?'[83] Lawyers have no excuse for their reluctance to adapt, since most have relevant experience. Three out of four barristers who participated in a Mencap survey[84] reported that they had represented a client with learning disability.

A Californian study[85] observed *habeas corpus* proceedings in which compulsory detentions in mental hospital were challenged. The author identified advocates' strategies to confirm the contention that the patient should not be released. Judges and lawyers on both sides generally acknowledged that one indicator of incompetence was 'crazy talk' during the patient's oral testimony. Others included a nervy, jumpy delivery, incoherence, or long pauses before answering questions. At the same time, all court personnel tended to assume that if a patient did not give evidence that was because he or she was incapable of doing so. It was observed that the questioning strategies of lawyers were designed on the one side (public defender) to prevent crazy talk, and on the other (district attorney) to elicit it. Thus the former tried to control the patient's testimony by asking questions to which the answer 'Yes' or 'No' was sufficient, and interrupting before the patient could say anything more. An example was 'Will you take your medicine?' The patient answered, 'Yes', but went on to say, 'If it didn't pass through the hands of too many Russians'. He was instantly interrupted by counsel talking through him, asking the next question. In retaliation, the district attorney tended not only to let patients talk, hoping they would 'hang themselves', but push them into crazy talk by not acknowledging answers that had actually been given. A one-word answer to a question might, therefore, result in total silence from the interlocutor, or in an interrogative 'Uh-huh?' Both tactics made patients think they should be saying more. Baffled, they would pause, and then often would follow a series of unrelated and/or irrelevant statements, which would confirm the view that the patient was not competent. If there was a hint of craziness in the testimony, for example, embarking on a discussion of rocket ships, the attorney would suddenly show interest, encouraging the witness to carry on. The irony, of course, is that the patient was actually trying to co-operate.

Where witnesses are completely unable to communicate orally by reason of mental or physical disability, an 'intermediary' who could 'translate' the questions from the lawyer into a form of language the witness can understand, and relay the answers back to the lawyers may be the solution.[86] The Youth Justice and Criminal

[82] See chapter eight.
[83] Sanders, Creaton Bird and Weber, above n.68, 58.
[84] *Barriers to Justice* (Mencap National Centre 1997).
[85] JA Holstein, 'Court Ordered Incompetence: Conversational Organization in Involuntary Commitment Hearings' (1988) 35 *Social Problems* 458.
[86] *Report of the Interdepartmental Working Group on the Treatment of Vulnerable or Intimidated Witnesses in the Criminal Justice System* (London, Home Office, 1998).

Evidence Act 1999[87] provides for the use of intermediaries. The function of this person will be similar to that of an interpreter translating into a foreign language. In terms of accuracy, the best intermediary for a child witness or adult with learning disability would be someone who knows the witness well. However, fears that the intermediary might distort or invent questions or answers, or even suggest answers to the witness in a way the tribunal cannot detect, has meant the introduction of a scheme for the accreditation of officially-recognised intermediaries, who will be trained in court procedures, on the basis of agreed criteria. Intermediaries must make a declaration that they will faithfully perform their function. It remains to be seen whether they will be trained with equal attention to the extraordinary versatility that will be required if they are to communicate with witnesses suffering from all kinds of physical and mental disability. The Act also provides for 'aids to communication'.[88] These are not defined at all, but interactive computer graphics may be a potential aid to communication for witnesses who are unable to express themselves orally. Researchers are currently working on projects in this area. These programmes would have to be simple to operate, and would have to be devised in such a way that there is no element of suggestion nor prejudice to the defendant in the graphic. Hence the depiction of a character representing the defendant would have to be carefully designed to avoid either a resemblance to the defendant where identity is in dispute, or some characteristic that could induce hostility in magistrates or jury.

Discrediting Witnesses

Advocates will seize in cross-examination on any matter that suggests a witness has been dishonest at other times. The suggestion is that a witness who would lie on a peripheral issue has lost credibility on the main issue. This could be seen as manifestations of the co-variation principle and the fundamental attribution error. Attribution theory would expect fact-finders to overlook information on the individual circumstances that might explain the lying behaviour, emphasising instead internal causes, the characteristics of the people involved.[89] Thus a general tendency to be dishonest will be assumed. But there seems to be little, if any, evidence of consistency in moral behaviour over diverse situations. There is 'no support for the widespread psychodynamic belief in ... a unitary entity of conscience or honesty'.[90] But at the same time, there is no empirical foundation for the belief that evidence of isolated praiseworthy deeds will produce a 'halo effect'

---

[87] Section 20; L Ellison 'Cross-Examination and the Intermediary' (2002) *Criminal Law Review* 114.
[88] S.30. Such device as the court considers appropriate with a view to enabling questions or answers to be communicated to or by the witness despite any disability or disorder or other impairment which the witness has or suffers from.
[89] RD Hausen and CA Lowe, 'Distinctiveness and Consensus:the Influence of Behavioral Information on Actors' and Observers' Attributions' (1976) 34 *Journal of Personality and Social Psychology* 425.
[90] W Mischel, *Personality and Assessment* (New York, Wiley, 1968) 26.

in the mind of the fact-finder. Lord Bingham doubts the value of cross-examination on dishonesty on collateral matters. Much must depend upon the witness's assessment of the importance of telling the truth in relation to a particular issue, and the explanation for the dishonesty.[91] Jurors in the New Zealand study did not automatically assume that a defendant who had lied at some point in the investigation must be guilty. Instead, they looked for a reason for it.[92]

However, it has been found that attacks on the character of the female victim of an alleged sexual offence are a better predictor of the verdict than the impression of the character of the accused. Even with strong evidence against the defendant, the most influential factor is her perceived trustworthiness.[93] Frequently, such attacks are couched in terms of the complainant's previous sexual behaviour. In simulated rape trials where the defence is consent, mock juries are reluctant to convict if they are told of the complainant's prior sexual history.[94] Her credibility is significantly diminished by evidence that she has been involved in a number of sexual relationships. In addition, jurors are more inclined to believe her to have been responsible for the incident, and even to denigrate the skill and competence of her trial attorney.[95] Cross-examination of the complainant is therefore crucial to defence tactics. Legislative attempts to prevent defence advocates generating this kind of prejudice, by devising a workable 'rape shield', have so far not been entirely successful.[96]

A question that suggests that a witness is of bad character may influence fact-finders irrespective of either the answer or its basis in fact. In one experiment, subjects listened to question and answer sessions in which the interrogator probed for evidence of either extraverted or introverted behaviour. The question might be: 'What do you do when you want to liven up a party?' (suggesting extraversion) or 'Have you ever felt left out of some social group?' (suggesting introversion). The subjects inferred that the witness actually possessed the character traits implied. In reality, all the witnesses were doing was answering the questions asked, whether or not these were situations that they had experienced.[97] It has been alleged that advocates in the United States ask questions that imply serious charges against witnesses, while knowing that there is little or no proof of them. Thus a rape complainant may be asked, 'Isn't it true that you have accused men of rape before?' where the advocate knows she has not. Although research indicates that this particular question has no effect on a mock jury, asking expert witnesses whether their work is poorly regarded

---

[91] Bingham, above n.37, 7.

[92] Young, Cameron and Tinsley, above n.7.

[93] AP Sealy and C Wain, 'Person Perception and Jurors' Decisions' (1980) 19 *British Journal of Social and Clinical Psychology* 7.

[94] K Cotton, 'Evidence Regarding the Prior Sexual History of an Alleged Rape Victim: its Effect on the Perceived Guilt of the Accused' (1975) 33 *University of Toronto Law Review* 165.

[95] E Borgida and N Brekke, 'Psycholegal Research on Rape Trials' in AW Burgess, (ed) *Rape and Sexual Assault* (New York, Garland, 1985).

[96] N Kibble, 'The Sexual History Provisions: Chartering a Course between Inflexible Legislative Rules and Wholly Untrammelled Judicial Decisions' (2000) *Criminal Law Review* 274.

[97] WB Swann, T Giuliano and DM Wegner, 'Where Leading Questions Can Lead; the Power of Conjecture in Social Interaction' (1982) 42 *Journal of Personality and Social Psychology*, 1025.

by colleagues seems to have significant impact, irrespective of whether the witnesses deny it, or whether the prosecution objects to the question.[98]

Demeanour

The adversarial system is built upon a conviction that the appearance and behaviour of a witness are crucial indicators of reliability. The result is an emphasis on oral testimony. Witnesses should give evidence in person so that the finder of fact can make an accurate assessment of their reliability. The rule against hearsay is the legal expression of this principle, requiring witnesses to appear in person and give evidence on oath. This allows observation of their demeanour while giving evidence and their reactions to being cross-examined. Hearsay evidence is now routinely admittd in civil trials, where the judge sits alone as the tribunal of fact.[99] Lord Bridge explained in *Blastland*:

> The rationale of excluding [hearsay] as inadmissible, rooted as it is in the system of trial by jury, is a recognition of the great difficulty, even more acute for a jury than for a trained judicial mind, of assessing what, if any, weight can properly be given to a statement by a person whom the jury may not have seen or heard and which has not been subject to any test of reliability by cross-examination ... The rule against admission of hearsay evidence is fundamental. It is not the best evidence and it is not delivered on oath. The truthfulness and accuracy of the person whose words are spoken to by another witness cannot be tested by cross-examination and the light which his demeanour would throw on his testimony is lost.[100]

In the United States it has been comparatively difficult to persuade the court to allow screens or closed-circuit television to protect vulnerable witnesses because of the importance of the constitutional right to confrontation.[101] The jury should be able not only to see witnesses' demeanour, but also to note their eye contact with the defendant. In the opinion, of the Supreme Court, this makes it more difficult for the witness to lie.[102] The Confrontation Clause does not of course, force witnesses to fix their eyes on the defendant, but it is thought that the triers of fact will draw their own conclusions if they do not.

The assumption that a tribunal can identify who is telling the truth in a courtroom depends upon two things a) that there are indicators that identify a liar or an occasion on which a person is lying, and b) that the tribunal knows what

[98] SM Kassin, LN Williams, and CL Saunders, 'Dirty Tricks of Cross-Examination: the Influence of Conjectural Evidence on the Jury' (1990) 14 *Law and Human Behavior* 373.
[99] Civil Evidence Act 1995.
[100] [1985] 2 All ER 1095,1099 quoting from *Teper v R* [1952] 2 All ER 447, Lord Normand at 449.
[101] 6th Amendment to the Constitution of the United States of America: 'the accused shall enjoy the right ... to be confronted with the witnesses against him'. It must be shown that the witness would be harmed by seeing the defendant in court *Maryland v Craig* 497 US 836 (1990). See chapter eight.
[102] *Coy v Iowa* 1085 Ct 2798 (1988).

these criteria are and acts upon them. This conviction is especially curious given that we live in a society in which deception is rife and to some extent socially necessary. In many social situations the person who is told a lie would prefer to believe it. There are also professional situations where someone does not want to know the truth.[103] For example, advocates often warn their clients not to admit guilt to them if they want to contest the charge in court. Lies are a major part of normal human communication, and are usually successful. Social relationships are facilitated by lies. People like the company of liars. Women tend to tell more other-oriented lies than men, and they teach their children to do the same when they are as young as three years old; it is polite, for instance, to pretend to like a present given by a relative.[104] Small children also have the ability to lie to avoid punishment; in one experiment three year olds were told not to peep while a new toy was being set up, but videotape revealed that ninety per cent did so. Only thirty-eight per cent admitted that they had. Of a group of five year olds subjected to the same test, every child who stole a look at the toy lied.[105]

For those who seek to measure the efficacy of lies or to identify common lying behaviour, laboratory experiments present obvious difficulties. To construct experiments which involve genuine lies requires considerable ingenuity. The commonest solution seems to be to ask subjects to watch a video and have some describing it honestly, while others describe something they have not in fact seen. However, the situation does not reproduce the stress that may be suffered by a liar who is anxious to be believed. Also, a group of randomly selected subjects may contain some individuals who are unused to lying, and will be poor liars who are easy to detect. Other will know little about the topic they are required to lie about. In most experiments, observers are alerted to the fact that some of the people they are required to appraise are lying, and they have to decide which.[106] That situation is not inevitably reproduced in a court of trial. However, courtroom fact-finders may have longer to observe the witness than an experimenter can arrange, and observers of experiments may not have the opportunity to test the witness's story by questioning. They do have the advantage, shared by a tribunal of fact in the courtroom, that exemption from the social obligation to interact with the speaker allows absolute concentration on his or her behaviour.

Although laboratory studies thus have limited generalisability to court proceedings, there has emerged sufficient data on lying behaviour severely to undermine belief in demeanour as a clue to honesty. 'Body language' appears to mislead as much as it informs. Liars do not necessarily cover their mouths with their hands, although many police manuals advise that they do.[107] Accomplished liars know that they should not fidget or appear tense. Research suggests that even

---

[103] Vrij, above n.39.

[104] M Lewis, 'The Development of Deception' in M Lewis and C Saarni, (eds) *Lying and Deception in Everyday Life* (New York, The Guilford Press, 1993).

[105] *Ibid.*

[106] Vrij, above n.39, 2.

[107] *Ibid.* 37.

children learn how to convince their listeners that they are telling the truth. The older they are, the more they know about how to deceive. Eight year olds asked by researchers to lie were found to use fewer body movements and to answer faster when lying than six year olds.[108] There is some evidence that if interrogators show signs of doubt, a liars' behaviour will instantly adjust to conform to the truthful stereotype, but this may only be true of certain kinds of liar.[109] Although many lay observers rely on indicators of dishonesty such as gaze aversion and smiling, these are unreliable and relatively easy to control. Research shows that people are able to modify facial expressions on command (though probably not under stress).[110] Nevertheless, some psychologists claim that there are external indicators of lying. Small movements of hand and foot may indicate an underlying nervousness. This is unlikely to be detected by the naked eye because of the outward composure deliberately maintained by any competent liar.[111] It has also been claimed that an expert can detect micro-expressions or simulated smiling, whereas a layman would see a micro-expression only if shown in slow motion.[112]

It is probably the case that there is no such thing as consistent 'lying behaviour', which can be detected objectively. 'Not all liars show the same behaviour in the same situation, and behaviours will differ across deceptive situations'.[113] Intelligence is a factor in being able to lie convincingly.[114] Bill Clinton, the former President of the United States, gave evidence before the Grand Jury on a notorious matter which had given rise to questions about his judgment and his credibility. On important points he became physically very still, sat up, and looked straight into the camera. Whether or not he was lying, he certainly 'wanted to make an honest impression'.[115] He employed the same behaviour whilst giving an interview to an American television news crew. He later conceded that the content of this interview was false.[116] According to Vrij, successful lying requires good preparation, the ability to think quickly, good acting, lack of guilt or fear, eloquence and a good memory. A high degree of intelligence means that the liar can afford to expend mental energy on controlling his or her demeanour. Vrij records a murder case where a suspect of low intelligence lied[117] in an interview with police officers.

---

[108] A Vrij and FW Winkel, 'Detection of False Statements in First and Third-Graders: the Development of a Nonverbal Detection Instrument' (1996) in G Davies, S Lloyd-Bostock, K MacMurran and C Wilson, *Psychology Law and Criminal Justice* (Berlin, de Gruyter, 1996).

[109] Vrij, above n.39, 52.

[110] M Zuckerman, DY Larrance, NH Spiegel and R Klorman, 'Controlling Non-Verbal Displays: Facial Expression and Tone of Voice' (1981) 17 *Journal of Experimental Social Psychology* 506.

[111] P Ekman P and WV Friesen, 'Non-verbal leakage and clues to deception' (1969) 32 *Psychiatry* 88.

[112] P Ekman, *Telling Lies: Clues to Deceit in the Marketplace* (New York, WW Norton, 1992); P Ekman, M O'Sullivan, M Friesen and KR Scherer, 'Face, Voice and Body in Detecting Deceit' (1991) 15 *Journal of Nonverbal behavior* 125.

[113] Vrij, above n.39, 52.

[114] *Ibid.*, G Köhnken, 'The evaluation of statement credibility: social judgment and expert diagnostic approaches', JR Spencer, R Nicholson, R Flin and R Bull, (eds) *Children's Evidence in Legal Proceedings* (Faculty of Law, University of Cambridge, 1990).

[115] Vrij, above n.39, 26.

[116] M Davis and D Hadkis, 'Demeanour and Credibility' (1995) 106 *Semiotics* 5.

[117] This was established by forensic evidence.

The videotape of the interview shows that when he lied, he averted his gaze, paused more, made more speech errors and spoke more slowly than when he was telling the truth. Constructing the lie probably required considerable effort from him. On the other hand, some professionals develop skill in hiding their emotions. In one experiment, nurses were required to watch videos with gruesome content. Some of them then described what they saw, pretending that it was pleasant. They turned out to be very effective deceivers.[118] Also, it seems that some people are so naturally credible that they tend to be believed whether they are lying or not.[119]

In everyday situations, Vrij suggests, we prefer not to rely on non-verbal behaviour as an indicator of truthfulness.[120] There may be other facts against which we can test the story for inconsistencies, and, indeed, this is probably the most accurate test for lying.[121] Failing that, from the United States across Europe, we look for a change in voice pitch, hesitations and speech errors, pauses, gaze aversion, fidgeting, smiling, and blinking. Police, lawyers and laymen[122] think that honest people speak in clear, steady tones. They believe people who keep a steady eye contact.[123] We expect an honest witness to be physically relaxed and positive. Such a person might nod agreement, and would vary facial expression and vocal intonation.[124] Good liars, however, know that this behaviour is required, and will adjust their demeanour accordingly.[125] They can even manufacture genuine or 'felt' smiles', knowing that 'false smiles', which use muscles not normally associated with smiling will be treated with suspicion.[126] Ethnic differences make it harder to detect liars. Body language associated with a particular culture may be misunderstood by observers from a different background.[127] Eye contact is regarded as impolite in some cultures. Black suspects are viewed with suspicion by white police officers, and tend to employ behaviours associated with lying whether lying or not.[128]

Failure to make eye contact, fidgeting, halting speech with long pauses and apparent nervousness probably have more to do with fear than with lying.[129]

---

[118] Ekman, above n.112.

[119] JE Hocking, JE Bauchner, EP Kaminski and GR Miller, 'Detecting Deceptive Communication from Verbal, Visual and Paralinguistic Cues, (1979) 6 *Human Communication Research* 33.

[120] Vrij, above n.39, 21.

[121] Köhnken, above n.114.

[122] HE Hocking , GR Miller and NE Fontes, 'Videotape in the Courtroom; Witness Deception' (1978) 14 *Trial* 52.

[123] Ekman, above n.112; KA Deffenbacher and EF Loftus, 'Do Jurors Share a Common Understanding Concerning Eye-Witness Behavior? (1982) 6 *Law and Human Behavior* 15.

[124] B Timney and H London, 'Body Language Concomitants of Persuasiveness and Persuasability in Dyadic Interaction' (1977) 3–4 *International Journal of Group Tensions* 48.

[125] GR Miller and JK Burgoon, 'Factors Affecting Assessments of Witness Credibility' in NL Kear and RM Bray, *The psychology of the Courtroom* (London, Academic Press, 1982), at 180.

[126] Ekman, above n.112, although Ekman believes there are micro-expressions to give the game away, above.

[127] P Ekman, ER Sorenson and WV Friesen, 'Pan-Cultural Elements in Facial Displays of Emotion' (1969) 164 *Science* 96.

[128] A Vrij and FW Winkel, 'Cultural Patterns in Dutch and Surinam Nonverbal Behavior: an Analysis of Simulated Police/Citizen Encounters' (1991) 15 *Journal of Nonverbal Behavior* 169.

[129] Vrij, above n.39: cf Miller and Burgoon, above n.125.

Being suspected of lying may itself cause agitation.[130] The demeanour of a witness in a trial could, therefore, lead the court badly astray. Witnesses may be nervous because of the number of people in the courtroom. They may be afraid of the consequences of being disbelieved. They may feel guilty, not because they are lying, but because of the content of their evidence, or its potential consequences. Stress is exacerbated by the witness's inability to escape from the situation.[131] But displaying signs of anxiety such as hesitation, looking away and speaking in a hesitant, subdued manner reduces the probability of being believed. Even in the calm atmosphere of a laboratory, success rates in lie detection is so low, that observers would probably do as well if they tossed a coin to decide who was telling the truth.[132] Looking at all the studies together, lies are detected between forty-five and sixty per cent of the time. University students are most often the participators in studies of lying, but their detection success rate is no worse than that of police officers, experienced or otherwise.[133] While it seems that some people have an individual talent for spotting deceit, [134] the only group apparently effective in it comprises people serving jail terms. Unlike 'experts', prisoners seem to recognise that physical repose is suspicious![135] This may be because in their daily lives they get more feedback than most people confirming whether their judgments of honesty are accurate. Lack of information to confirm or disprove everyday social judgments of honesty may explain why detection rates are generally so low, even when the observer knows the speaker well.[136]

It is easier to detect lies told by children than lies told by adults, because deception requires sophisticated cognition and social skills. Hence adults recognise lying more readily in young children than older ones.[137] However, the success rate is still little better than chance. In Westcott's study,[138] the overall accuracy rate was only fifty-nine per cent. Only one child was correctly identified as truthful by all the raters who saw him. Here, the children either went on a Natural History Museum trip or saw an edited video recording of it. Some of each group were asked to lie about whether they went on the visit or saw the video. In another study, eleven year olds successfully duped barristers and students[139] when

---

[130] Ekman, above n.112, 39.

[131] Penman, above n.69.

[132] Miller and Burgoon, above n.125.

[133] Vrij, above n.39,74.

[134] Ekman, above n.112.

[135] A Vrij and GR Somin, 'Lie Experts Beliefs about Non-Verbal Indicators of Deception' (1996) 20 *Journal of Nonverbal Behavior* 65.

[136] TR Levine, SA McCormack and HS Park, 'Accuracy in Detecting Truths and Lies: Discounting the 'Veracity Effect'' (1999) 66 *Communication Monographs* 125.

[137] BM De Paulo, 'Nonverbal Behavior and Self-Presentation; a Developmental Perspective' in RS Feldman and B Rimer, (eds) *Fundamentals of Nonverbal Behavior* (Paris, Cambridge University Press, 1991) 351–97; RS Feldman, L Jenkins and O Popoola, 'Detection of Deception in Adults and Children via Facial Expressions' (1979) 50 *Child Development* 350.

[138] HL Westcott, GM Davies and BR Clifford, 'Adults' Perception of Childrens' Videotaped Truthful and Deceptive Statements' (1991) 5 *Children and Society* 123.

[139] J Jackson, '*Truth or Fantasy: the Ability of Barristers and Laypersons to Detect Deception in Children's Testimony*' (Paper presented at the APLS Biennial Conference, Hilton Head Island, S Carolina USA, 1996).

pretending to describe watching a video of chimpanzees. The lying children displayed chilling cleverness. When asked whether they had enjoyed the film they tended to say 'No' more frequently than the children who had actually seen it, and then used their avowed lack of interest to explain why they could not supply details of the film. Observers relied most heavily on verbal cues, tending to believe the children who supplied the most detail. They also relied on factors such as long pauses before answering, averted eye contact, hesitancy, 'lying smiles' and nervous smirks, and confidence. Ironically, the most confident children were in fact lying.[140]

Some years ago naïve faith in technological development encouraged flirtations with truth drugs and lie detector machines, but experience has since proved that they are not reliable indicators of honesty. They are in fact simple devices which measure the level of moisture on the palms of the hands, and so may indicate nervousness, but nothing more.[141] Methods used to deceive the machine include biting the tongue or wiggling the toes in order to confuse one's physiology. Such techniques were allegedly used to great effect by Aldrich Ames, a Soviet spy who defeated American polygraph testing in both 1986 and 1991.[142] Polygraphs are used in Canada, Israel and Japan, but nowhere more than in the United States, although courts in some states will not accept polygraph evidence.[143] In the United Kingdom, a working group produced such a devastating report on polygraph machines that the Government of the day abandoned any attempt to introduce them as a source of evidence.[144] Courts have tended to dismiss evidence so obtained on technical grounds,[145] creating the impression that polygraph evidence is inadmissible in England and Wales.[146] Recently, however, two American polygraph examiners conducted trials in three police areas in England. They tested convicted paedophiles, who were asked by probation officers whether they were having unsupervised contact with children. As a result, 'significant action' was taken in three cases to prevent them reoffending, and the Home Office is said to be considering a pilot scheme elsewhere.[147] Yet there is little support for polygraphs amongst forensic psychologists, and even polygraph specialists disagree as to the reliability of various methods.[148]

---

[140] Westcott, Davies and Clifford, above n.138.

[141] L Saxe, 'Science and the GKT Polygraph: a Theoretical Critique' (1991) 3 *Current Directions in Psychological Science* 69.

[142] R Wiseman, speaking at annual meeting of the British Association for the Advancement of Science, Leicester, September 2002, *Daily Telegraph* 9 September 2002.

[143] CJ Patrick and WG Iacono, 'Validity of the Control Question Polygraph Test: the Problem of Sampling Bias' (1991) 76 *Journal of Applied Psychology* 229.

[144] Report of the Working Group of the British Psychological Society on the Use of Polygraphs (1986) 39 *Bulletin of the British Psychological Society* 81: see P Cohen, 'Lie Detectors on Trial' (1997) *New Scientist* 15 May 1997.

[145] As inadmissible previous consistent or hearsay statements.

[146] DW Elliott, 'Lie Detector Evidence: Lessons from the American Experience' in E Cambell and L Waller, (eds) *Well and Truly Tried* (Sydney, Law Book Co, 1982).

[147] *Daily Telegraph* 9 September 2002.

[148] Vrij, above n.39, 172.

Demeanour and the Courts

Notwithstanding the empirical evidence that the demeanour of witnesses is unlikely to lead fact-finders to an accurate assessment of their credibility, courts continue to give it central importance. It has been said that jurors are more able than judges to assess the credibility of witnesses, because they are likely to be

> of similar background to the defendant (and witnesses) and/or to have had experiences which are sufficiently close to that of the defendant to enable them to take a view on a person's possible responses in those circumstances.[149]

Nevertheless, judges are prepared to give considerable weight to their own assessment of a witness's credibility. In *Re DH*,[150] a mother suffering from Munchausen's Syndrome by Proxy had lost custody of her son to his father after she was seen on videotape harming the boy. The father and social services opposed the mother having any contact with the child. Wall J overrode their objections, having been struck 'by the mother's basic honesty and straightforwardness'. He noted that during questioning about her husband 'her eyes flashed', and that she asked to leave the court while the videotape was played. He believed her statement that she would not harm her child again. Similarly, a judge required to decide whether a particular ship had been deliberately scuttled by the crew dismissed powerful evidence that they had indeed sabotaged their own ship for the insurance money. He was persuaded to the contrary by the evidence of the second mate, who testified that the ship had struck a piece of floating wreckage: 'He gave his evidence fairly and frankly, and with great reticence. In my judgment, that was a witness of truth'.[151] In *Pickford v ICI*,[152] the House of Lords acknowledged the importance of the deportment of an expert witness. The issue was whether a typist's disabling condition was physical rather than psychological. It was held that where expert evidence conflicts, demeanour is a legitimate way of resolving the case.

Where judges find themselves sitting in a criminal case without a jury, they may be less content to make categorical judgments based on demeanour. Jackson and Doran found that judges in the Diplock Courts preferred to examine the content of the story for internal consistency and plausibility.[153] The same caution in criminal cases was exercised by the jurors surveyed in New Zealand.[154] They took account of both content and demeanour. Witnesses who seemed frank, forthright and genuine, and who gave consistent evidence were generally believed. If witnesses contradicted themselves, were defensive or evasive, or became annoyed during cross-examination, they were generally regarded with suspicion. But witnesses

---

[149] Home Office *Juries in Serious Fraud Trials: A Consultation Document* (Home Office London 1998) 7.
[150] [1994] 2 FCR 3.
[151] *La Compania Martiartu of Bilbao v Royal Exchange Assurance* (1922) Ll.L.Rep 186, 188–89.
[152] [1998] 1 WLR 1189.
[153] Jackson and Doran, above n.31.
[154] Young, Cameron and Tinsley, above n.7.

who were found to have contradicted themselves or to have told lies were not necessarily disbelieved entirely, if a plausible explanation was apparent. In general, jurors did not want to rely entirely on their assessment of the witness's credibility, and wanted 'hard facts'. Even where they believed the complainant to the point where they felt convinced of the defendant's guilt, they were reluctant to convict, presumably because they felt they might be wrong.

Lord Bingham acknowledges that a witness's performance in the witness box probably reveals nothing in the commonest kind of case, which consists of two witnesses contradicting each other and appearing equally plausible. However, he claims that there are occasions when demeanour does identify a liar. For a judge might recognise a type of rogue he has encountered before, or there might be a very strong impression that a particular witness is lying.[155] More recently, however, Sir Robin Auld sufficiently doubted the importance of demeanour to recommend a reduced role for the hearsay rule.[156] It was seen above that the rule against hearsay derives its authority largely from the belief that the credibility of witnesses must be tested in court; unless a witness can be cross-examined in front of the tribunal of fact, dishonesty or mistake could go undetected. However, there are exceptions to the rule, allowing the hearsay statement of an absent witness to be adduced if circumstances suggest that person spoke truthfully. One of these exceptions concerns the 'dying declaration'. This should be made by someone

> at the point of death, and when every hope of this world is gone; when every motive for falsehood is silenced, and the mind is induced by the most powerful considerations to speak the truth; a situation so solemn and awful is considered by law as creating an obligation equal to that which is imposed by a positive oath administered in a court of justice.[157]

Being at this 'state of extremity' is thought to inspire honesty. 'No person who is immediately going into the presence of his maker will do so with a lie on his lips'.[158] Consequently it must be shown that the declarant at the time had a 'settled hopeless expectation of death'.[159] Whether or not this conviction has any empirical validity, its logic breaks down in that the exception applies only to homicide trials and the victim's statement accounts for the (fatal) injury.[160] Another exception to the rule against hearsay is *res gestae*.[161] It holds that an utterance that is spontaneous is unlikely to be deliberately misleading. Absolute contemporaneity is not required, if the event remains overwhelmingly at the forefront of the victim's mind, so that the danger of fabrication is minimal. The test is

---

[155] Bingham, above n.37, 8.
[156] Auld, above n.4 pp 547–8.
[157] *Woodcock* (1789) 1 Leach 500, per Eyre CB.
[158] *Osman* (1881) 15 Cox CC 1 per Lush J.
[159] *Perry* [1909] 25 TLR 676.
[160] *Woodcock* (1789) 1 Leach 500; *Mead* (1824) 2 B&C 605.
[161] The statement is part of the 'thing in issue', or the event which the trial concerns, whether it be the crime, or the making of a contract.

whether the event was so unusual, startling or dramatic as to dominate the thoughts of the witness, so that his or her utterance was an instinctive reaction to that event, thus giving no opportunity for reasoned reflection.[162]

The existence of these exceptions suggests that, despite its intrinsic unreliability, demeanour is of paramount importance in the legal system. The obsession appears to be with uncovering malice, rather than exposing mistake. The fact that, where a witness is absent, there can be no cross-examination aimed at uncovering errors (for example, of identification) seems to be regarded as relatively unimportant. Yet it may be the case that where a person is subject to stress, the potential for errors of fact is increased. Both *res gestae* statements and dying declarations (where the person has just received a fatal injury and knows it) involve people exposed to dramatic events. In *Bedingfield*,[163] for example, the defendant's wife was seen by witnesses to enter her room. She left it again shortly afterward, her throat horribly cut, and said to one of them, 'Oh dear, aunt, see what Bedingfield has done to me'. She died subsequently. Her statement would have been admissible as a dying declaration had she exhibited a settled, hopeless expectation of death (which, unfortunately, she failed to do) or as a *res gestae* statement had it been sufficiently spontaneous.[164] Legal enthusiasm for 'heat of the moment' statements[165] ignores empirical findings that stress has a negative effect on human powers of description and recall.[166] Clifford and Holling asked subjects to watch a film. Some saw a scene in which a woman in the street was asked for directions, and others one in which she was thrown against a wall and her bag stolen. Subjects who saw the violent incident could remember fewer details.[167] In fact, it seems that violence reduces memory even for events which occurred before the attack took place.[168] Weapon focus studies show that people pay more attention to the weapon than the surrounding circumstances.[169]

Ethical constraints make it difficult for psychologists to reproduce severe stress.[170] Data drawn from real events appears to contradict laboratory findings.

---

[162] *Andrews* [1987] 1 AER 513.

[163] (1879) 14 Cox CC 341.

[164] At the time of this decision, courts required absolute contemporaneity. In *Andrews*, above n.162, the emphasis shifted to spontaneity. Mrs Bedingfield's statement would be admissible today as part of the *res gestae*.

[165] Not all dying declarations are made immediately following the infliction of the injury; the timing depends upon how long it takes the victim to die. Some, however, will be 'heat of the moment' statements and would also have been part of the *res gestae*.

[166] BR Clifford and R Bull, *Psychology of Person Identification* (Routledge and Kegan Paul, Boston, 1987); BL Cutler and SD Penrod, *Mistaken Identification: The Eyewitness, Psychology and the Law* (Cambridge, Cambridge University Press, 1995).

[167] BR Clifford and C Hollin, 'Effects of Type of Incident and the Number of Perpetrators in Eyewitness Testimony' (1981) 66 *Journal of Applied Psychology* 352.

[168] EF Loftus and HJ Burns 'Mental Shock can Produce Retrograde Amnesia' (1982) 10 *Memory and Cognition* 318.

[169] EF Loftus, GR Loftus and J Messo, 'Some Facts about Weapon Focus' (1987) 11 *Law and Human Behavior* 55; NM Steblay, 'A Meta-Analysistic Review of the Weapon Focus Effect' (1992) 16 *Law and Human Behavior* 43.

[170] PB Ainsworth, *Psychology, Law and Eyewitness Testimony* (Chichester, Wiley, 1998) 37.

The survivors of a disaster on the River Thames, where a pleasure boat collision killed fifty-one people, had fairly accurate memories for the details even months afterwards.[171] In Cutshall and Yuille's study of real crimes of violence, witnesses' memories became more detailed and accurate over time. They were not amenable to suggestion. Violent robberies were remembered better than non-violent ones. More details were supplied by witnesses to crimes where a weapon was used than where none was used. They also furnished a better description of the attacker. One explanation for this may be that extreme stress could result in 'flashbacks' afterwards, enhancing the witness's memory. If so, the more serious the crime, and the more caught up in it the witness, the greater the reliability of the evidence. However, it seems that, despite the quality of their descriptions, Cutshall and Yuille's subjects did not make more accurate identifications when asked to recognise the perpetrator at a parade.[172] It is possible that they had been pressed by police interviewers to supply more and more information, with the attendant possibility that, while similar in content, they had become increasingly inaccurate.[173]

Refusal to Testify

Any defendant who refuses to testify runs the risk that fact-finders will assume that reluctance to speak indicates guilt. In England, the defendant in a criminal trial cannot be compelled to give evidence.[174] In Continental trials, accused persons cannot decline to be questioned, but they can decline to answer. If they do elect to explain themselves, they do so unsworn. In most legal systems, no adverse inferences may be drawn from a refusal to answer all or any of the questions put. There is considerable psychological pressure to answer, however, because unfavourable common-sense inferences are almost inevitable, given that the refusal always relates to a particular question.[175] Yet a defendant may have very good reason to decline to give evidence. A poor performance in the witness box may sufficiently undermine his or her perceived credibility to lead the fact-finder to infer guilt. And while it is true that prosecution witnesses suffer a great deal of stress while giving evidence in court, and have to satisfy a higher standard of proof than the accused, they do not run the risk of being convicted of a criminal offence with the attending consequences. Accused persons stand at risk of a criminal penalty which could in their terms be very serious. In addition, they could lose their job, family and friends.

---

[171] J Thompson, T Morton and L Fraser, 'Memories for the Marchioness' (1997) 5 *Memory* 615.

[172] JC Cutshall and JC Yuille, 'Field Studies of Eyewitness Memory of Actual Crimes' in D Raskin, (ed) *Psychological Methods in Criminal Investigation and Evidence* (New York, Springer-Verlag, 1989).

[173] PA Tollestrup, JW Turtle and JC Yuille, 'Actual Victims and Witnesses to Robbery and Fraud: an Archival Analysis' in DF Ross, JD Read and MP Toglia, (eds) *Adult Eyewitness Testimony: Current Trends and Developments* (Cambridge, Cambridge University Press, 1994).

[174] Criminal Evidence Act 1898, s.1(1).

[175] MR Damaska, 'Evidentiary barriers to conviction and two models of criminal procedure: a comparative study' (1973) 121 *University of Pennsylvania Law Review* 506.

The Criminal Justice and Public Order Act 1994 allows the tribunal of fact in criminal trials to draw such adverse inferences 'as appear proper'[176] if the defendant declines to give evidence, unless guilt is not in issue, or it appears to the court that the 'physical or mental condition of the accused makes it undesirable for him to give evidence'.[177] Thus the legal system has reasserted its emphasis on demeanour and presentation, relying more than ever on a probably imaginary human ability to distinguish lies from the truth. Accused persons are therefore in an unenviable position. They face the risk that hesitancy and nervousness will undermine their testimony, and must attempt to display the fluency and confidence that tends to ensure people are believed. To some extent the courts have mitigated the impact of the 1994 provisions by demanding that an inference of guilt may not be drawn if parts of the prosecution case have so little evidential value that they do not call for an answer. But where aspects of the evidence clearly call for an explanation which the accused ought to be in a position to give, if an explanation exists, then a failure to give any explanation may as a matter of common sense allow the drawing of an inference that there is no other explanation than that the accused is guilty. Thus, evidence that the defendant had been in a car linked with a shooting did not call for an answer from him, being highly circumstantial. Evidence that linked him directly with the shooting itself did call for an answer, and failure to provide one entitled the jury to infer guilt.[178]

A nervous defendant who decides not to testify because of fear of giving a poor performance is therefore placed in a quandary. The judicial climate is very hostile to an inadequate defendant. In *Friend*,[179] the defendant, who was accused of murder, had the mental age of a nine-year-old child. On the ground that a nine-year-old child could give evidence, the judge refused to rule that Friend's mental condition made it undesirable for him to do so. Hence the jury was instructed that they might draw adverse inferences from his failure to testify. The Court of Appeal upheld his conviction, although if Friend had been aged only nine he could not have been tried at all, since children are only criminally responsible at the age of ten. It is not surprising that, since these provisions were enacted, very few defendants in England and Wales refuse to give evidence. The figure was already low in magistrates' courts, so the change is most significant in Crown Courts.[180]

Particular Witnesses

Does the perceived credibility of a witness depend upon the attributes of the fact-finder? Although women may be less active during group discussion than men,[181]

---

[176] S.37(3).
[177] S.37(1).
[178] *Murray* (1993) 97 Cr App R 151.
[179] [1997] 2 All ER 1011.
[180] T Buck, R Street and D Brown, *The Right to Silence and the Impact of the Criminal Justice and Police and Criminal Evidence Act 1994* HORS 199 (London, Home Office, 2000).
[181] Arce, Fariña, and Sabral, above n.34.

it appears that in general the gender of jurors has little effect on the verdict.[182] However, many advocates are convinced that female jurors are more inclined to disbelieve complainants in rape cases. Denigration of victims may be an inevitable incident of a just world-driven attribution of responsibility.[183] But women in general fail to convince as witnesses because of their tendency to employ 'powerless' speech styles.[184] Blacks and children are also likely to be disbelieved because of their characteristic use of powerless language.[185] 'Powerful' language suggests confidence and reliability.[186] The prejudice of individual jurors may also detract from the perceived credibility of some witnesses; there are reports from real jurors of racism having affected verdicts.[187] Stereotypical expectations may apply not only to the category of witness but to the kind of crime alleged. Women who testify that they suffered sexual assault may not be believed unless there they show evidence of distress. Jurors generally appear to have an expectation that a genuine rape victim should be in a highly emotional state.[188] Similarly, children who have been abused should be distraught.[189] In the absence of signs of distress, either in the courtroom itself or immediately after the alleged crime, complainants may be seriously misjudged. Women who have been assaulted are as likely to respond in a 'controlled' fashion (subdued and calm) as 'expressively' (crying, restless).[190] In *Taylor*,[191] an American case, expert evidence to explain rape trauma syndrome to the jury was admitted to prevent them from being misled by the absence of visible signs of distress following the alleged rape. But there is a danger that prosecution lawyers will pander to the stereotype. An advocate who considers that the evidence of a complainant in tears is more likely to convince the jury will be unenthusiastic about special measures in the courtroom that are designed to reduce stress for the witness. Certainly, a number of prosecution lawyers have in the past

---

[182] G Kelte and VJ Konečni, 'Communication Channels and Gender: Differences in Decoding and Integration of Cues in Legal Decision-Making' in G Davies, S Lloyd-Bostock, M K MacMurran and C Wilson, (eds) above n.29.

[183] See chapter two.

[184] For example the frequent use of intensifiers such as 'so', 'very' and 'surely'; use of hesitations such as 'well', 'you know'.

[185] WM O'Barr, *Linguistic Evidence: Language, Power and Strategy in the Courtroom* (New York, Academic Press, 1982).

[186] Straightforward language, fewer adjectives, rational and assertive.

[187] D Barber and G Gordon, *Members of the Jury* (London, Wildwood House, 1974).

[188] FW Winkel and L Kopelaar, 'Perceived Credibility of the Communicator: Studies of Perceptual Bias in Police Officers Conducting Rape Interviews' in F Lösel , D Bender and T Bleisener, (eds) *Psychology and Law: International Perspectives* (New York, Walter de Gruyter, 1992).

[189] E Borgida, AW Gresham, MB Kovon and PC Regan, 'Children as Witnesses in Court: the Influence of Expert Psychological Testimony' in AW Burgess, (ed) *Child Trauma: Issues and Research* (NewYork, Garland, 1992) 131.

[190] A Burgess and L Homstrom 'Rape Trauma Syndrome' (1974) 131 *American Journal of Psychiatry* 981. 'Rape trauma syndrome' has been said to be a subtype of post-traumatic stress disorder; AA Stone, 'Post Traumatic Stress Disorder and the Law: Critical Review of the New Frontier' (1993) 21 *Bulletin Academy of Psychiatry and the Law* 23.

[191] 75 NY 2d 277; 552 NE 2d 131.

failed to request special measures for child witnesses. Parliament has responded by enacting a presumption in favour of special measures in their case.[192]

There are some studies which suggest that attractive witnesses may expect to have the sympathy of the court, but the evidence inconclusive.[193] For example, it has been said that in rape trials where if the evidence is ambiguous, the defendant is more likely to be found guilty if he is unattractive and the victim attractive, than he is if he is attractive and she is unattractive.[194] At the trial of John Blott, a police officer, his undoubted good looks did not prevent him from being convicted in 1998 of raping several women. His defence was that they consented to sexual intercourse, and in support of this claim argued that someone who could so easily attract women had no need to rape. But the evidence of the complainants was that, although they had initially readily agreed to a date with Blott, he then deliberately humiliated and then raped them. The women were believed. The verdicts against him were consistent with findings that criminal defendants benefit from their attractiveness unless it is suggested that they used their looks to commit the crime.[195] Some work has been done to see whether certain kinds of appearance may be linked by jurors to certain kinds of crime.[196] It has been claimed that people with baby faces with large round eyes are more likely to be found to be negligent in relation to selling a hazardous product than those with more mature faces. Immaturity may be associated with carelessness, whereas those with mature faces are thought to be more likely than innocent-looking people to commit fraud.[197]

The law has a range of preconceptions about the credibility of witnesses. The corroboration rules resulted from suspicion about certain kinds of witness who were for many years thought to be intrinsically unreliable. The evidence of children, for example, was particularly distrusted, especially if they were very young.[198] Although the traditional corroboration rules are now consigned to history,[199] a vigorous lobby having claimed that children do not make up stories of abuse,[200] it may still be difficult to persuade fact-finders to convict on the basis of children's

---

[192] See chapter eight.

[193] FC Dane and LS Wrightsman, 'Effects of Defendants' and Victims' Characteristics on Jurors' Verdicts' in NL Kear and RM Bray, (eds) *The Psychology of the Courtroom* (London, Academic Press, 1982).

[194] Ibid; cf JJ Stewart, 'Defendant's Attractiveness as a Factor in the Outcome of Criminal Trials: an Observational Study' (1980) 10 *Journal of Applied Social Psychology* 348. But see B Thornton, 'Effect of Rape Victims's Attractiveness in a Jury Simulation' (1977) 3 *Personality and Social Psychology Bulletin* 666.

[195] Stewart, above n.194.

[196] DS Berry and LZ McArthur, 'Perceiving Character in Faces: the Impact of Age-Related Craniofacial Changes in Social Perception' (1986) 100 *Psychological Bulletin* 3.

[197] H Sigall and N Ostrove, 'Beautiful but Dangerous: Effects of Offender Attractiveness and Nature of the Crime in Juridic Judgments' (1975) 31 *Journal of Personality and Social Psychology* 410.

[198] See JR Spencer and R Flin, *The Evidence of Children: the Law and the Psychology* (London, Blackstone, 1993).

[199] See chapter eight.

[200] See JR Spencer, 'Child Witnesses and the Law of Evidence' [1987] *Criminal Law Review* 76; [1988] *New Law Journal* 147.

testimony. In a study carried out on behalf of the Home Office, physical abuse cases attracted a far higher proportion of guilty pleas than allegations of sexual abuse, possibly because physical evidence would be available in many cases of violence. Out of eight contested prosecutions for the rape of a child, only one resulted in a conviction, and that was for a lesser charge.[201] American college students believe that children under six are particularly prone to tell lies, second only to politicians in their perceived dishonesty.[202]

Complainants in sexual cases have also long been regarded with suspicion, and judges traditionally had to warn the jury against convicting on the strength of the complainant's evidence alone. The reasoning was of this nature:

> The evidence of Lady Wishfort complaining of rape may be dangerous because she may be indulging in undiluted sexual fantasy. A Mrs Frail making the same allegation may need corroboration because of the danger that she does not wish to admit the consensual intercourse of which she is ashamed.[203]

This view is not exclusive to men. The Heilbron Report, the work of a woman judge, says: 'We are not unaware of the fact that from time to time women do make false charges from a variety of motives'.[204] There are eminent forensic practitioners who appear to concur.[205] They may be as guilty of subscribing to myth as the numerous Scottish police officers who reported to researchers that many allegations of rape are false. When asked, they were unable to recall instances of unquestionably false complaints that they had dealt with personally.[206] The Home Office concedes that it is difficult to know to what extent, if any, false charges are made.[207] In answer to allegations from police surgeons who claimed that at least a third of rape allegations are false, Adler replies that the only methodologically sound study[208] is that of the New York Sex Crimes Analysis Unit, which examined all reports of rape in New York over two years. False allegations accounted for about two per cent of rape complaints — a figure comparable with unfounded allegations of crimes generally.[209] Despite the abolition of the requirement for a corroboration warning in sexual cases,[210] the high level of acquittals in contested rape trials in England and Wales[211] suggest that traditional scepticism has not been overcome.

---

[201] G Davis, L Hoyano, C Keenan, L Maitland and R Morgan, *An Assessment of the Admissibility and Sufficiency of Evidence in Child Abuse Proceedings*, (London, Home Office, 1999).

[202] B Kintz, 'College Students' Attitudes about Telling Lies' (1977) *Bulletin of the Psychonomic Society* 490.

[203] *Kilbourne* [1973] AC 729, per Lord Hailsham at 748.

[204] *Report of the Advisory Group on the Law of Rape* (1976 Cmnd 6352).

[205] S Smith and FS Fiddes, *Forensic Medicine* (London, Churchill, 1955).

[206] G Chambers and A Millar, *Investigating Sexual Assault*, (Edinburgh, HMSO, 1983).

[207] Home Office, *Sexual Offences, Consent and Sentencing* (HORS No 54).

[208] Z Adler, *Rape on Trial* (London, Routledge and Kegan Paul, 1987) 25.

[209] *Report of the New York Sex Crimes Analysis Unit*, quoted in P Patullo, *Judging Women*, (London, NCCL, 1983).

[210] S.32(1) Criminal Justice and Public Order Act 1994.

[211] 75% acquitted: J Harris and S Grace, *A Question of Evidence? Investigating and Prosecuting Rape in the 1990's*, Home Office Research Study 196 (London, Home Office, 1999). The figure is particularly striking in view of the low proportion (about 20%) of reported rapes that are prosecuted.

CONSTRUCTING A STORY

Jurors have to contend with evidence presented to them in the manner and order dictated by a constellation of procedural and evidential rules. This results in a massive collection of information offered usually in jumbled temporal sequence, and with gaps in the depiction of events. Jury deliberations appear to begin with an information search as they attempt to unravel the narrative, so procedural and legal matters are dealt with towards the end of the discussion.[212] Bennett and Feldman[213] suggest that the narrative jurors try to construct is modelled on the detective stories with which they are familiar. Their research combined prolonged observations not only of court proceedings, but also of the informal discussions and behaviour of participants. In addition they conducted experiments prompted what they saw. They discovered that only rarely did the weight of the evidence dictate the verdict. Where cases were difficult to resolve, the juror used a combination of two tests for the evidence: did it happen that way? could it have happened that way? The authors concluded that a narrative is accepted as true if it presents a coherent central action and a setting that makes the action understandable. Evidence is fitted together by jurors within a story framework that dictates a chronology. Where the evidence leaves gaps, the story will fill them, but if the plausibility of the story depends on understandings drawn from experience, then jurors who came from different social worlds may disagree about the meaning and the plausibility of the same stories.

Research led by Professor Hastie has elaborated on Bennett and Feldman's story thesis and provided empirical evidence for it. In a well-known study designed to discover how jurors react to this problem, sixty-nine different mock juries were asked to assess the same case, presented on video. It was a murder case based on a real trial. According to legal experts, the only proper verdict was second-degree murder, but there were three other possible verdicts, and thirty-eight per cent of jurors selected those. When the jurors explained what they thought had actually happened, it was found that this depended on which facts they recalled.[214] They had selected facts to make a plausible story, and then the story itself filled any gaps in the evidence. In fact, forty-five per cent of the components of the story they accepted were mere inferences. Hastie and his colleagues concluded from this that deviant verdicts are associated with poor comprehension, together with poor memory for the salient facts of the case, the legal definitions of the crimes and the details of the evidence of individual witnesses. The mock jurors who chose different verdicts had constructed different stories,[215] but it was not clear whether the story dictated the verdict or was an *ex post facto* justification for the verdict.

---

[212] KL Hansen, EG Schaefer and JJ Lawless, 'Temporal Patterns of Normative, Informational and Procedural-Legal Discussion in Jury Deliberations' (1993) 14 *Basic and Applied Social Psychology* 33.
[213] WL Bennett and MS Feldman, *Reconstructing Reality in the Courtroom* (London, Tavistock, 1981) 171.
[214] Hastie, R, Penrod, S, and N Pennington, above n.30. But see ET Higgins and JA Bargh, 'Social cognition and social perception' (1987) 38 *Annual Review of Psychology* 369.
[215] N Pennington and R Hastie, 'Evidence Evaluations in Complex Decision Making' (1986) 51 *Journal of Personality and Social Psychology* 242.

The influence of the need for narrative was seen in a later study where individual mock jurors were most likely to convict if the prosecution case was presented as a story, but the defence case was presented in witness order. They were most likely to acquit where the defence case was presented as a story and the prosecution case was not. Where neither side had a story format, the results were indeterminate. Participants also felt more confident of the decision, and found the evidence stronger, when presented with a story.[216] Clearly, the traditional serial calling of individual witnesses prevents events from being described in the sequence in which they originally occurred. According to Pennington and Hastie, jurors try to select, from the welter of facts they have heard, the story that appears most coherent in terms of completeness, consistency and plausibility.[217] Suppose, for example, the defendant lives in an isolated rural area and keeps a loaded shotgun by his bed. He shoots a burglar dead, and claims that he did so in fear of his life, since he and his neighbours have been repeatedly broken into at night with no protection from the police who are based miles away. They may make deductions from world knowledge,[218] such as large farmers are hard to frighten (or not). Heuristics will influence the judgement, but Pennington and Hastie believe that the reasoning process is more sophisticated than a rush into stereotyping. They suggest that inferential reasoning proceeds by steps, which are associated with 'certainty conditions', such as typicality (how typical a farmer is the defendant? how typical a burglary was it?).[219] To this the juror adds reasoning by analogy — how would I feel? The decision-maker constructs an intermediate picture of the event and that is the basis of the final decision.

Lay jurors, and to some extent, magistrates, listen to evidence without knowledge of its legal significance (which they are told at the end of the trial).[220] Yet it seems that judges, who understand the relationship of items of evidence to the legal issues, also operate a story model to give meaning to the evidence before them. According to Wagenaar,[221] this may lead to error, and to convictions which are unsafe. Wagenaar's work is based on judicial decision-making in The Netherlands; since judges there give reasons for their decisions, their reasoning processes are less opaque than jury verdicts in British trials. His team found that before a judge will accept a story, it must be tied to reality by means of evidence (which is itself only another narrative which may or may not be true). The ultimate anchor, however, is common sense or heuristical belief, causing excessive reliance on narrative coherence and stereotypes. One of his examples is that of a

---

[216] *Ibid.*

[217] N Pennington and R Hastie, 'Explanation-Based Decision Making: Effects of Memory Structure on Judgement' (1988) 14 *Journal of Experimental Psychology: Learning, Memory and Recognition* 521.

[218] Pennington and Hastie, above n.215.

[219] Cf the 'representativeness' heuristic: A Tversky and D Kahneman, 'Extensional Versus Intuitive Reasoning: the Conjunction Fallacy in Probability Judgment' (1983) 90 *Psychological Review* 293.

[220] See chapter five.

[221] WA Wagenaar, PJ van Koppen, and HM Crombag, *Anchored Narratives: the Psychology of Criminal Evidence* (Hemel Hempstead, Harvester Wheatsheaf, 1993).

person who has been shot dead. Beside his dead body is a gun bearing John's fingerprints. This in itself cannot incriminate John unless some other evidence suggests that this gun was the murder weapon. The additional evidence may be scientific in nature and, to be accepted, rests on an assumption that ballistic experts generally tell the truth. On the other hand, the link between the gun and the killing may consist of no more than a belief that, in general, guns found by the corpses of those shot dead are the ones used for the killing. Wagenaar argues that triers of fact like to anchor stories in evidence that is supported by general rules or common sense propositions. This becomes dangerous when a story is so plausible that it is anchored directly to the belief structure without any intermediate level of evidence. This could lead to the conviction of one person even when there is another equally likely, or even more likely, suspect. Just as alarmingly, highly diagnostic evidence can be omitted from the anchoring structure without affecting the perceived strength of what remains. Wagenaar observes that judges will explain what evidence convinced them, but not the common-sense assumptions they relied on. Yet the strength of the evidence depends entirely on the rule chosen as anchor, whether it be that forensic scientists make few mistakes, or that innocent men do not confess.

One of Wagenaar's own examples is the case of *Henkemans*,[222] who said he had come to Amsterdam using an air ticket given to him by a friend whose name and address he could not remember. The police, acting on a tip-off, observed him arrive at the airport. He was seen immediately to visit two Chinese professional drug-dealers in a hotel. These men left, carrying a suitcase. Their house was searched, and heroin discovered there, but no trace of heroin could be found in the suitcase or on the defendant Henkemans. Nevertheless, he was convicted of supplying heroin, although the *actus reus* of the offence was not anchored at all. The case appears to confirm the importance of a narrative that is convincing, even if it does not necessarily provide anchors on the issues which, from a legal point of view, are crucial in a criminal case, namely, identification, *actus reus* and *mens rea*. In *Henkemans*, the lack of evidence on those issues had no impact because the prosecution story was so good. In an English case, a jury was equally persuaded by a good story. In *Yalman*[223], the defendant met his elderly father at Stansted airport. Yet he did not approach his father on his arrival, acknowledging him only from a distance. They met up later, at the exit. Yalman explained this by saying that they had had a disagreement. The father's suitcase contained heroin. There was evidence at Yalman's flat that he was a user of heroin. Yalman was convicted of importing a Class A drug into England. His claim to have been at the airport innocently required the jury to accept a weak narrative, involving a son who behaves in a way sons generally do not. The prosecution's story, that father and son had a prior arrangement designed to avoid suspicion, provided a more convincing explanation for his actions.

---

[222] *Ibid.*, 48.
[223] [1988] 2 Cr App R 269.

Jackson and Doran endorsed Wagenaar's findings. The Belfast judges they observed tended to sum up in terms of a comparison of rival stories. Where there were contradictions and conflicts of credibility, allegations were compared against the judge's own ideas of likely behaviour — for example, would most people have informed the police straight away in that situation? Judges employ case materials that could be considered conducive to story-construction, for example, knowledge of other crimes. In the New Zealand Jury Project, it was discovered that some jurors expected the trial to follow a story format, and therefore took inadequate notes of a witness's testimony on the assumption that the witness would re-appear at a later stage. Many jurors found that the order of presentation of evidence militated against their understanding of the narrative. They used the story they constructed to fill evidential gaps, but, unfortunately, in some cases the story they wanted to flesh out was largely irrelevant.[224] Although they were willing to change one version of the story for a new one in the light of new facts emerging s the trial progressed, the later version was often significantly influenced by the content of the earlier.[225] They would have been helped by advance notice of the content of the defence story, for example, had the defence had presented a summary of their case before they began.

Common sense as the ultimate anchor of the narrative selected by the tribunal of fact could allow prejudice and stereotyping to dictate the verdict. The plausibility of the story, as it accords with the fact-finder's heuristical assumptions, may dictate which witnesses are believed more than the way they present themselves in the witness box. The important question may be the extent to which the particular testimony fits into a coherent narrative, which itself will be convincing if it complies with common sense assumptions about the way people behave and events unfold. Lord Bingham describes a case he heard about how a ship came to be damaged. There was a conflict of testimony between a seaman and his First Officer. The seaman said that when he was due to fly out to join his new ship, bound for India, he went with his wife and children to the airport. There he met the First Officer, also travelling to meet the ship. The party went for a meal. He alleged that his wife expressed concern about how he would cope with the heat in India, to which the First Officer replied that she should not worry, as he proposed to run the ship aground before they got there, so that he could earn extra overtime. In court, the First Officer denied that he had said this. As judge, Lord Bingham took the view that it was highly unlikely that the First Officer would make such a statement in front of a family he did not know.[226] Although not impossible, the seaman's story sounded highly improbable.

A melodramatic story may prove irresistible to the tribunal of fact. In 2001, Nicholas Kay was tried for murdering his wife, who had disappeared in 1992.[227] No body has ever been found. According to her sister, Rochelle, Rhonda Kay vanished

---

[224] Young, Cameron and Tinsley, above n.7 para.5.30.
[225] *Ibid.*, para.3.13.
[226] Bingham, above n.37, 14.
[227] *Daily Telegraph* 6 October 2001.

the day after she found her husband in bed with their lodger, Karen Scott. Kay denied all knowledge of his wife's whereabouts, but burnt or sold her clothes and possessions within two days of her disappearance. Although Mrs Kay had apparently ejected her from the house, Scott returned the next day, and she and Kay were married three years later. In 1999, police placed a listening device in their home while they were on holiday.[228] Rochelle telephoned Kay on their return. On police instructions, she told him that Rhonda's remains had been found. She ended her call, 'I hope they get you this time, you bastard.' Subsequently, Kay was heard to talk with Karen Scott about a body in a particular lake, discussing whether it would be possible to obtain forensic evidence from it. He mentioned a plastic bag, adding, 'It would be too small. It was all in bits. Once the tendons have rotted it will separate and disperse'. When Scott expressed concern that forensic evidence would linger in his van and on the bedroom walls, he replied, 'I had a hell of job getting the carpet sorted; I must've been at it for an hour.' Police searched the lake in question, but found nothing. Later, Kay claimed that the couple had suspected that the house was bugged, and staged the conversation as a joke. But the strength of the prosecution story was so strong that it overrode his explanation, the lack of a body, and the absence of any evidence as to how Rhonda died. The jury convicted Kay of manslaughter, a conclusion based on their belief that Rhonda was dead, that her husband had caused her death, and that he had caused her death with a criminal degree of culpability.[229]

In *Blastland*,[230] the defendant was charged with the murder of a boy, K. He suggested that the murderer was another man, M, who had been in the vicinity while Blastland had been with the boy. Several witnesses had observed M, before K's body had officially been found, to arrive home mud stained, announcing that a boy had been killed in the woods. The defence wished to adduce evidence of this to suggest that the reason for M's knowledge was that he had killed K himself. The House of Lords upheld the trial judge's view that this evidence, designed to support a defence narrative in which M was the murderer, was inadmissible. The rival story was irrelevant. Direct evidence against M would have been admissible, but it is not in order for the defence to construct a circumstantial case of this kind against someone who is not on trial. This kind of reasoning puts the defence in severe difficulty. Wagenaar has observed that anchored narratives may explain how evidence that suggests that the defendant is not guilty, and even that someone else is, may be disregarded. The anchoring construction consists of evidence that connects the narrative to general beliefs. Only the evidence that fits this purpose is selected. Thus it can happen that only a small portion of the evidence is used, the rest being ignored. The defence need to be able to present an alternative story 'which accommodates the incriminating facts in an innocent manner'.[231]

---

[228] A lawful operation with required permissions.
[229] Nicholas Kay received a prison sentence of six years.
[230] [1985] 2 All ER 1095.
[231] Wagenaar, van Koppen and Crombag, above n.221, 58.

In the case of *Shonubi*,[232] the determination of the defendant's sentence involved a judgment of his credibility. The defendant explained his earlier trips between Nigeria and New York as visits to relatives. The prosecution argued that he had been smuggling heroin, although they had no evidence of this. Judge Weinstein employed most of the methods of assessment of witness veracity discussed in this chapter. Shonubi was guilty of both inconsistency and deceit, in that he had changed his story several times and had lied to the customs officer. His demeanour struck the judge as 'brazen'; he 'vigorously' instructed his lawyers throughout the case, and insisted on giving evidence in court despite being advised not to do so. This behaviour, perceived as reckless by Judge Weinstein, led him to infer recklessness in other matters — such as swallowing enormous quantities of heroin. He had no doubts whatever that Shonubi's evidence was untrue. These assessments were supported by the persuasive power of a good story over the weak one offered by the defence. Shonubi's story was anchored in implausibility. Students do not in general have spare cash for regular flights between Africa and America.

The American Supreme Court recognised the importance of narrative reasoning in *Old Chief v US*.[233] The defendant was charged with being a convicted felon in possession of a firearm. The defendant had a conviction for a serious assault. He preferred to admit that he was a convicted felon rather than have the prosecution adduce evidence that he was, because of the potentially prejudicial effect of the nature of his previous offence. The Supreme Court upheld the defendant's right to make the admission. Justice Souter said:

> The evidentiary account of what a defendant has thought and done can accomplish what no set of abstract statement ever could, not just to prove a fact but to establish its human significance... Thus the prosecution may fairly seek to place its evidence before the jurors, as much to tell a story of guiltiness as to support an inference of guilt, to convince the jurors that a guilty verdict would be morally reasonable as much as to point out the discrete elements of the defendant's legal fault ... There lies the need for evidence in all its particularity to satisfy the jurors' expectations about what proper proof should be. Some such demands they bring with them to the courthouse, assuming, for instance, that a charge of using a firearm to commit an offense will be proven by introducing a gun in evidence. A prosecutor who fails to produce one, or some good reason for its failure, has something to be concerned about.[234]

The danger here appeared to be, in part at any rate, that the jury would be drawn into weaving the additional facts, the details of the prior offence, into a new narrative in which the defendant would play a villainous role. Lempert[235] imagines

---

[232] (1993, *US v Shonubi* (Court of Appeals): 998 F.2d; 1993 US App.; referred for sentence: 895 F. Supp 460; 1995 US Dist) see above chapter 1.
[233] 519 US 172 (1997).
[234] 519 US 172 (1997) 187–9.
[235] RO Lempert, 'Narrative Relevance, Imagined Juries and a Supreme Court Inspired Agenda for Jury Research' (2002) 21 *St Louis University Public Law Review* 15

the jury craving for facts of marginal relevance as part of their dependency on colour and texture. A richly textured story might be even more likely to fill evidential gaps than a plain one. It would engage jurors' attention and demonstrate the moral context in which their decision is to be made. The desire for detail could induce an expectation in the jury that certain items of evidence will be produced; if they are not forthcoming, the party who would be responsible for producing it may be regarded with suspicion.

There are good reasons, then, for producing evidence which is not strictly relevant, but explains the background of the story. For example, photographs of a bloody crime scene may not have any evidential bearing, but the brutality of the image may give meaning to the evidence. It may enhance jurors' appreciation of the coherence of the prosecution case, and help them maintain interest in the trial. Lempert suggests that the provision of film footage, as opposed to a verbal description, of a mercy killing carried out by Dr Jack Kervorkian (Doctor Death), the euthanasia campaigner, may have been the reason for his conviction for murder by a Michigan jury in 1999. He had been acquitted in four previous cases.[236] The obvious danger, however, is that this kind of evidence could lead to emotional over-reaction or distraction. This was found in the New Zealand study, where jurors who took exhibits with them into the jury room were frequently unsure of their relevance, and started playing with them .[237] However, jurors said they found maps and photographs useful and wished that they had more of these to give them a picture of the events in question. At Rosemary West's trial, the jury requested a visit to the house where the bodies were found.[238]

The damaging effect of defeated juror expectations may colour their reaction to a defendant who elects not to give evidence in court. Lawyers have long feared that adverse inferences are drawn even in systems where, in law, silence may not be taken as evidence of guilt. But gaps in the story can arise from the operation of the law itself, in the form of exclusionary rules of evidence. The hearsay rule may leave many a juror wondering, 'What did he say next?' Probably for this reason, prosecutors habitually lead evidence of the defendant's replies to police questions. The practice is now so well established that the House of Lords has invented new legal categories for the evidence to occupy.[239] Yet there is no legal obligation on the prosecution to do this, and the interview may not advance their case if no admissions were forthcoming. Indeed, it may have little or no evidential significance.[240] In some cases, this evidence actually undermines the prosecution case, since any defence mentioned in the self-serving part of the defendant's statement immediately becomes a live issue in the trial.[241] Yet prosecutors routinely choose

---

[236] *Ibid.*
[237] Young, Cameron and Tinsley, above n.17, para.2.46.
[238] H Souness, *Fred and Rose* (London, Warner, 1995).
[239] See J McEwan, *Evidence and the Adversarial Process*, 2nd edn. (Oxford, Hart Publishing, 1998) 245–48.
[240] The defence could adduce them as previous consistent statements to bolster the credibility of a defendant whose testimony in court is to the same effect.
[241] *Duncan* (1981) 73 Cr App R 359; *Sharp* [1988] 1 All ER 65.

to produce unhelpful police interviews, in the belief that not to do so could alienate the court, as magistrates may conclude that something is being hidden from them.[242] As the story develops, an instinctive reaction is to wonder what the defendant said when accused of the crime. The technical labels lawyers want to attach to it are of no interest to the finder of fact.

Similarly, magistrates or jurors might find it disconcerting, in a case concerning conspiracy or joint enterprise, that one of the parties is nowhere to be seen. Case law has recognised that there are circumstances when it is necessary to explain the absence of the other defendant from the dock. For example, in *Bennett*,[243] the charge was theft. The co-defendant had at an earlier hearing pleaded guilty to an allegation that she, a shop worker, passed goods to Bennett for less than the true price The jury at Bennett's trial did not need this information in order to reach a verdict, but the Court of Appeal held that to omit information about the earlier guilty plea would bewilder them. Yet proof of the co-defendant's conviction inevitably involved recitation of all the details,[244] including Bennett's role, and so this information was very damaging. The same problems may arise in conspiracy trials. If A is on trial for conspiring with B, the prosecution could adduce evidence that B has already admitted and been convicted of conspiring with A. Courts seem to fear that fact-finders will wonder where B is, and punish the prosecution for the lack of information.[245]

---

[242] Personal communications by prosecutors to author.

[243] [1988] *Criminal Law Review* 686.

[244] S.75 Police and Criminal Evidence Act 1984.

[245] Where excessive prejudice is caused by providing such information to the jury, the court may exclude it under s.78 Police and Criminal Evidence Act 1984.

5

The Layman and the Law

JUDGE JEROME FRANK dismissed the efforts of the jury:

> While the jury can contribute nothing of value so far as the law is concerned, it has
> infinite capacity for mischief, for twelve men can easily misunderstand more law in
> a minute than the judges can explain in an hour.[1]

Despite this apparent contempt, the legal system expects lay fact-finders to
perform some very specific, and often complex, mental tasks. Juries are directed at
the end of the trial on the law they are to apply. This will include an explanation
of the issues to be tried, and instructions on the significance of the evidence they
have heard. There may be items of evidence that they hear D but must be directed
to disregard, or at least, to disregard on a particular issue. Magistrates are advised
by their clerk on the law, but have to make decisions as to admissibility themselves.
Any inadmissible evidence they heard on the *voir dire*[2] they should disregard as
they arrive at a verdict. At the end of each trial, then, fact-finders become aware of
the correct categorisation for each of the various pieces of information they have
heard. Each item should be placed neatly in its appropriate pigeonhole. There
should be no cross-fertilisation or contamination of information held within this
tidy mental structure. The law requires the thought processes of decision-makers
to be mechanistic, in following an orderly sequence.

JUDICIAL INSTRUCTIONS ON EVIDENCE

Some judicial instructions involve particularly abstruse distinctions. One example
applies when two defendants are tried together. During police interview Smith
accused Brown of being involved. The interview evidence is admitted to show
how Smith reacted to being accused himself, but is not to taken as evidence of
Brown's involvement. (Used in that fashion it would be hearsay). Another complex hearsay direction has to be given where a woman testifies that she was raped
by Green. It transpires that before the trial she told someone that Green raped her.
If she said this at the first reasonable opportunity that presented itself after the

---

[1] *Skidmore v Baltimore & Ohio Railroad* 167 F 2d 54 [2d Cir 1948].
[2] 'Trial within a trial' at which the admissibility of evidence is considered.

alleged rape, it may be admissible as evidence of her consistency, thus supporting her credibility as a witness at the trial.[3] However, the jury must be warned that the out-of-court statement, or 'recent complaint', is not evidence that she was raped by Green. It is only evidence of her consistency and thus supports her testimony, which is the actual source of evidence of Green's guilt. Not surprisingly, jurors appear to find this distinction unintelligible. Sealy's study selected mock jurors from a pool of persons eligible for jury service. They were played audiotapes which reconstructed real trials. Of the mock jurors who heard the judicial direction on 'recent complaint' direction, not one juror could in pre-trial discussion, explain what it meant, and few remembered it at all. Nevertheless, giving the jury the instruction increased the chance of acquittal or conviction for a lesser offence, in contrast to cases where the complaint was repeated without its relevance to consistency being explained.[4] This suggests that without the instruction the evidence was being used for the illegitimate purpose of providing evidence against the defendant.

Pickel found that subjects (students of psychology) successfully ignored hearsay when instructed to do so irrespective of whether a legal explanation was given.[5] However, the scenario he constructed employed a piece of evidence that arguably was not hearsay at all. The case concerned someone accused of stealing from his former employer. A witness testified that the defendant, referring to the former employer, said, 'Elliott just fired me'. That evidence is hearsay only if admitted to show that the defendant had been sacked (something outside the witness's personal knowledge) but it was perfectly admissible to show the defendant's state of mind and, therefore, possible motive. The use to which the jury was directed to put the evidence probably only reflected jurors' their views about its probative value. Jurors are probably more aware of the limitations of genuine hearsay evidence than lawyers think. Mock jurors seem to consider hearsay to be less reliable than oral testimony, with or without judicial admonishment.[6] In Sealy's study,[7] mock jurors understood the corroboration principle fairly well, and could make a reasonable attempt at explaining it. However, the warning backfired and increased the conviction rate.

> So while a remembered and reasonably well understood instruction works counter to its intention, an apparently unintelligible and unnoticed instruction tends to affect verdicts in the manner anticipated in the legal justification.[8]

---

[3] *Osborne* [1905] 1 KB 551.

[4] AP Sealy, 'Instructional Sets in Trials of Rape' in PJ van Koppen and G van den Heuvel, (eds) *Lawyers on Psychology, and Psychologists on Law* (Amsterdam, Swets and Zeitlinger, 1988); cf TR Carretta and RL Moreland, 'The direct and indirect effects of inadmissible evidence' (1983) 13 *Journal of Applied Social Psychology* 291.

[5] KL Pickel, 'Inducing Jurors to Disregard Inadmissible Evidence: a Legal Explanation does not Help' (1995) 19 *Law and Human Behavior* 407.

[6] P Miene, E Borgida and R Park, 'The Evaluation of Hearsay Evidence: a Social Psychological Approach' in NJ Castellan, (ed) *Individual and Group Decision-Making: Current Issues* (Hillsdale, New Jersey, Erlbaum, 1993).

[7] Sealy, above n. 4.

[8] *Ibid.* at 157.

This may be due to the fact that in warning that a conviction without corroboration might be dangerous, the judge would then review, piece by piece, the evidence, which could, as a matter of law, corroborate the complainant.[9]

Research into the effect of judicial instructions upon jurors has tended to concentrate on identification evidence.[10] In the wake of psychological research demonstrating the unreliability of identification evidence, fact finders in many jurisdictions are warned that they should treat it with caution. Nevertheless, faith in the eyewitness appears to survive a judicial warning of the weaknesses of identification evidence.[11] Cutler and Penrod found that the judicial instructions on identification evidence in frequent use in the United States had little effect on their mock juries. Juror sensitivity to the factors affecting the reliability of eyewitness evidence was not increased. Manipulation of the timing and content of the instructions did not increase their impact.[12] Jurors who have heard the testimony of an eyewitness come to accept the prosecution case and become critical of the defendant's testimony, even if the eyewitness is subsequently discredited.[13] Alarming results were obtained in Loftus' study; jurors still believed an identification witness later found to be very short-sighted and not to have been wearing his spectacles.[14] However, her findings have been contradicted by subsequent research, which gave the eyewitness's visual limitations more emphasis.[15] It may be that evidence of the risk of eyewitness unreliability must be given particular prominence. Jurors' attention appears better engaged if an expert witness gives evidence that not only explains that witness confidence is not an accurate indicator of reliability, but also sets out the kind of physical conditions which reduce the accuracy of identification evidence.[16] Overall reliance on the eyewitness testimony does appear to be reduced, although jurors may nevertheless be unable to distinguish between accurate and inaccurate identifications.[17]

The rules of evidence assume that should the triers of fact become aware that the defendant has bad character or a criminal record, they will be prejudiced and less likely to reach the correct decision on the facts. Chapter six investigates the

---

[9] The 'recency effect', see below.

[10] See chapter eight.

[11] WA Wagenaar, PJ van Koppen, and HM Crombag, *Anchored Narratives: the Psychology of Criminal Evidence* (Hemel Hempstead, Harvester Wheatsheaf, 1993); KD Williams, EF Loftus and KA Deffenbacher, 'Eyewitness testimony' in DK Kagehiro and WS Laufer, (eds) *Handbook of Psychology and Law* (New York, Springer-Verlag, 1992).

[12] BL Cutler and SD Penrod, *Mistaken Identification: The Eyewitness, Psychology and Law* (Cambridge, Cambridge University Press, 1995) 255–64.

[13] DM Saunders, N Vidmar and EC Hewitt, 'Eyewitness Testimony and the Discrediting Effect' in S Lloyd-Bostock and BR Clifford, (eds) *Evaluating Witness Evidence* (Wiley, Chichester, 1983). See SM Kassin, and LS Wrightsman, *The American Jury on Trial* (New York, Hemisphere,1988) 136.

[14] 68% convicted whereas 18% would have convicted on the same evidence minus the eyewitness: EF Loftus, 'Reconstructing Memory: The Incredible Eyewitness' (1974) 8 *Psychology Today* 116.

[15] See A Kapardis, *Psychology and Law* (Cambridge, Cambridge University Press, 1997) 66.

[16] Cutler and Penrod, above n.12, 225–51.

[17] GL Wells, RCL Lindsay and JP Tousignant, 'Effects of Expert Psychiatric Advice on Human Performance in Judging the Validity of Eyewitness Testimony' (1980) 4 *Law and Human Behavior* 275.

accuracy of this view and the way the law tries to balance the risk of prejudice against the importance of admitting probative evidence. At this point, it is sufficient to note that there are circumstances in which fact-finders do become aware of the accused's former bad character. Most Anglo-American systems allow cross-examination on the criminal record of defendants who 'throw away the shield'[18] by bringing in evidence of their own good character, or by attacking the character of a witness for the prosecution. Where such cross-examination is allowed, the law seeks to limit the prejudicial effect by insisting that its relevance is confined to the issue of the credibility of the defendant's own oral evidence. The jury must be warned not to use previous convictions as evidence of guilt. They must consider them in relation to the defendant's credibility on oath irrespective of the nature of the criminal record and its relationship to the current charge.[19] Given that the earlier offences could range from grievous bodily harm to living off immoral earnings, it is not surprising that juries find it difficult to comply with judicial instructions on this issue. It has been found that, irrespective of guidance from the trial judge, mock jurors were more ready to convict where the defendant had previous convictions. Yet their perception of the defendant's credibility appeared to be unaffected. The illegitimate use of the criminal record as an indicator of guilt may occur because juries are irrationally prejudiced by it. That is the trial lawyer's view. Equally, it could be the product of a comprehension failure for which the legal system is itself to blame, in its insistence on an unworkable dichotomy between the issue of the defendant's credibility and the issue of guilt.[20] A third possibility is that the belief that earlier criminality is relevant to guilt is a rational response untainted by prejudice.[21]

Joining counts together, so that the defendant is accused of a range of criminal activity, is thought to create bias, increasing the probability of conviction even when the offences are unrelated. A judicial direction to treat the cases separately appears not to negate the biasing effect.[22] Intrusion from one case to the other is greatest when the joined charges are similar as opposed to dissimilar. Tanford and Penrod[23] in fact found significant joinder effect only when cases involved offences of the same type, either 'identical' (as with three service station burglaries) or 'similar' (as with three burglaries at different kinds of premises). These findings may provide support for the 'interference theory' of memory. This theory is derived from memory experiments in which subjects are required to learn two lists of words simultaneously and then recall items from one of the lists. The result

---

[18] Law Commission, *Evidence in Criminal Proceedings: Previous Misconduct of a Defendant* Consultation Paper No 141 (London, HMSO 1996); Law Commission *Evidence of Bad Character in Criminal Proceedings* Law Com No 273 Cm 5257 (London, Stationery Office, 2001).
[19] See chapter six.
[20] See J McEwan, *Evidence and the Adversarial Process*, 2nd edn. (Oxford, Hart Publishing, 1998) 40–43.
[21] See chapter six.
[22] KS Bordens and IA Horowitz, 'Information Processing in Joined and Severed Trials' (1983) 13 *Journal of Applied Social Psychology* 351.
[23] S Tanford , S Penrod and R Collins, 'Decision Making in Joined Criminal Trials: the Influence of Charge Similarity, Evidence Similarity and Limiting Instructions' (1985) 9 *Law and Human Behavior* 319.

is confusion between the lists. Where a person learns material from two different sources simultaneously, therefore, there is a possibility that they will forget the source. Jurors may thus become confused between offences where they hear evidence of more than one. As the percentage of anti-defendant intrusions increases, so does the perceived guilt of the defendant. But Tanford and Penrod are not themselves convinced that there is a relationship between measures of confusion (intrusion) and guilt assessment. Nor have all researchers found confusion of evidence to explain the increased conviction rates in joined trials.[24] Another possibility is simple accumulation of evidence; evidence from one case reinforcing evidence in another. Tanford and Penrod found an accumulative effect, but Bordens and Horowitz did not. The alternative explanation is that jurors who hear of alleged criminality on other occasions infer a criminal disposition, which in turn provides extra evidence to add to the prosecution's case. None of the studies clearly and unambiguously establish a causal link between inferences of criminality and guilt judgment. Tanford has shown that the defendant in a joinder trial is seen as more dangerous, less likeable and less believable, but could not demonstrate that this led to an inference of guilt.[25] In the New Zealand study, jurors simply were confused by alternative counts, either thinking they should convict of both or acquit of both.[26]

Illegally obtained evidence is normally excluded.[27] Jurors thus are entirely unaware of it, whereas magistrates will discover its nature at the *voir dire*. In a simulation where the case concerned a civil suit for damages in respect of an illegal police search of private property, the level of damages awarded by the mock jurors was affected by whether or not the victim of the search was discovered to have committed a serious offence. If jurors were specifically told to disregard this evidence, the outcome was the same.[28] In contrast, a study which used students as mock jurors found that knowledge of inadmissible evidence did not prejudice the verdict. Subjects were provided with a transcript of a fatal armed robbery case. In one version, illegal wiretapping evidence contained an admission of guilt by the defendant. The students who heard the inadmissible evidence were more likely to believe the defendant to be guilty, but this did not inevitably influence them to find him guilty. In oral discussions, they would remind each other, if need arose, that they should not rely on the evidence.[29] Given that their discussions were

---

[24] KS Bordens and IA Horowitz, 'Joinder of Offences,: a Review of the Legal and Psychological Literature (1985) 9 *Law and Human Behaviour* 339.

[25] S Tanford, 'Decision Making Processes in Joined Criminal Trials, (unpublished doctoral dissertation, University of Wisconsin 1985); see Bordens and Horowitz, above n. 24.

[26] W Young, N Cameron and Y Tinsley, *Juries in Criminal Trials*, Law Commission of New Zealand Preliminary Paper 37, Vol 2, (Wellington, New Zealand, 1999) 7.23.

[27] S. 76 Police and Criminal Evidence Act 1984 describes when confessions should be excluded because of the way they have been obtained. S. 78 gives judges a discretion to exclude evidence of any kind if to admit it would make the trial unfair.

[28] JD Casper, K Bendedict and JL Perry, 'The Tort Remedy in Search and Seizure Cases: a Case Study in Juror Decision Making (1988) 13 *Law and Social Inquiry* 279.

[29] TR Carretta and RL Moreland, 'The Direct and Indirect Effects of Inadmissible Evidence' (1983) 13 *Journal of Applied Social Psychology* 291.

audiotaped, and that students might be anxious to please the researchers, this might strike a cynic as too good to be true. However, illegally obtained evidence did influence some verdicts. Sue, Smith and Caldwell[30] conducted an experiment where mock jurors heard a weak prosecution case. In that condition no guilty verdicts were returned. If they varied the conditions so that the jurors heard a damning piece of evidence, a judicial warning that it should be ignored was likely to be disregarded. However, the methodology employed may have influenced this outcome, by introducing the inadmissible piece of evidence last, creating the risk of a possible 'recency effect'. Wolf and Montgomery observed in their study that guilty verdicts were more likely if the judge gave a warning in the summing up, than they were if the evidence was simply ruled inadmissible at the time it was presented with no further judicial comment being made. The warning, therefore, appears to backfire, by reminding the jury of something they heard earlier, but might successfully have dismissed from their minds during the trial.[31]

At common law it is the right of an accused person at a trial not to give evidence, and to decline to answer police questions. Parliament has made substantial inroads into this right for England and Wales.[32] In New Zealand, however, judges who comment on the accused's failure to give evidence must still point out that it is the right of any accused person not to do so, and that it may not be used as evidence of guilt.[33] Jurors in the New Zealand study claimed they had understood and absorbed the judicial direction on the right to silence. In only eight cases was the defendant silent at interview, and jurors were mostly unaffected by it. Twenty defendants elected not to give evidence at the trial. Jurors in all but six of these cases maintained they gave no weight to this. But in those six, they thought silence indicated guilt, and seemed not to refer to the trial judge's direction.[34] Whether the reaction of the New Zealand juries was affected by the strength of the prosecution case is not clear from the report.[35] In simulations, psychologists have found evidence of significant bias, both during deliberations and in relation to verdict, where the defendant elects not to testify, despite a warning against drawing adverse inferences.[36]

In some cases the scale of media coverage leads to fears that jurors will be unable to dismiss the publicity from their minds, making a fair trial impossible. In 1999 the mass murderer, Doctor Harold Shipman, was spared further prosecution

[30] S Sue, RE Smith and C Caldwell, 'Effects of Inadmissible Evidence and Decisions of Simulated Jurors: a Moral Dilemma' (1973) 3 *Journal of Applied Psychology* 345.

[31] S Wolf, DA Montgomery, 'Effect of Inadmissable Evidence and Level of Judicial Admonishment to Disregard on the Judgments of Mock Jurors' (1977) 7 *Journal of Applied Social Psychology* 205.

[32] Criminal Justice and Public Order Act 1994 ss 34–7 incl.

[33] *Bathurst* [1968] 2 QB 99.

[34] Young, Cameron and Tinsey, above n.26.

[35] Judges have limited the drawing of adverse inferences to cases where the prosecution evidence is relatively strong, see chaper four.

[36] DR Shaffer and T Case, 'On the Decision not to Testify on One's Own Behalf: Effects of Withheld Evidence' (1982) 42 *Journal of Personality and Social Psychology*, 353. Leaving gaps in the narrative gives scope to the jury to fill them with their own version: see chapter four.

because it was thought that a second trial would be prejudiced by the massive media coverage of his first trial. In less notorious cases, judges may consider it sufficient to warn the jury to disregard media discussion of the case. Simon exposed experimental subjects to pre-trial publicity of a murder case. This was either 'sensational' or 'conservative'. The sensational coverage did produce stronger pre-trial attitudes, but early instruction to disregard it and concentrate on the evidence cancelled out this effect.[37] In California, the effect of media coverage of three criminal cases seemed to make subjects more disposed to convict, however. Pre-trial knowledge of the case was a better predictor of the verdict than general attitudinal and demographic factors.[38] Kramer also found that pre-trial publicity was difficult for jurors to ignore.[39] Researchers concede, however, that publicity may have varying effect, according to how much individuals choose to expose themselves to the news. Also, experimenters tend to expose subjects to it in a way that might not replicate life.[40] In the New Zealand study, only two jurors acknowledged any influence from pre-trial publicity. Researchers asked prospective jurors what they knew of the case before it began, and found knowledge derived from media coverage to be hazy. In one case there had been a lot of publicity about the defendant, who had been tried before. All the jurors knew of this and referred to it. But the verdict appeared to rest on the considerable personal credibility of the chief prosecution witness.[41]

JUDICIAL INSTRUCTIONS ON STANDARD OF PROOF

In every case, the decision must be based on the standard of proof appropriate to the matter being tried. In criminal cases, a conviction depends upon the prosecution case being proved beyond reasonable doubt. Failing that, the defendant should be acquitted. Do finders of fact understand what is meant by reasonable doubt? It seems unlikely, given that lawyers have trouble with the definition. Judicial attempts to produce one have resulted in such confusion that the Court of Appeal advises reticence. It is best merely to say that the jury should be so satisfied that they feel sure,[42] or the judge should tell them to satisfy themselves beyond all reasonable doubt without further elaboration.[43] In the United States,

---

[37] RJ Simon, 'Murders, Juries and the Press — does Sensational Reporting Lead to Verdicts of Guilty?' (1966) 3 *Trans-Action* 40.

[38] E Constantini and J King, 'The Potential Juror: Correlate Causes of Judgment' 1980 15 *Law and Society Review* 9.

[39] GP Kramer, NL Kerr, and JS Carroll, 'Pre-Trial Publicity, Judicial Remedies and Jury Bias' (1990) 14 *Law and Human Behavior* 409.

[40] JS Caroll, NL Kerr, JJ Alfini, FM Weaver, RJ MacCoun and V Feldman, 'Free Press and Fair Trial: the Role of Behavioral Research' (1986) 10 *Law and Human Behavior* 187.

[41] Young, Cameron and Tinsley, above n. 26, 7.46–7.50.

[42] *Kritz* [1950] 1 KB 82; *Walters v The Queen* [1969] 2 AC 26.

[43] *Hepworth and Fearnley* [1955] 2 QB 600.

interpretation varies from state to state, with models ranging from 'an abiding conviction or belief' in the guilt of the accused[44] to the most explicit version:

> such proof as precludes every reasonable hypothesis except that which it tends to support, and is proof which is wholly consistent with the guilt of the accused.[45]

Variations in language may affect the readiness of juries to convict. Mock trials staged for the London Jury Project of the London School of Economics resulted in a significantly lower conviction rate where the jury were told that they 'must feel sure and certain on the evidence that the accused is guilty',[46] than where they were told:

> You should be sure beyond a reasonable doubt and by a reasonable doubt I mean not a fanciful doubt that anyone might use to avoid an unpleasant decision, but a doubt for which reasons can be given.[47]

Most British and some American judges think it best to avoid giving a definition of beyond reasonable doubt, leaving it to juror common sense to fix the appropriate level of certainty. This may make the prosecution task more difficult than if a definition were provided. In a survey by Montgomery,[48] respondents who were given the preferred English direction on standard of proof were far more likely to believe they had to be one hundred per cent sure than those provided with the most explicit of the American directions. The absence of a definition clearly affects verdicts as much as the terms of any definition that is provided. In one study, mock jurors were directed in one of three different ways. They were either given a definition described as ('stringent' or 'lax'), or were merely told the standard of proof, with no definition at all. Those who heard it defined in the most stringent terms produced the lowest conviction rate, followed by those given no definition, with the greater number of convictions returned following the 'lax' definition.[49] In the New Zealand study, most jurors were simply told the standard of proof without further elaboration. They tended to operate a standard of between seventy-five per cent and ninety-five per cent, although some applied fifty per cent or a hundred per cent.[50] However, there was no evidence of this leading to perverse verdicts, so far as the researchers could tell. In cases where the burden of proof shifted to the defence, the New Zealand jurors became very confused. Although the correct standard in such cases is proof on the balance of probabilities, some applied the criminal standard.[51]

---

[44] Washington State. See JW Montgomery, 'The Criminal Standard of Proof' (1998) *New Law Journal* 582.
[45] Eg., Georgia, *Yearwood* 401 SE 2d 558.
[46] *Kritz*, n.42.
[47] AP Sealy and WR Cornish, 'Juries and the Rule of Evidence' (1973) *Modern Law Review* 208.
[48] Montgomery, above n.44.
[49] NL Kerr, RS Atkin, G Strasser, D Meek, RW Holt and JH Davies, 'Guilt beyond a Reasonable Doubt: Effects of Concept Definition and Assigned Decision Rule on the Judgments of Mock Jurors' (1976) 43 *Journal of Personality and Social Psychology* 282.
[50] Young, Cameron and Tinsley, above n. 26, para. 7.18.
[51] *Ibid.*

It has been argued that expressing the standard in terms of a percentage would be more helpful to lay fact-finders.[52] However, judges themselves appear unable to agree on a numerical equivalent, giving a criminal standard varying between eighty and a hundred per cent. This finding comes from a study by Simon and Mahan, in which no unanimity was found on the civil or criminal standard of proof amongst judges or jurors.[53] There is some evidence that juries adopt a sliding scale according to the seriousness of the offence.[54] This would be consistent with a defensive attribution only if they were more likely to convict where the offence is serious, but the opposite appears to be the case. Montgomery's subjects seemed to be heavily influenced by the seriousness of the offence, when they were more likely to acquit in the face of the evidence. They were more likely to convict on less evidence where the offence was trivial.[55] A sliding scale may be legitimate; Holroyd J, in *Sarah Hobson*,[56] stated: 'The greater the crime, the stronger the proof required for the purpose of conviction'. The introduction of causing death by driving offences as an alternative to gross negligence manslaughter was an acknowledgment of jurors' reluctance to convict of the latter, more serious, offence.[57]

REASONS FOR DISOBEDIENCE

Obstinacy?

Why is it so difficult for jurors to observe directions on the law? An obvious possibility is that they simply do not understand what they are being instructed to do; this issue will be discussed below. But however well a jury understand a judicial direction, they retain the power to ignore it. There is a machinery to protect the defendant from an entirely perverse conviction. Where the evidence against an accused is very weak, the trial judge has the power to stop the case. The verdict is a 'directed acquittal'. A case should be withdrawn from the jury if the prosecution cannot produce sufficient evidence to constitute a case to answer. But trial judges are not expected to form a view of the credibility of the prosecution witnesses unless no reasonable jury could convict on the strength of their testimony.[58] The procedure tends to be reserved for cases where, for technical reasons, the prosecution

---

[52] MJ Saks, 'What do Jury Experiments Tell Us About how Juries should Make Decisions?' (1997) 6 *Southern California Interdisciplinary Law Journal 1*; DK Kagehiro, 'Defining the Standard of Proof in Jury Instructions' (1990) *Psychological Science* 194.

[53] RJ Simon and L Mahan, 'Quantifying Burdens of Proof: a View from the Bench, the Jury and the Classroom' (1971) 5 *Law and Society Review* 319.

[54] *Ibid.*

[55] Montgomery, above n. 44.

[56] (1823) 1 Lewin 261; cf. *Bater v Bater* [1951] P 35.

[57] Originally in Road Traffic Act 1956 s.8.

[58] *Galbraith* [1981] 2 All ER 1060.

cannot be allowed to proceed. But there is nothing to stop a jury returning an acquittal in the teeth of an apparently unanswerable prosecution case. Some argue that in a democracy, the jury's role, if they consider the law to be unjust, is to flout legal requirements and return a verdict of not guilty. In the United States, this as regarded as a constitutional right even by judges, and there are demands that juries should be reminded of it of it in the summing up.[59] The intervention of the jury is seen as a protection for the citizen against oppression by public authorities.[60] In the United Kingdom there is less enthusiasm in legal circles for jury nullification. Sir Robin Auld thinks it anti-democratic insofar as it defeats the will of Parliament.[61]

The effect of police and prosecutor discretion before trial may prevent a case that elicits a great deal of sympathy from being brought to court. But with unpopular laws, the jury has the last say. The 'British Aerospace Case' involved four defendants who freely admitted breaking in to private property and deliberately damaging aircraft there. Their motive was to mount a political protest against the Government selling arms to East Timor during a bloody conflict. They were acquitted in 1996. More famously, a civil servant named Clive Ponting was acquitted in 1985 of an offence against the Official Secrets Act 1911, despite admitting, during the course of the trial, that he had passed on secret papers. The papers referred to the sinking of the Argentine battleship, 'General Belgrano', during the Falklands conflict between Britain and Argentina. The trial judge had told the jury in the strongest terms that the defendant Ponting, who declared that he judged his action to be in the national interest, had no defence. This may have backfired on the judge.[62] An alternative explanation could be that the jury would have acquitted anyway out of sympathy with Ponting's views.

A factor which may affect willingness to convict is the seriousness of penalty — all decision-makers have the potential to be affected by this, from academics who are aware that a particular student needs an Upper Second, to the juror who knows that the defendant stands at risk of capital punishment. The starker the choice, the more the adjudicator may be tempted into a judgment designed only to avoid an outcome thought to be unconscionable. The tendency of harsh outcomes to distort the decision-making process has been seen above in the manipulations of the legal and medical professions in problematic criminal cases such as infanticide, and 'diminished responsibility' euthanasia. Jurors are often willing participants in the defeat of legal doctrine. In 1981, a paediatrician, Dr Leonard Arthur,[63] was tried for the attempted murder[64] of a newborn Downs'

---

[59] JB Weinstein, 'Considering Jury Nullification: When May and Should a Jury Reject the Law to Do Justice?' (1993) 30 *American Criminal Law Review* 239.

[60] *Ibid.*

[61] Sir Robin Auld, *Criminal Courts Review* (London, HMSO, 2001) www.criminal-courts-review.org.uk para 5.10.

[62] See below.

[63] *Arthur* (1981) 12 BMLR 1.

[64] Problems in proving causation led the prosecution not to proceed with a murder charge.

Syndrome baby boy who had been vehemently rejected by his parents. The doctor had given instructions that the child receive 'nursing care only', water, but no food. He prescribed a sedative to prevent suffering. The child died. He was acquitted. Similarly, Kalven and Zeisel found jurors reluctant to convict in cases of self-defence or defence of property.[65] In the New Zealand research, however, sympathy or prejudice distorted the outcome in only six cases. In one case, jurors acquitted because they were very worried about the impact of a conviction on the community, a concern in fact based on a fundamental misunderstanding of the law.[66]

The phenomenon of jury nullification, or acquittal in the face of the evidence, has attracted attention from psychologists in recent years[67]. Perverse acquittal may result if the jury feels that the sentence (or the fact of conviction) is simply too severe.[68] An example observed by Professor Lloyd-Bostock[69] involved an Oxford hot-dog salesman who was provoked by some youths. He admitted wounding one of them. The trial judge ruled out provocation as a defence, because the charge was not one of homicide. The jury nevertheless returned a verdict of not guilty. The explanation could be a reaction to the inflexibility of the law, which allows provocation as a defence only to a murder charge. Jurors do not like constraint, as an experiment into restricted options demonstrates. Mock jurors either had a free choice between a finding of first degree murder, second degree murder or manslaughter, or they were told that if they were not convinced of murder, they must acquit. They were given transcripts of the trial evidence; where they had a free choice, there was only one acquittal. Where they were limited to murder or acquittal, the number of acquittals rose.[70]

'Reactance theory' suggests that people act in response to the elimination of a previously held freedom. A state of psychological arousal, directed towards restoring that freedom, is induced.[71] Wolf and Montgomery suggest that jury nullification could be a manifestation of psychological reactance; they are happy to accept a ruling on the law, but not to take orders. They suggest that the style of the trial judge's instructions is more important than the content.[72] Pickel[73] believes that

---

[65] H Kalven and H Zeisel, *The American Jury* (Chicago, University of Chicago Press, 1966).

[66] Young, Cameron and Tinsley, above n.26, para. 7.11.

[67] IA Horowitz, 'The Impact of Jury Nullification Instruction on Verdicts and Jury Functioning in Criminal Trials' (1985) 9 *Law and Human Behavior* 23; R Weiner, K Habert, G Shkodriani and C Staebler, 'The Social Psychology of Jury Nullification: Predicting when Jurors Disobey the Law' (1991) 21 *Journal of Applied Social Psychology* 1379.

[68] R Arce, 'Evidence Evaluation in Jury Decision-Making' in R Bull and D Carson, (eds) *Handbook of Psychology in Legal Contexts* (Chichester, Wiley, 1995).

[69] S Lloyd-Bostock, 'The Jury in the United Kingdom: Juries and Jury Research in Context' in G Davies, S Lloyd-Bostock, K MacMurran and C Wilson, (eds) *Psychology Law and Criminal Justice* (Berlin, de Gruyter, 1996).

[70] N Vidmar, 'Effects of Decision Alternatives on the Verdicts and Social Perceptions of Simulated Jurors (1972) 22 *Journal of Personality and Social Psychology* 211.

[71] JW Brehm, *A Theory of Psychological Reactance* (New York, Academic Press, 1966).

[72] S Wolf, DA Montgomery, 'Effect of inadmissable evidence on the decisions of simulated jurors: a moral dilemma' (1977) 3 *Journal of Applied Social Psychology* 213.

[73] Pickel, above n.5.

the situation is rather more complicated. The jury will disregard a judge's instructions if they are unsympathetic to the rationale, and therefore the effect of admonishment in a hearsay case might be different from a judicial instruction in a bad character case. If the judicial direction is regarded as fair, as they were in the hearsay case, they are more likely to be followed. Alternatively, willingness to comply may depend on the jury's own cost-benefit analysis. It has been found that if the prosecutor's case is strong, the jury is more ready to adhere to a direction to disregard an item of evidence, having plenty of other evidence to base a conviction on. But if the case is weak, they are more likely to rely on the inadmissible evidence.[74] The tendency of adversarial systems to exclude various items of evidence may backfire in jury trials. The New Zealand jurors thought evidence was being deliberately withheld[75] and that, in consequence, the story they were trying to construct was incomplete. Sometimes this was construed as counsel trying to stop damaging evidence coming in. Otherwise they were mystified as to the reason. Some resorted to speculation as to what the missing evidence might have been. Thus the issue may have been given more emphasis rather than less.

Incomprehensibility of Instructions

Irrespective of exclusionary rules, if questions thought relevant by fact-finders are not asked by the advocates, the case will be perceived to contain evidential gaps. Magistrates become used to asking questions *via* the Chair. Lawyers have traditionally been reluctant to allow juror participation through the asking of questions. The editor of Archbold has written:

> The practice of inviting a jury to ask questions is generally speaking to be deprecated. Jurors are not familiar with the rules of evidence and might ask questions which are difficult to deal with.[76]

But Heuer and Penrod found that asking questions of witnesses promoted juror understanding of the facts, and increased their confidence in the verdict. Permitting the jurors to ask questions did not cause problems for the advocates. They did not raise questions counsel had deliberately omitted to ask. If one of their questions was refused on the grounds of admissibility, no offence was taken, and the jury did not draw adverse inferences against the party who had made objection. However, taking the opinion of the trial judge as the measure, the authors doubted that the quality of the verdict was improved.[77] Jurors in the

---

[74] Sue, Smith and Caldwell, above n. 30.
[75] Young, Cameron and Tinsley, above n. 26, para. 4.8.
[76] P Richardson, (ed) *Archbold Criminal Pleading, Evidence and Practice* (London, Sweet and Maxwell, 2001) 8.250.
[77] L Heuer and S Penrod, 'Increasing Juror Participation in Trials through Note-Taking and Question Asking' (1996) 79 *Judicature* 256.

New Zealand survey were unimpressed by the advocacy of some barristers, and thought there were questions the witnesses should have been asked, but were not. Some of them did not ask questions because they felt intimidated by the procedure, or they thought it was not allowed. The researchers observed occasions when it would have been helpful to allow jury questions because counsel had not clarified the issue.[78] The Law Commission of New Zealand suggests that jurors should be told at the outset both that they are entitled to ask questions, and that sometimes it may not be possible to answer them.[79]

All trials involve hours of listening to oral evidence, and some are factually complex. Some cases last for weeks or even months. Yet, in Northern Ireland, jurors are apparently not encouraged to take notes,[80] although the facility exists. Many lawyers are unenthusiastic about jurors writing notes during the trial, on the ground that they would be too occupied in the process to observe the witnesses, thus missing crucial aspects of their demeanour whilst giving evidence.[81] In fact, Darbyshire reports that sometimes jurors, who initially would have liked to make a record, give up the attempt because they cannot watch the reactions of witnesses and take notes at the same time.[82] In a study by Heuer and Penrod,[83] judges were asked to assess trials they were hearing in relation to the complexity of the evidence, the quantity of the evidence, and the complexity of the law. Some of them were asked to stress, at the close of each witness's evidence in chief and cross-examination, that the jurors should ask questions if they wished. Others were asked to allow the taking of notes. The rationality of their verdicts[84] was not enhanced by juror note-taking nor by the asking of questions. The jurors felt that asking questions made them more confident on the law, but they were no more confident in the verdict than those who had not asked questions.

The inability of most people to take accurate notes at speed has much to do with the limited usefulness of jury note-taking. The impossibility of keeping up was reported by the jurors in the New Zealand survey. The oral nature of the proceedings caused juries to struggle to recollect evidence. They reported difficulties in concentrating on the testimony, much of which they found protracted and dull, a problem exacerbated by the slowness of pace and the long pauses necessary for the stenographer to keep a record. Jurors found it difficult to remember who said what. In sixteen out of the forty-eight trials studied, they asked, at the deliberation stage, for testimony to be read back to them. Those that had made notes

---

[78] Young, Cameron and Tinsley, above n. 26 para. 4.14.

[79] Law Commission, *Juries in Criminal Trials*, Report 69 (Wellington New Zealand 2001) 366–7.

[80] J Jackson, 'Juror Decision-Making in the Trial Process' in G Davies, S Lloyd-Bostock, K MacMurran and C Wilson, (eds) *Psychology Law and Criminal Justice* (Berlin, de Gruyter, 1996).

[81] Usefulness of demeanour evidence discussed, chapter four.

[82] P Darbyshire, 'The Lamp that shows that Freedom Lives: Is It Worth the Candle?' (1971) *Criminal Law Review* 740.

[83] L Heuer and S Penrod, 'Trial Complexity: a Field Investigation of its Meaning and its Effects' (1994) 18 *Law and Human Behavior* 29; L Heuer and S Penrod, 'Jury Decision-Making in Complex Trials' in R Bull and D Carson, (eds) *Handbook of Psychology in Legal Contexts* (Chichester, Wiley, 1995).

[84] The measure being the opinion of the trial judge.

found them useful, but many had been unable to do it. In the jury room, notes were pooled and used to resolve disputes about the content of testimony. The fullest notes were heavily relied on, although in fact some were inaccurate. This gave undeserved influence to the fastest writers. Many jurors commented, unprompted, that they wished they could have had access to the trial judge's notes of evidence.[85] Certainly, access to a transcript would help them remember the provenance of evidence. It has been found that when people recall information, they are often unable to recall its source.[86] During the course of a trial this could have been an advocate, a witness, or the judge.

Long trials pose practical problems for jurors with work or family commitments, creating the risk that they are reluctant to deliberate for longer than is necessary.[87] The trial of Kevin and Ian Maxwell for fraud in relation to the misuse of Mirror Group pension funds, lasted twelve months.[88] The Serious Fraud Office reported that the average length of trial it prosecutes is six months, ensuring, observed *The Times*, that the jurors would have to come from the 'unemployed or unemployable'.[89] The longer the trial, the more likely professionals are to ensure that they are excused from serving on the jury on grounds of hardship.[90] Where trials go on for a long time, there is a greater risk that personality clashes between members of the jury will impede their ability to work together. This problem is exacerbated by the considerable proportion of their time that they spend sitting around together while the lawyers argue technical points behind closed doors.[91] In *Ongle*,[92] two members of the jury complained that friction was affecting their concentration. The trial judge questioned all twelve jurors in open court, talked to them, and then exhorted them to go away and sort out their differences. The Court of Appeal agreed that he was right not to have questioned them separately. One wonders how frank unhappy jurors would be in this context.

The most serious difficulty faced by advocates of trial by jury is the weight of empirical evidence indicating that jurors simply do not understand the law that they are expected to apply. It has been found that juries conscientiously try to follow instructions,[93] but, if they cannot understand them, they use some form of common sense justice, or what ordinary people think the law should be.[94]

---

[85] Young, Cameron and Tinsley, above n. 26, para. 3.9.
[86] MK Johnson, JD Bransford and SK Solomon, 'Memory for Tacit Implications of Sentences' (1973) 98 *Journal of Experimental Psychology* 203; MK Johnson and CL Kaye, 'Reality Monitoring' (1981) 88 *Psychological Review* 67.
[87] Darbyshire, above n. 82.
[88] *R v Lord Chancellor ex p Maxwell* [1996] 4 All ER 751.
[89] *The Times*, 5 March 2001.
[90] M Levi, *The Investigation , Prosecution and Trial of Serious Fraud*, Royal Commision on Criminal Procedure Research Study No 14, (London, HMSO, 1993).
[91] Darbyshire, above n. 82; Young, Cameron and Tinsley, above n. 26.
[92] [1993] 4 All ER 533.
[93] WW Steele and EG Thornburg, 'Jury Instructions: a Persistent Failure to Communicate' (1988) 67 *North Carolina Law Review* 77.
[94] NJ Finkel, *Commonsense justice: jurors' notions of the law* (Cambridge Mass, Harvard University Press, 1995).

Most juries appear to be considerably at sea on the legal issues.[95] In a study of mock jurors, Ellsworth found that although they spent a fifth of deliberation time discussing the law, only about half of their statements were correct and a fifth were seriously in error. Yet the same jurors were quite competent in their grasp of the facts.[96] Mock jurors who watched a lawsuit for negligence had no greater understanding of the issues where they received judicial instructions than if they got none at all. The legal issue, admittedly, was a complicated one, involving the definition of proximate cause. However, they got confused on the matter of contributory negligence and tended to reach verdicts inconsistent with their own findings. The authors devised a simpler set of instructions, which helped slightly.[97] The New Zealand study recorded high levels of misunderstanding of the trial judge's directions. Although they did their best, jurors went astray in all but thirteen of the forty-eight trials. They struggled with the definition of the offence itself. They were confused as to the meaning of intention, being unable to distinguish purpose from intent, which they took to mean premeditation.[98] Also, they were often not sure at what point in the story they should be looking at intent, and the trial judge often did not explain this. Some American research paints a similarly depressing picture of jury understanding. Tanford sent questionnaires[99] to persons who had actually served on juries and also to people who had been selected for jury service, but ultimately did not serve on a jury.[100] Those who had acted as jurors and therefore had heard a judicial summing-up had a significantly better awareness of jurors' duties and of procedural rules. But they were more often wrong than right in relation to questions on the burden of proof. As far as the substantive law was concerned, those who had sat in real criminal cases knew no more about the legal issues that arose in the cases they had actually heard than others who had not sat at all. Where the case had been complex their scores were particularly poor. There was a slight increase in comprehension if the judge had given a plain English response to requests for help, but some jurors said they felt they should not ask for help. But Tanford's results show that lawyers have no reason to disparage the jury. Lawyers who had served on juries got only about seventy per cent of the legal questions right.

In general, the law that jurors are expected to apply is explained to them at the end of the trial. In complicated trials, jurors may receive some legal education as they go along. In the Maxwell fraud trial, for example, the prosecutor supplied

---

[95] A Reifman, SM Gusick and PC Ellsworth, 'Real Jurors' Understanding of the Law in Real Cases' (1992) 16 *Law and Human Behavior* 539; A Elwork, B Sales and JJ Alfini, *Making Jury Instructions Understandable* (Charlottesville, VA, Mitchie 1982); PC Ellsworth, 'Are Twelve Heads Better than One?' (1989) 52 *Law and Contemporary Problems* 205; R Hastie, SD Penrod and N Pennington, *Inside the Jury* (Cambridge, Mass, Harvard University Press, 1983); L Severance, and EF Loftus, 'Improving the Ability of Jurors to Comprehend and Apply Jury Instructions' (1982) 17 *Law and Society Review* 153.
[96] Ellsworth, above n.95.
[97] Elwork, Sales and Alfini, above n. 95.
[98] Young, Cameron and Tinsley, above n. 26 para. 7.14.
[99] These were rather abstract.
[100] JA Tanford, 'The Law and Psychology of Jury Instructions' (1990) 69 *Nebraska Law Review* 71.

them at the outset with a booklet explaining the law on limited companies. This was perceived by the lawyers involved to be a complicated case, yet a high level of rationality was observed in a study which ran the evidence from the trial before mock jurors. They were presented with the same evidence in the same way as the original jurors. In the main, they understood the case reasonably well. During regular interview sessions with the researchers, most mock jurors were found to employ good quality reasoning.[101] Yet many lawyers consider that fraud is too difficult for laymen, and have consistently argued that, in fraud cases, a tribunal consisting of a judge and a small number of specially qualified lay members should replace jury trial.[102] Against the prosecutor's wishes, the Court of Appeal decided that the number of issues to be presented in the Maxwell trial dictated that the counts on the indictment should be severed, so that they be tried before different juries.[103] In the *Blue Arrow* case,[104] which lasted one hundred and eighty-four days prior to the jury retiring, the Court of Appeal commented that the case had become unmanageable, and quashed all convictions on the ground that the volume and complexity of the issues presented to the jury created the risk of a miscarriage of justice.

Perhaps the special attention paid to fraud trials, with its emphasis on making the evidence and the law accessible to jurors has in fact, ironically, made them rather easier to understand than certain other trials which involve complex issues. The prosecution in 1992 of Roy Wharton, Chairman of the Castlegate group of companies, represented a breakthrough in the presentation of complicated fraud in the Crown Court. The commercial dealings were so complex that the transfer bundle[105] amounted to seventeen thousand pages. There were seven and a half tons of unused material. New computer software enabled the prosecution to reduce this mass of paper to two files. The financial dealings were demonstrated to the jury on screens, which judge and advocates could highlight with a light pen. A new facility allowed the transcript of the oral evidence being typed by the court stenographer to be shown simultaneously on screen, so that the trial was not slowed down to enable manual note-taking by the lawyers. The trial judge, May J, thought that this reduced the trial length by between a quarter and a third. It freed all participants from having to keep track of reams of paper. All the lawyers involved considered that it also enabled the jury to concentrate on key issues such as dishonesty.[106] By the time the Maxwell brothers found themselves on trial, courts had developed considerable experience in using technology to improve jury understanding. Excluding juries from particular kinds of trial, such as fraud

---

[101] TM Honess, M Levi and EA Charman, 'Juror Competence in Processing Complex Information: Implications from a Simulation of the Maxwell Trial' (1998) *Criminal Law Review* 763.
[102] *Report of the Fraud Trials Committee* (London, HMSO, 1986); cf Auld, n. 61 para. 5.173–5.906; White Paper, *Justice For All* CM5563 (London, The Stationery Office, 2002) 28–31.
[103] *R v Lord Chancellor ex p Maxwell,* above n.88.
[104] *Cohen* [1992] *New Law Journal* 1267 (largely unreported).
[105] The prosecution case submitted to establish that there was a case to answer.
[106] C Miskin, 'Watch His Honour's Light Pen' [1995] *New Law Journal* 648.

trials, is probably a less appropriate response to complexity than giving them more information pre-trial, and presenting evidence more clearly. The New Zealand researchers found that fraud was not in itself necessarily problematic. The greatest difficulty for jurors was encountered in multiple-count cases, such as manslaughter. These results provide some support for Lempert's contention that the length and density of factual evidence is less confusing for jurors than legal complexity.[107]

In general, too little is done to ensure that juries have sufficiently understood instructions on the law. Confusion about the meaning of judicial instructions is particularly understandable in those cases where jurors have returned to the judge to ask for elucidation. Frequently, judges will do no more than repeat what was said in the first place, refusing to explain or paraphrase.[108] Legal language relies heavily on long sentences containing many subclauses. This makes oral delivery very difficult to follow. Lawyers are also wont to employ a large number of double negatives as well as nouns contracted from a verb. 'The doing of which' is a common phrase found in legislation. If standard instructions are rewritten in simpler language compliance rises.[109] Charrow and Charrow[110] tested the effect of rewriting standard judicial instructions. They used more conventional vocabulary and sentence structure. They found that the legal predilection for sentences containing a subordinate clause in the passive caused major comprehension problems. Linguistic complexity seemed to have a more adverse effect on comprehension than conceptual complexity. Once the instructions had been redrafted into simpler language, there was a significant increase in jurors' ability to recall the law, although they still tended to be inaccurate. However, the greater the conceptual complexity, the greater the improvement when the instruction was rewritten. Darbyshire notes the complicated language used in American written instructions to juries in comparison with those drafted for the Judicial Studies Board of England and Wales. However, even there, sentences may contain five clauses. The circuit judges who devise these do not consult psychologists and linguistics experts.[111] It seems to increase jurors' confidence in their grasp of the law if they are given written instructions to take with them into the retiring room, but there is little evidence that it actually helps them understand.[112] Pattern instructions may be effective in reminding jurors of concepts with which they are familiar, but do not improve comprehension of new, difficult or counter-intuitive laws.[113]

---

[107] R Lempert, 'Civil Juries and Complex Cases: Let's Not Rush to Judgment' (1981) 80 *Michigan Law Review* 68.

[108] Severance and Loftus, above n.95.

[109] BD Sales, A Elwork and J Alfini, 'Improving comprehension for jury instruction' in BD Sales, (ed) *Perspectives in Law and Psychology Vol 1, The Criminal Justice System* (New York, Plenum, 1977).

[110] RP Charrow and VR Charrow, 'Making Legal Language Understandable: a Psycholinguistic Study of Jury Instructions' (1979) 79 *Colombian Law Review* 1306.

[111] P Darbyshire, A Maugham and A Steward, *What Can the English Legal System Learn from Jury Research Published Up to 2001?* Criminal Courts Review, www.criminal-courts-review.org.uk.

[112] L Heuer and SD Penrod, 'Instructing Jurors: a Field Experiment with Written and Preliminary Instructions' (1989) 13 *Law and Human Behavior* 409.

[113] Sales, Elwork and Alfini, above n.95.

The answer may be to provide jurors with flow charts, as recommended by the New Zealand Law Commission. Indeed, one of the juries in their study constructed their own on a whiteboard. Those juries who were unable to structure their discussion around the legal issues foundered badly.[114] Auld suggests that judges produce guidance in the form of a series of questions and answers to facilitate structured jury discussion.[115]

In the United States, judges can advise on the law but not comment on the facts. Model directions generally come from books of approved jury instructions[116] and define jurors' duties, the rudiments of procedure and explain the burden of proof. This is highly abstract. Where the judge sums up on fact and law, as in the United Kingdom, it is often possible to combine the two in a way that is more case-specific, which may make it easier to apply the law to the facts. For example it might be possible to reduce the contentious issue down virtually to a simple, 'If you believe Mrs Smith the defendant is guilty'. However, the New Zealand jurors seemed to find the judge's summing up of the facts unhelpful, considering it repetitive. A third of them thought it indicated what the judge's view of the case was, particularly the passages where he gave the model directions on what inferences they could draw from facts, as with the effect of lies or silence by the accused. In reality, there was no correlation between jurors' interpretation of the judge's view and his or her real opinion. Jurors actually appeared to be seeking reassurance that the judge agreed with them; there was a distinct correlation between what jurors considered to be the judge's preference and their own.[117]

In fact, the legal attitude to juries is ambivalent. Despite the oft-repeated reservations that have been expressed about the appropriateness of jury trial in fraud cases, and the dismissive tone of comments such as Jerome Frank's, quoted above, courts repeatedly express great confidence in the ability of the lay fact-finder to unravel evidence in the light of the technical rules. The usefulness of this alternative posture is that it justifies the law in preserving abstruse definitions and distinctions, and these, in consequence do not afford grounds for overturning convictions on appeal. In *G (a Minor)*,[118] the Divisional Court was untroubled by the fact that magistrates had heard evidence of a previous indecent assault by a twelve year old boy who was, in the instant case, accused of indecent assault against a young girl. Evidence of the earlier offences was adduced to rebut the presumption of *doli incapax*,[119] the argument being that after the furore that followed a previous episode, the defendant must have known that what he was doing was wrong. The defence argued that to inform the Bench of the earlier offence would be

---

[114] Law Commission of New Zealand, above n.79.

[115] Auld, above n.61, para. 8. 24.

[116] Tanford, above n.101.

[117] Young, Cameron and Tinsley, above n. 26 para. 7.32.

[118] *The Times* 27 November 1997.

[119] The presumption, that a child of between ten and fourteen has insufficient knowledge of right and wrong to be held liable for criminal offences. Abolished, s.34 Crime and Disorder Act 1998.

prejudicial, in that they might use it to infer guilt. It was held that magistrates were entirely able to separate the issue of guilt from that of *doli incapax.*

TRIAL STRUCTURE

The structure of trials presents jurors with problems judges do not share. Juries listen to evidence sometimes over considerable periods of time, without having a legal context in which to place it. By the time an explanation is provided of the legal significance of the evidence, it has all been heard. The jury must recall it to mind and fit it within the legal framework.[120] This has been compared with

> telling jurors to watch a baseball game and decide who won without telling them what the rules are until the end of the game.[121]

Jackson and Doran noted that in a trial for rape, an expert gave evidence that there was no abrasion in the woman's vagina. The jury passed the judge a note asking whether rape could be committed in the absence of a sexual assault. Judge said that he would explain what rape was at the end of the trial.[122] It is scarcely surprising, therefore, to find that if a judicial summing-up simultaneously reminds jurors of some evidence they heard but instructs them to disregard it, the admonishment appears to be counter-productive.[123]

We gave seen above that warning the jury to disregard evidence they heard about some time ago, and may have partly forgotten about until reminded,[124] may backfire. Research supports the possibility of a recency effect.[125] Such a phenomenon should give the defence an advantage, since they present their case last. Most studies do suggest a recency effect; the later information is provided, the more influence it has.[126] Against this, one experiment discovered that a quarter of mock jurors had reached a decision early in a trial simulation. After that, the effect of the testimony was merely 'to change their certainty'.[127] Kassin and Wrightsman suggest that where subjects are making judgments about people, their early attitudes

[120] J Jackson, above n.80.

[121] T Grove, *The Juryman's Tale* (London, Bloomsbury, 2000) The problems was succinctly expressed by Kassin and Wrightsman: 'When was the last time you heard the rules of a game after you had played it?' Kassin and Wrightsman, above n.13, at 144.

[122] J Jackson and S Doran, *Judge Without Jury: Diplock Trials and the Adversary System* (Oxford, Clarendon, 1995).

[123] Wolf and Montgomery, above n. 72; S Lloyd-Bostock, above n.69; Tanford, above n.100; Hastie, Penrod, and Pennington, above n.95.

[124] L Walker, J Thibaut and V Andreoli, 'Order of Presentation at Trial' (1972) *Yale Law Journal* 216.

[125] Sue, Smith and Caldwell, above n.30; Sealy, above n.4.

[126] CA Insko, 'Primacy versus Recency as a Function of the Timing of Arguments and Measures' (1964) 69 *Journal of Abnormal and Social Psychology* 381; N Miller and DT Campbell, 'Recency and Primacy in Persuasion as a Function of the Timing of Speeches and Measurements' (1959) 59 *Journal of Abnormal and Social Psychology* 1; EA Lind, 'The Psychology of Courtroom Procedure' in NL Kear and RM Bray, *The Psychology of the Courtroom* (London, Academic Press, 1982).

[127] HP Weld and ER Danzig, 'A Study of the Way in which a Verdict is reached by a Jury' (1940) 53 *American Journal of Psychology* 518.

tend not to shift. Hence, if first sight of a chronically unattractive defendant produces an adverse reaction, or if fact-finders learn at an early stage that he has confessed to the police, the defence have major hurdles to overcome.[128] In their study, jurors had decided on their verdicts by a point around the middle of the trial. Consequently, if the judge's direction on the burden of proof was delivered after all the evidence had been heard, it had very little effect. Where the instruction was given at the beginning of the trial, the conviction rate fell significantly. It may be the case that these experiments created their own recency effect, however. The mock jurors were repeatedly interviewed to see if there was any shift of opinion. The interviews themselves may acted as reminders, and distorted the reasoning process.

It is most unlikely that court verdicts can be explained entirely either in terms of the recency effect or the reluctance of fact-finders to move from first impressions. Research into the effect of manipulating the order of arguments is inconclusive.[129] The crucial determinant may be the combination of the order of evidence presentation, together with the relative strength or weakness of the evidence for each side.[130] Horowitz and Borderns experimented with trial structure in a simulation of a tort action involving multiple claims for damages alleged to be caused by chemical pollution.[131] One set of mock jurors dealt with all the issues on one unitary trial, where causation, liability and the quantum of damages were all heard together. Others dealt with separate issues; for instance, they might try the matter of causation on its own. In the latter case, the plaintiff tended to be less successful. Thus the complexity of the trial affected the verdict. However, so also did the order of presentation of evidence. Most advocates, in fact, favour ordering their own case in a weak to strong sequence designed to achieve maximum impact.[132] The likelihood of a recency effect may depend also on the length of the trial:

> A long trial brings recency to the fore, as the 'availability heuristic' dictates that we are more likely to utilise this more recent information in our decisions about the case as they are more easily available to our short-term memory.[133]

In a short trial, initial interpretations tend to be reinforced. The first person to introduce an explanation of events has the opportunity to suggest sequences of actions in the form of stories supporting his argument.[134]

---

[128] Kassin and Wrightsman, above n.13.

[129] M King, *Psychology In or Out of Court* (London, Pergamon, 1986) 86; S Lloyd-Bostock, above n.69.

[130] Walker, Thibaut and Andreoli, above n.124.

[131] IA Horowitz and KS Bordens, 'An Experimental Investigation of Procedural Issues in Complex Tort Trials' (1990) 14 *Law and Human Behavior* 269.

[132] Walker, Thibaut and Andreoli, above n.124.

[133] D Bartlett and A Memon, 'Advocacy' in R Bull and D Carson, (eds) *Handbook of Psychology in Legal Contexts* (Chichester, Wiley, 1995) at 545.

[134] S Lloyd-Bostock, *Law and Practice in Applications of Psychology to Legal Decision-Making and Legal Skills* (Leicester, British Psychological Society, 1988).

Judges who are reluctant to allow juries a second viewing of videotaped evidence seen earlier in the trial appear to have the possibility of a recency effect in mind. The videotape would have been used in lieu of the evidence in chief of a child (usually a prosecution) witness. Although videotapes provide accurate records of child witnesses' testimony and demeanour, it is thought that replaying them may induce the jury to place excessive reliance on them. If they should ask to be reminded of the child's evidence, the judge is enjoined to read from his or her written note, as would be the practice with ordinary oral testimony. If the jury particularly want to be reminded of the witness's demeanour, the video may be replayed but should be watched in court with judge, counsel and the defendant present. The judge should instruct the jury not to give the evidence disproportionate weight. Also, to maintain a fair balance, the judge should, afterwards, remind the jury from his or her own notes of the terms of the cross-examination, whether the jury ask for it or not.[135]

The structure of adversarial trials, according to Wagenaar, creates another significant bias, in all cases favouring the prosecution. The prosecutor selects the level of analysis, determines the narrative and chooses the anchors which operate as the court's starting-point. The result is an allegedly anchored narrative which the defence have to challenge. Although it is open to the defence is to produce an alternative narrative, the adversarial context place obstacles in their way.[136] This was certainly true in *Blastland*,[137] where a rival narrative offered by the defence was deemed irrelevant because of insufficient anchoring. Thus the choice of narratives offered to the jury may be limited. In addition, the order in which evidence is presented may make construction of a story difficult for the fact-finder. This was the experience of the jurors participating in the New Zealand survey.[138] Significantly, they also signally failed to understand the nature and purpose of the adversarial trial, and thought the task was to uncover the truth rather than weigh up the rival merits of two competing versions of events.[139] The quest for the most convincing narrative available, as opposed to the case which defence and prosecution advocates actually wish to plead, may explain why jurors ask questions which seem irrelevant to many lawyers.

CONCLUSION

Much of the difficulty jurors experience with legal concepts is inflicted on them by the legal system itself. Procedures could be made far more conducive to rational decision-making. Auld recommends that at the outset the jury should be given a copy of the charge, as Scottish juries are. But they should also have, at the

---

[135] *Rawlings and Broadbent* [1995] 1 All ER 680.
[136] Wagenaar, van Koppen and Cronbag, above n.11, 209–10.
[137] [1985] 2 All ER 1095. See above chapter four.
[138] Young, Cameron and Tinsley, above n.26 para. 3.14.
[139] *Ibid.,* para. 1.14.

beginning of the trial, a summary of the case and issues arising (as agreed by counsel) so that there would be no need for a long summing up on the law.[140] In Heuer and Penrod's experiment,[141] some of the participating judges gave juries advice on the law before the evidence was heard. The judges were more satisfied with the final decisions than were judges in trials where this procedure was not followed. In a libel case brought in 1984-5 by General Westmoreland against CBS, which took five months to hear, the judge allowed counsel to offer interim summaries at regular intervals. They tended to last only a few minutes and both sides thought it a useful procedure.[142] In New Zealand, there have been changes of practice following the publication of the jury survey. These centre upon making the information provided to juries accessible and manageable. Comprehension and memory are assisted by much greater reliance on visual and written aids.[143] Unlike lawyers in the United Kingdom, lawyers in New Zealand apparently have managed without rancour to identify at the outset what are the basic issues to be dealt with in the trial, and present these in a non-partisan way. Informing and assisting jurors may be a more constructive way forward than abandoning jury trials altogether.[144]

---

[140] Auld, above n.61, para.11.22. There is already provision for this in serious fraud cases, Criminal Justice Act 1987 s.9.
[141] Heuer and Penrod, above n.112.
[142] EA Lind and TR Tyler, *The Social Psychology of Procedural Justice* (New York, Plenum, 1988) 136.
[143] Y Tinsley, Paper presented to the Criminal Law Group, SLS Conference, Leicester de Montfort, September 2002.
[144] See White Paper *Justice For All* (London, Stationery Office, 2002).

6

The Criminal Process and Personality

PERSONALITY AS PROOF OF GUILT

ON OCTOBER 24TH, 1983, the Laitner family held a wedding reception for their elder daughter in a marquee in their garden. There were signs that someone had lain in the grass nearby for a considerable period, watching the party. That night, after the bride and groom had departed and the family had gone to bed, a man broke into the house. He woke up the bride's sister, Nicola, who had been a bridesmaid, pulled her out of bed, and raped her. He then dragged her through the house, past the murdered bodies of her parents and brother. He raped her again in the garden, and left her there. Nicola Raitner identified Arthur Hutchinson as that man. He had a string of convictions for violent sexual offences, and had escaped from custody. He had been living rough. His defence was that Nicola consented to intercourse and that someone else murdered the family. The jury was not told of his criminal history or that at the time of the murders, he was on the run. Nevertheless, they probably observed his mental instability when, during cross-examination, he pointed to a local journalist, who was at the time sitting in the Press Gallery, and accused him of the murders.[1]

Failing particular probative value, evidence of the defendant's criminal history is likely to be excluded from an Anglo-American adversarial trial. This is partly because the logic of adversarial proceedings suggests that the purpose of the trial is to test the strength of the prosecution evidence. Yet, in 2001, when Barry George was tried for the murder of Jill Dando, a well-known television presenter,[2] the prosecution adduced, in support of a weak identification case, evidence that George tended to develop obsession with famous people, even to the extent of changing his name to that of one of his heroes. Further, he was an isolated and lonely figure. The jury were not informed, however, of his previous convictions for sexual offences, nor of instances of his stalking and harassing women in the past. It seems that part, although not all, of his character was in issue, and was thought to suggest guilt. What was the jury to infer from this evidence? No expert witness advised them on the relevance of George's personality to the question of his guilt. It was not established what proportion of people who become fixated on famous individuals go on to murder the object of their affections. Courts discuss the

---

[1] *Hutchinson* (1986) 82 Cr App R 51.
[2] *George, The Times* 30 August 2002; see chapter eight.

admissibility and significance of 'disposition' evidence entirely on the basis of intuitive judgments about its probative value. This depends to a large extent on the degree to which the behaviour or circumstances are perceived as unusual. We have seen in chapter one that this judgment is founded upon heuristics. But whether or not 'personality', if it exists, can be accurately identified in order that predictions may be based on it, remains to be established in both law and psychology.

The extent to which personality should be considered relevant to decisions of guilt or innocence has increasingly become the focus of debate. Psychologists interested in the investigation or crimes, and, at the other end of the criminal process, in the sentencing of offenders, have carried out work on the relationship between personality and criminal activities. Saks and Hastie[3] argue that since personality or trait is not a reliable predictor of future behaviour for sentencing purposes, testimony about a defendant's general traits or dispositions would be unreliable and undermine judgment. However, criminal courts do use aspects of personality as indicators of guilt. For example, failure to answer questions in police interview may be used as evidence against the accused, as may refusal to give evidence during the trial. Evidence of 'reaction' to being accused of an offence is deemed helpful evidence for the jury.[4] On the other hand, a suspect who willingly confesses during police interview has also supplied evidence indicative of guilt. If it transpires that he or she is so compliant that admissions are worthless, the law must provide a mechanism to prevent a possible miscarriage of justice.

Offender Profiling and Disposition

While lawyers anxiously debate the probative value of the defendant's disposition, criminal investigators are involved in a similar controversy about the usefulness of offender profiling as an investigative tool. The assumption that there are certain personality constants that determine behaviour is highly controversial. However, the expert profiler is now a familiar character not only in police dramas on television and in films, but also in high profile investigations such as the disappearance and murders of Holly Wells and Jessica Chapman in Cambridgeshire in August 2002. English and American police have consulted offender profilers from as long ago as 1880, when the 'Jack the Ripper' murders were being investigated. More recently, David Canter assisted in the 'Railway Murders', of which Michael Duffy was convicted in 1986.[5] Profiles are constructed from statistics comprising the common characteristics of particular kinds of offender. Part of the theory is that behaviour is exhibited at a crime scene. Informed interpretation of crime scene evidence may allow inferences to be drawn about the offender. It is assumed that

---

[3] MJ Saks, R Hastie, *Social Psychology in the Courtroom* (New York, Van Nostrand, 1978).
[4] *Storey* (1968) 52 CR App R 334; *Pearce* (1979) 69 Cr App R 365.
[5] D Canter, *Criminal Shadows: Inside the Mind of the Serial Killer* (London, Harper Collins, 1994). Duffy's accomplice, David Mulcahy, was not convicted until 2001.

certain personality types exhibit similar behavioural patterns, knowledge of which can assist in the investigation of the crime. This information can come from clinical experience, research and the statistical analysis of offender databases. It is acknowledged that not all crimes lend themselves to this technique; the most suitable offences are those where suspects' behaviour at the scene reveals important information about themselves.[6] It is thought that arson and sexually motivated crimes offer the most information. The Federal Bureau of Investigation in the United States (FBI) tends not to use profiling for non-arson criminal damage, robbery-related violence, or for drug-induced crimes, since drugs usually alter personality.[7] It is unusual for analyses of women to appear in profiling literature.

There have been many claims for the success for offender profiling,[8] but reports of accuracy vary from forty-six per cent[9] to eighty per cent.[10] Success is difficult to measure; an offender who is caught may or may not fit the profile, but that depends on how his personality is assessed at that later stage. Sceptics have claimed that the reported accuracy of profiles is unsurprising, given that the hypotheses they present combine statements of the obvious with common sense assumptions that any experienced detective could make. McCann, however, denies that profiling consists of little more than 'best guesses', claiming that it has become a 'systematic process', based on (in the United States at any rate) a large amount of computer-stored factual information.[11] He stresses that profiling is at a preliminary stage of development, but seems to regard any problems as organisational in nature, requiring more co-operation at the investigation stage. Professor Canter, a well-known English profiler, argues that the FBI base their profiles on too small a group of offenders. His method is more scientific, and shows the importance of locale and the average distance offenders travel to commit their crimes.[12] Even so, the emphasis on 'pathological' crimes inevitably limits the size of the population of offenders studied. Despite reservations in some quarters, the practice of using profiles seems to be growing. For England and Wales, there is a chief police officers' committee which 'accredits' profilers, although not on any scientific basis. Some police officers use unaccredited profilers because

---

[6] JT McCann, 'Criminal Personality Profiling in the Investigation of Violent Crime' (1992) 10 *Behavioral Sciences and the Law* 475.

[7] *Ibid.*

[8] RH Morneaux , RR Rockwell, *Sex, Motivation and the Criminal Offender*, (Springfield Illinois, Charles C Thomas, 1980); RK Ressler, AW Burgess, CR Hertman, JE Douglas and A McCormack, 'Murderers who Rape and Mutilate', (1986) 1 *Journal of Interpersonal Violence* 273; RR Hazelwood and JE Douglas, 'The Lust Murderer' (1980) 49 *FBI Law Enforcement Bulletin* 18; JE Douglas, AW Burgess, 'Criminal Profiling' (1986) 55 *FBI Law Enforcement Bulletin* 9; JE Douglas, RK Ressler, AW Burgess and CR Hartman, 'Criminal Profiling from Crime Scene Analysis, (1986) 4 *Behavioral Sciences and the Law* 401; D Canter, 'Offender Profiles' (1989) *The Psychologist* 12–16.

[9] AJ Pinizzotto and NJ Finkel, 'Criminal Personality Profiling: an Outcome and Process Study' (1990) 14 *Law and Human Behavior* 215.

[10] RR Hazelwood, 'The Behaviour-Oriented Interview of Rape Victims: The Key to Profiling' (1983) 51 *FBI Law Enforcement Bulletin* 1; McCann, above n.6.

[11] McCann, above n.6.

[12] Canter, above n.5.

they know them and have confidence in them. Some are psychologists or psychiatrists. Some are police officers.

The FBI has been criticised for its espousal of offender profiling, on the ground that there is no theoretical base for it in psychology.[13] The fundamental objection to offender profiling, which applies equally to similar fact 'disposition' evidence, is that psychology has not established what human personality is, nor whether personality governs how people behave.[14] The insistence on internal causes is redolent of the fundamental attribution error. Trait theory assumes that people behave according to their innate disposition; its critics argue that behaviour is situationally specific. For example, a child who lies at school might not do so at home; a child who cheats in examinations might not do so in sports.

> Character evidence used as a basis for predicting human behaviour is useless ... Thus, the assumption upon which character evidence is deemed admissible does not exist. The legal conclusion therefore ought to be that evidence of character has no probative value.[15]

To the argument that there are traits, such as aggressiveness, that are consistent across situations, sceptics cite such individuals as Heinrich Himmler, who opposed hunting on the grounds that every animal has a right to life.[16]

Trait theorists certainly cannot predict with confidence a single instance of behaviour, but claim that there is a generalised tendency for a person to behave in a certain way across a number of events. This does not imply that particular behaviour will be displayed on all occasions, even in the same situation. Alker[17] contends that where behaviours differ, interaction between personality and situation is the most significant source of variance. He argues that severely disturbed persons may be more influenced by their personalities and less by situations than others. Where a personality is abnormal it appears to be a better predictor of behaviour than the situation.[18] This could explain the amenability of crimes such as hostage taking, anonymous letter writing, threats of violence, rape, arson and serial sexual homicide for offender profiling. Apparently indifferent to the theoretical debate, professional profilers appear to ignore theory and simply use available

---

[13] JL Jackson and DA Bekerian, 'Does Offender Profiling have a Role to Play?' in JL Jackson and DA Bekerian, (eds) *Offender Profiling: Theory, Research and Practice* (Chichester, Wiley, 2000).
[14] JCW Boon, 'The Contribution of Personality Theories to Psychological Profiling' in JL Jackson and DA Bekerian (eds) *Offender Profiling: Theory, Research and Practice* (Chichester, Wiley, 2000).
[15] R Spector, Impeaching the Defendant by his Prior Convictions and the Proposed Federal Rules of Evidence: a Half Step Forward and Three Steps Backward [1970] *Loyola University Law Journal*.
[16] DP Bryden and RC Park, 'Other crimes evidence in sex offense cases' (1994) 78 *Minnesota Law Review* 529.
[17] HA Alker, 'Is Personality Situationally Specific or Intrapsychically Consistent?' (1972) 40 *Journal of Personality* 1; see reply, NS Endler, 'The Person versus the Situation; a Response to Alker' (1973) 41 *Journal of Personality* 287.
[18] RA Prentky and RA Knight, 'Identifying Critical Dimensions for Discriminating amongst Rapists' (1991) 5 *Journal of Consulting and Clinical Psychology* 643; PH Gebhard, PJ Gagnon, WB Pomeroy and CV Christiansen, *Sex Offenders*, (London, Heinemann, 1965).

data on offenders and personal experience to try to construct profiles that work.[19] Professor Davies contends that since methodology was improved,

> the usefulness of trait information in predicting behaviour is no longer controverted by members of the psychological community.[20]

She concludes that it is possible to predict human behaviour, but only when there is considerable information about the individual to be assessed. Even a lay person, given information about someone's past behaviour, is enabled to predict his or her future actions 'with a significant degree of accuracy.'[21]

Rightly or wrongly, the law of evidence assumes that there are constants of character. Credibility, or the lack of it, is assumed to be stable across time and situations.[22] It is thought legitimate in the courtroom to examine under the forensic microscope every character flaw a witness may have. Yet it is thought dangerous to expose defendants in a criminal trial to the risk to the same treatment. It is not permissible to appeal merely to prejudice; disposition evidence is admissible only if it directly incriminates the defendant:

> It is undoubtedly not competent for the prosecution to adduce evidence tending to show that the accused has been guilty of criminal acts other than those covered by the indictment, for the purpose of leading to the conclusion that the accused is a person likely from his criminal conduct or character to have committed the offence for which he is being tried. On the other hand, the mere fact that the evidence tends to show the commission of other crimes does not render it inadmissible if it bears upon the issue whether the acts alleged to constitute the crime are designed or accidental, or to rebut a defence which would otherwise be open to the accused.[23]

The crucial issue, therefore, is just how probative is this defendant's disposition? If a unique *modus operandi* permeates the defendant's criminal history, the answer is relatively clear. The legal approach to a hallmark may be seen in the famous passage from *DPP v Boardman*:[24]

> Whilst it would certainly not be enough to identify the culprit in a series of burglaries that he climbed in through a ground floor window, the fact that he left the same humorous limerick on the walls of the sitting room, or an esoteric symbol written in lipstick on the mirror, might well be enough. In a sex case … whilst a repeated homosexual act by itself might be quite insufficient to admit the evidence as

---

[19] Boon, above n.14.
[20] SM Davies, 'Evidence of Character to Prove Conduct: a Re-Assessment' (1991) 27 *Criminal Law Bulletin* 504, 516.
[21] *Ibid.*, 517.
[22] See chapter four.
[23] *Makin v A-G for New South Wales* [1894] AC 57: per Lord Herschell at 65.
[24] [1975] AC 421.

confirmatory of identity or design, the fact that it was alleged to have been performed wearing the ceremonial head-dress of a Red Indian chief or other eccentric garb might well in appropriate circumstances suffice.[25]

Courts have found it much more difficult to deal with cases where it is argued that the defendant's personality is in itself probative of guilt. *Thompson*[26] illustrates the problem. Two boys reported that a man had committed acts of gross indecency with them. They told police that they had a rendezvous with him, and the police attended at the relevant time and place with the boys. When Thompson arrived, they identified him as the offender. Thompson claimed that they had the wrong man; yet at his premises were numerous pornographic photographs of young boys. It was held that Thompson's sexual preference was relevant to the issue of the accuracy of the boys' identification, making the evidence more probative than it was prejudicial. There was no 'striking similarity' or pattern between a series of offences, no unique *modus operandi*, merely an inclination to homosexual paedophilia. Given that Thompson had arrived at the rendezvous, and that the boys identified him, this was adjudged abnormal and sufficiently unusual to be probative of guilt. It made the possibility of a mistake by the boys more remote. Yet the significance of Thompson's proclivities was discussed and evaluated by the House of Lords entirely in the absence of any statistical data or expert evidence on the subject.

Despite the precedent set in *Thompson*, courts have been wary of making judgments about personality. In *Beggs*,[27] the defendant, a student, brought home for the night a man he met at a gay club. The dead body of this man was discovered in the morning in Beggs' room. Beggs alleged that the man had made unwanted homosexual advances to him during the night, so he had defended himself by slashing his throat with a razor blade. Beggs was tried for murder, pleading self-defence. The prosecution obtained permission at the trial to add to the murder count several charges of wounding in respect of a series of incidents involving male students who shared a house with Beggs. He appeared to have a practice of prowling the premises at night and cutting into the legs of sleeping men. The trial judge agreed that the wounding charges should be heard together with the murder charge, by the same jury. The prejudice that hearing of Beggs' activities would induce in the jury was outweighed by its probative value. It might cast a different light on his claim to self-defence, in that the jury might decide that Beggs' tastes had escalated from cutting the legs of a man asleep to cutting his throat. However, the Court of Appeal decided that the jury should not have been informed of the non-fatal incidents,[28] which were insufficiently probative. As far as the homicide was concerned, the injury was to a different part of the body, and was more serious;

---

[25] *Ibid.*, Lord Hailsham 454.
[26] [1918] AC. 22. p 235.
[27] (1990) 90 Cr App R 430.
[28] Tried as a series of wounding charges jointly with the murder charge.

also, the victim was not a student. Beggs' conviction for murder was quashed on the ground that hearing of the wounding charges might have unduly prejudiced the jury. Certainly, they convicted him. This might have been a consequence of prejudice, or it may be that jurors thought his unusual practices suggested a more likely explanation of the death than his story that he needed to repel homosexual advances from a man he brought home from a gay club. They may have thought that someone who derives a thrill from the infliction of slight wounds might well progress into more extreme violence. If so, they were right. Beggs has recently been found guilty in Scotland of the sexual assault and murder of a youth whose body had been decapitated and dismembered. The police are currently investigating the possibility of other murders, having found what appears to be the blood of seventeen different men at Beggs' flat.[29] Support for the English jury derives from more than hindsight; there are research findings, as we shall see below, that corroborate the view that someone with Beggs' predilections is likely to escalate the level of his violence. Hence, it is remarkable that the Scottish jury who convicted him more recently were not told of any of the evidence from the previous trial. Presumably that was also thought more prejudicial than probative.

In *Thompson* Lord Sumner explained that not all criminal personalities are probative:

> Persons ... who commit the offences now under consideration seek the habitual gratification of a particular perverted lust, which not only takes them out of the class of ordinary men gone wrong, but stamps them with the hall-mark of a specialised and extraordinary class as much as if they carried on their bodies some physical peculiarity... Experience tends to show that these offences against nature connote an inversion of normal characteristics which, while demanding punishment as offending against social morality, also partake of the nature of an abnormal physical propensity. A thief, a cheat, a coiner, or housebreaker is only a particular specimen of the genus rogue, and, though no doubt each tends to keep to his own line of business, they all alike possess the by no means extraordinary characteristic that they propose somehow to get their living dishonestly. So common a characteristic is not a recognisable mark of the individual.[30]

The quotation from Thompson suggests that a propensity to commit burglary is too unexceptional to indicate guilt. However, it may not be impossible to develop profiles on burglars. It has been suggested that patterns may be identified by collating data on *modus operandi*, location, proximity, time of day and relationship with the victim.[31]

Comparing *Beggs* and *Thompson* suggests that judges believe that there is such a thing as a paedophile personality but not a murderous one. There is some evidence

---

[29] *The Times* 15 October 2001.
[30] Above n.26, at 235.
[31] JA Stevens, 'Standard Investigatory Tools and Offender Profiling' in JL Jackson and DA Bekerian, (eds) *Offender Profiling: Theory, Research and Practice* (Chichester, Wiley, 2000).

that they are right. Pinizotto and Finkel found that professional profilers produced more accurate descriptions of sex offenders than detectives or students, but could not do so for homicide.[32] They suggest that the difference is arises from the impossibility, in the latter instance, of gaining information from the victim.[33] But, doubting that even sex offenders have similar characteristics, Prentky and Knight have observed:

> Offenders with widely varying family and developmental experience, psychological profiles, psychiatric diagnoses and criminal histories have been treated as a cohesive, homogeneous group by virtue of the presence of sexual coercion in their offences. Their sexual offences have varied markedly with respect to numerous features ... [D]espite this manifest diversity, rapists have frequently been viewed as a homogeneous class of offenders. The discrepancy between the myth of their homogeneity and the reality of their heterogeneity has led inevitably to considerable inconsistency in research on these offenders.[34]

They conclude that the multivariable approach of some profilers who seek to counter this complexity will succeed only if the right variables are selected in the first place, in anticipation of results. Also, investigation into subjects' criminal backgrounds involves the obvious problem that official criminal records may represent only the tip of the iceberg. At the same time, self-report may be unreliable for a variety of reasons. Thus profiles may be based on a small, unrepresentative proportion of offences committed, or on fictitious crimes boasted of in self-report.

If the science in this area is uncertain, does that mean that we should allow the fact-finder to proceed in utter ignorance of the history and character of the defendant in a criminal trial? McCann suggests that where joinder is the issue, expert evidence would be appropriate to link several crimes together, thus implicating a serial offender.[35] Similarities between offences have been used in this way in trials where the defendant is charged with several joined offences, and identification is an issue in each one. In *Black*,[36] there was clear evidence of the defendant's guilt in relation to one charge of abducting a little girl, since she was found in the van he was driving. It was held that the jury was entitled to use similar fact evidence to establish a link between that crime and three other offences of which he was accused, the abduction and murder of three girls. All the victims were pre-pubescent, all were abducted from a public place on fine summer days and then transported for many miles, all wore white socks, had their shoes removed and were indecently assaulted. Defendants could benefit as well as suffer disadvantage from this kind of linkage, for example, if the defendant is clearly innocent of at least one crime in a series of crimes which appear to be the work of one person.

---

[32] Although here professionals showed more expertise, such as the amount of detail in their reports.
[33] Pinizotto and Finkel, above n.9.
[34] Prentky and Knight, above n.18.
[35] Above, n.6.
[36] [1995] *Criminal Law Review* 640.

The *Makin* principle offers no guidance to suggest to judges when and in what way a particular kind of personality might be probative of guilt. A vast body of case law has developed in which unusual features or striking similarities have been used to justify the admission of 'similar fact' evidence. But cases where the offender leaves a 'signature' are rare and are unlikely to constitute crimes for gain. It is no coincidence that while offender profiling has burgeoned in areas such as child abuse, sex offences and murder, similar fact evidence, requiring features that take the case out of the common run, tends also most commonly to be found in such cases. If, indeed, there are identifiable common characteristics within these groups of offender, the question arises whether the fact-finder should be acquainted with them as a matter of routine. What is known about those who commit crimes of this nature?

Murderers

Recent trials have supplied interesting examples of the kind of evidence thought to suggest that someone is capable of killing. At the trial of Rosemary West, wife of the notorious serial murderer, Frederick West (who committed suicide before his trial), the court heard a wide range of evidence about the defendant's personality. The prosecution had to establish that this unremarkable-looking mother of several children was complicit in her husband's abduction, torture, rape and murder of young women, including his own daughter. The trial judge allowed them to lead evidence of the brutal way she had treated her children. The jury also heard that she had enjoyed a lesbian relationship with a neighbour, that she had worked as a prostitute, and that she had helped to force one of her teenage daughters also into prostitution. The rationale for this appeared to be that she was such a perverted personality as to be capable of anything, yet the Court of Appeal considered that there was no risk that the jury would have been unduly prejudiced.[37]

This decision presents a baffling contrast with the collapse of the prosecution case against Colin Stagg.[38] He was charged with the murder of Rachel Nickell on Wimbledon Common. His presence near the scene at the time she was stabbed to death in the presence of her young child was insufficient on its own to implicate him in her killing. But it was known that, in correspondence with a woman pen friend, Stagg had displayed a taste for violent sexual fantasies. He appeared to have an interest in Satanism. He had a previous conviction for indecent exposure. Paul Britton, a forensic psychologist and specialist in offender profiling, was due to give evidence for the prosecution explaining the significance of Stagg's personality, given the circumstances of Rachel Nickell's death. Ognall J refused to allow this, or

---

[37] *West* [1996] 2 Cr App R 574.
[38] M Fielder, *Killer on the Loose. Inside Story of the Rachel Nickell Murder Investigation* (London, Blake Publishing, 1994).

to allow any of the disposition evidence to be admitted.[39] Yet Stagg's personality fitted closely to the profile of the sadistic sexual murderer (below), giving his presence close to the scene considerable significance. In his case, the prosecution had a far stronger scientific claim for the admissibility of the disposition evidence than they did at the West trial. There is little evidence of personality traits that can be associated with female murderers. Most murder cases are domestic in nature, with no suggestion that the perpetrator had an unusual personality. In these cases, offender profiling is thought impossible and unnecessary. Profilers have tended to concentrate on those cases where the victim appears to be randomly selected and sadism is the motive.[40] Female killers are rarely involved in this kind of case.

According to Morneaux and Rockwell,[41] the sadistic murderer does not 'come from nowhere and disappear into nothingness'; he tends to be male, and his history typically includes sex offences, not necessarily violent in nature.[42] In a study of imprisoned rapists carried out by Grubin and Gunn,[43] those who had killed their victims were not significantly more prone to mental illness than the other rapists, and were not particularly sexually disturbed. However, they were more socially isolated. They had more previous convictions for sex offences, and these were more likely to have been for rape. But men who rape and then murder may differ from the 'sadistic murderers', who tend to exhibitionism in relation to the killing.[44] Unlike rapist-murderers, they get their sexual satisfaction from the killing itself. It is rare for rapists to perform sexual acts after killing their victims, whereas the sadistic murderer frequently does. Rendering the woman unconscious or dead before intercourse suggests the offender's inability to function with living or conscious persons. The classic portrait of the sadistic sexual murderer is of a confused, disorganised person, possibly with mental problems. He is likely to be introverted, timid, over dependent on his mother, possibly the victim of abuse or neglect as a child, socially isolated, and who may have attempted suicide. Sexually inexperienced but sexually deviant, he may have stolen women's clothes or been a voyeur in adolescence. Since he is incapable of approaching women in normal way, he has a rich, sadistic, fantasy life.[45]

---

[39] Matters were complicated by the manipulations of a woman police officer who pretended to be Stagg's penfriend, and struck up a relationship with him. She was advised throughout by Paul Britton. Evidence obtained by this means was excluded as a breach of the Police and Criminal Evidence Act 1984, since Stagg was effectively undergoing police interview without realising it and without a caution.

[40] RP Brittain, 'The Sadistic Murderer' (1970) 10 *Medicine Science and the Law* 198.

[41] Above, n.8,119.

[42] Cf Brittain above n.40.

[43] D Grubin and J Gunn, *The Imprisoned Rapist and Rape* (London, Institute of Psychiatry, 1990).

[44] Ressler, Burgess, Hertman, Douglas and McCormack, above n.8; RP McCullock, PR Snowden, PJ Wood and HE Mills, 'Sadistic Fantasy, Sadistic Behaviour and Offending' (1973) 143 *British Journal of Psychiatry* 20.

[45] Douglas, Ressler, Burgessand Hartman, n.8; Hazelwood and Douglas, n.8; JP de River, *The Sexual Criminal: a psychoanalytical study* (Springfield Illinois, Charles C Thomas, 1956); it has been argued, however, that this classic picture may be more appropriate to serial sexual murder; RA Prentky, AW Burgess, F Redous, A Lee, C Hartman, R Reisler and J Douglas, 'The Presumptive Role of Fantasy — Serial Sexual Homicide' (1989) 146 *American Journal of Psychiatry* 887.

Serial killing is not common, and poisoning is very rare.[46] Cordess[47] has only four case histories from which to draw his admittedly 'tentative conclusions' as to the characteristics of 'the poisoner'. He concentrates on the mass poisoner, who is more likely to have identifiable personality traits than the poisoner with a financial motive. The most prolific serial killer in English legal history, however, is a poisoner. Dr Harold Shipman[48] in many respects conforms to Cordess's profile of the multiple poisoner. Poisoners tend to have been interested in chemicals from an early age. They are mostly male. They are often medical staff. The killings are motivated by power seeking and a desire for notoriety. A feeling of profound inadequacy may lead to serial killings because of the need to repeat. The offenders are not generally psychotic, but frequently have borderline personality disorders. They tend to be introspective, solitary and studious. However, Cordess goes on to list other characteristics which are, as far as is known, less pertinent to Shipman's case. The poisoner's history may feature early episodes of cruelty, perhaps involving the poisoning of animals. There may have been a fascination with Nazism, the occult or demonology. Whether this kind of information has sufficient scientific basis to justify acquainting the jury with it may be a matter for argument. What is clear, however, is that too few women have become involved with serial sadistic murders committed by their male partners for any consistent personality profile to be created. Rosemary West's trial proceeded on the entirely unscientific assumption that a woman who could be so cruel to her own children betrayed the Madonna portrait of popular imagination, and was capable of anything.[49]

Rapists

Is there an identifiable class of men who commit rape? One problem is that the class depends upon the legal definition, and this may change over time. For example, in England and Wales a recent ruling by the House of Lords on marital rape[50] extends the class 'rapist' so that the victim's husband might be included. In 1994, the offence of rape was redefined to include cases with a male victim,[51] thus widening the category and possibly altering the personality profile. Offender profilers have been unable to identify a consistent psychological profile or set of characteristics that discriminate between sexual offenders and others.[52] A Dutch study

---

[46] S Cordess, 'Criminal Poisoning and the Psycopathology of the Poisoner' (1991) 1 *Journal of Forensic Psychiatry* 213.

[47] *Ibid.*

[48] Dame Janet Smith: *The Shipman Inquiry: First Report* www.the-shipman-inquiry.org.uk/reports.asp. See chapter one.

[49] See chapter three.

[50] *R v R* (1992) 94 Cr App R 216.

[51] Criminal Justice and Public Order Act 1994, s.142.

[52] JR Conte, 'The Nature of Sexual Offences against Children' in CR Hollins and K Howells, (eds) *Clinical Approaches to Sex Offenders and their Victims* (Chichester, Wiley, 1991).

found rapists have similar criminal careers to those of bank robbers, but different personalities. Robbers tend to act with others, and are professional criminals. Rapists are more isolated, both socially and in their offending.[53] Research into the characteristics of rapists fails to demonstrate any pattern in their criminal histories. There are studies that show that they generally do have criminal records, but that sexual offences do not predominate.[54] On the other hand, Groth,[55] in his sample of rapists, found a high incidence of previous convictions for sexual offences. If anything, he argues, these under-represent involvement in sexual offending, given the low incidence of reporting, prosecuting and conviction in sexual cases. Over three-quarters of his Florida sample and nearly half of that in Connecticut admitted to one or more undetected rapes.[56] In a major British study, Grubin and Gunn[57] examined the careers of a hundred and forty-two men imprisoned in six different prisons. Ten per cent had records which included seriously violent offences, and there was also violence in a number of the thefts, but this was rarely directed at women. Overall, thirty per cent had been previously convicted for sex offences, and ten per cent had a previous conviction for rape. Seven had previous sex convictions of an aggressive kind. However, of the men the authors identified as serial rapists, nearly fifty per cent had previous convictions for sexual offences. There was also a greater tendency to use weapons. The use of violence is something that evolves and increases over time.

Gebhard found that violent rapists were more prone than other rapists to have previous convictions for sexual offences, from writing obscene graffiti, indecent exposure, to rape itself.[58] Offender profiling in rape cases tends to concentrate on the 'sadistic' or aggressive rapist, where a more antisocial history is likely to be found.[59] Some profilers include past acts such as cruelty to animals as predictors of the antisocial or psychopathic personality of sadistic rapists.[60] Exhibitionism[61] used to be perceived as harmless, but now can be seen in some cases to be merely the starting point of a sex offender's career.[62] In one study,[63] which may suffer

[53] JL Jackson, P van den Eshof and EE de Kleuver, 'A Research Approach to Offender Profiling' in JL Jackson and DA Bekerian, (eds) *Offender Profiling: Theory, Research and Practice* (Chichester, Wiley, 2000).
[54] Gebhard, Gagnon, Pomeroy and Christiansen, above n.18; KL Soothill, C Way and TCN Gibbens, 'Rape Acquittals' (1980) 43 *Modern Law Review* 159.
[55] AN Groth, RF Longo , HB McFadin, 'Undetected Recidivism in Rapists and Child Molesters' (1982) 28 *Crime and Delinquency* 450.
[56] *Ibid.*
[57] Grubin and Gunn, above n.43.
[58] Gebhard, Gagnon, Pomeroy and Christiansen, above n.18; Morneaux and Rockwell, above n.8; de River, above n.45; N Walker and S McCabe, *Crime and Insanity in England Vol II* (Edinburgh, Edinburgh University Press, 1973); R Bluglass, 'Indecent Exposure in the West Midlands' in DJ West, *Sexual Offenders in the Criminal Justice System,* (Cambridge, Cambridge Institute of Criminology, 1980).
[59] Prentky and Knight, above n.18; Gebhard, Gagnon, Pomeroy and Christiansen, above n.18.
[60] Morneaux and Rockwell, above n.8; de River, above n.45.
[61] Indecent exposure, or 'flashing'.
[62] RM Holmes, *Sex Crimes* (California, Sage, 1991).
[63] GG Abel, JV Becker, J Cunningham-Rather, MS Mittelman, JJ Rouleau, 'Multiple Paraphiliac Diagnoses among Sex Offenders' (1991) 16 *Bulletin of the American Academy of Psychiatry and the Law* 153.

from an over-representation of the most serious and extreme sex offenders, of the hundred and twenty-six subjects who had raped an adult woman, forty-four per cent had been involved with female non-incestuous paedophilia, fourteen per cent with male non-incestuous paedophilia, and twenty-four per cent in female incestuous paedophilia. Twenty-eight per cent had a record for exhibitionism, and eighteen per cent for voyeurism, eleven per cent in frottage and ten per cent in sadism. There was a much higher rate of diagnosed paraphiliac behaviour among the serial offenders, leading to the conclusion that they were more disordered sexually.[64] Grubin suggests that a longstanding history of sexual deviance or sadistic fantasies are important prognostic signs of the sadistic rapist.[65] Langevin also suggests a connection with sadomasochism and fetishism in the case of the most violent rapists.[66] For while most rapists are not sexually isolated,[67] do not lack for consenting sexual partners and are not particularly aroused by stimuli depicting forceful sex as opposed to scenes of mutually enjoyable sex, those with the most violent histories are aroused by violence.[68] According to American research, escalation of violence is to be expected of the sadistic rapist.[69] Groth in his well-known description of anger and power rapes[70] predicts that the power-rapist is likely to carry on and on because reality does not live up to the fantasy. He may also escalate aggression. The anger-rapist, on the other hand, is probably triggered by conflicts in his relationships with the women in his life. The victim may be elderly, and he may kill. This kind of rape is less common than power rapes.[71]

Hence, although it seems impossible to paint a picture of the criminal history of a 'typical' rapist, there is evidence that aggressive or sadistic rapists are more likely to have previous convictions for sexual offences. The profile might therefore legitimately have served as evidence against Arthur Hutchinson. His personality and criminal career would have been entirely probative on the question of the veracity of Nicola Laitner's assertion that she did not consent to sexual intercourse with him. It certainly would been more helpful on that issue than counsel's attempt to break her down over the course of a day-long cross-examination.

---

[64] Grubin and Gunn, above n.43.

[65] D Grubin, Editorial, 'Sexual Sadism' (1994) 4 (1) *Criminal Behaviour and Mental Health* 3.

[66] R Langevin, D Paitich and A Russon, 'Are Rapists Anomalous Aggressive or Both?' in R Langevin, *Erotic Preference, Gender Identity and Aggression in Men* (New Jersey, Erlbaum Assoc., 1985).

[67] ML Cohen, R Garafolo, R Boycher, D Seghorn, 'The Psychology of Rapists' (1971) 3 *Seminars in Psychiatry* 307; GG Abel, JV Becker, MS Mittelman, WD Murphy, 'Self-Reported Sex Crimes of Nonincarcerated Paraphiliacs' (1987) 2 *Journal of Interpersonal Violence* 3.

[68] WL Marshall, 'The Classification of Sexual Aggressives and their Associated Demographic, Social, Developmental and Psychological Features', in SN Verdun-Jones, AA Keltner, (eds) *Sexual Aggression and the Law* (Criminology Research Centre, Simon Fraser University, 1983); M Baker and R Morgan, *Sex Offenders: a Framework for the Evaluation of Community-Based Treatment* (London, Home Office, 1990).

[69] Ressler, Burgess, Hertman, Douglas and McCormack, n.8.

[70] AN Groth, AW Burgess and LL Holmstrom, 'Rape, Power, Anger and Sexuality' (1977) 134 *American Journal of Psychiatry* 1239; D Canter and R Heritage, A Multivariate Model of Sexual Offending Behaviour: Developments in 'Offender Profiling' (1990) 1 *Journal of Forensic Psychiatry* 185.

[71] Langevin, Paitich and Russon, above n.66.

Paedophiles

The House of Lords decision in *R v P*[72] represents a judicial belief there is such a thing as a disposition to commit incest. A father who committed incest with one daughter was considered so likely to done the same with another that evidence of his offences against the first daughter was admissible to show his guilt in relation to the second. The judgment is to some extent supported by Waterhouse's Scottish study in which researchers interviewed five hundred and one convicted sex abusers of children.[73] However, although acts of incest amongst children of the same family are relatively common, they found little reason to assume that incestuous fathers and stepfathers will offend outside the home. Only fourteen per cent of offenders in that group had previous convictions for sex offences against children. Most of the offences were against girls.[74] It seems, then, that incest offenders are not necessarily paedophile. They are less deviant sexually, and less recidivist, than stranger-abusers of children. They tend to live apparently normal lives.[75] Barbaree[76] reports less deviant sexual arousal with incest offenders, although other researchers have found otherwise.[77] Clinical accounts of incest families show that frequently both parents were brought up in chaotic, dysfunctional families of origin.[78] About a third of the Scottish cohort reported having been victims of sexual abuse themselves.

Stranger abuse is more likely to take place against boys than girls, and violence is more likely to be used outside the family. Offenders are more likely than incest offenders to have previous convictions for sexual offences against children. In the Scottish study, fifty per cent of stranger abusers reported having been victims of sexual abuse as children.[79] But Waterhouse argues that not all stranger abusers are genuinely paedophile. Paedophile abusers are sexually drawn to children, whereas random abusers appear to include children and women in violent attacks. Frequently their offences against children are associated with alcohol. They claim not to be sexually attracted to children, and to have been taken aback by the sexual content of the crime. Satisfaction is derived from cruelty, rather than sex.

---

[72] [1991] 3 All ER 337.

[73] L Waterhouse, RP Dobash and J Carnie, *Child Sexual Abusers* (Edinburgh, Scottish Office Central Research Unit, 1994).

[74] Cf. Conte, above n. 52.

[75] Waterhouse, Dobash and Carnie, above n.73.

[76] HE Barbaree and WL Marshall, 'Erectile Responses among Heterosexual Child Molesters, Father-Daughter Incest Offenders, and Matched Non-Offender' (1989) 21 *Canadian Journal of Behavioural Science* 70.

[77] Research which finds multiple paraphilias amongst incest offenders indicating that incest offenders are likely also to have committed other paedophile offences outside the family: Abel, Becker, Cunningham-Rather, Mittelman and Rouleau, above n.63; GG Abel and JL Rouleau, 'The Nature and Extent of Sexual Assault' in WL Marshall, DR Laws and HE Barbaree, *Handbook of Sexual Assault* (New York, Plenum, 1990).

[78] VL Quinsey, 'The Assessment and Treatment of Child Molesters; a Review' (1977) 18 *Canadian Bar Review* 204; Abel, Becker, Cunningham-Rather, Mittelman and Rouleau, above n.63; RF Hanson, JA Lipovsky and BE Saunders, 'Characteristics of Fathers in Incest Families' (1994) 9 *Journal of Interpersonal Violence* 155.

[79] Waterhouse, Dobash and Carnie, above n. 73.

Waterhouse's team concludes that violence inspires sexual excitement in this group, making random abusers the most dangerous offenders they interviewed. Their backgrounds generally consisted of unhappy, abusive childhoods. Many had been placed in care or youth custody. They were likely to have delinquent histories, and were often violent with women. Their marriages were brief in duration. In contrast, paedophiles are sexually attracted to, and fantasise about, children. They may randomly engage stranger children, or use institutional authority they have over children to secure sex. A sub-group in this category, the committed paedophiles, rarely have stable adult sexual relationships, and find establishing a rapport with adults difficult. Most have had unhappy childhoods and have attempted suicide. The majority had experienced unemployment and when, employed, tended to engage in unskilled casual work. Sometimes they were homeless. The other group, latent paedophiles, were more stable in their relationships and work. In order to gain access to children, paedophiles often took jobs or performed voluntary work involving children. Otherwise, they might simply linger near parks or swimming pools.

Gebhard[80] found that aggressive heterosexual offences against children were associated with more previous convictions than those of any other sex offenders. Indeed, if the victim were aged under fifteen, the record was dominated by sex offences. There was a strong likelihood also that there had been other offences against female children, with and without the use of violence. Homosexual offences against children are also associated with a large number of previous convictions for sex offences. Abel and Rouleau[81] conclude that non-familial molesters of boys exhibit the most deviant behaviour, have the highest offence rates and are the most recidivistic of all offenders involved in 'contact' sex offences. Nevertheless, the predictive power of criminal history and personality remains still weak. Although the behaviour of child molesters is highly repetitive,[82] current theory and supporting data do not provide an adequate basis for the confident assessment of 'propensity' toward sexually deviant behaviour.[83] For investigative purposes, disagreements as to personality typology have frustrated the compilation of profiles. For instance, Groth's distinction between regressed and fixated child molesters[84] has been challenged.[85]

---

[80] Gebhard, Gagnon, Pomeroy and Christiansen, above n. 58.

[81] Abel and Rouleau, above n. 77.

[82] RI Lanyon, 'Theories of Sex Offending' in CR Hollins and K Howells, (eds) *Clinical Approaches to Sex Offenders and their Victims* (Chichester, Wiley, 1991).

[83] Although the Lord Chief Justice suggested on BBC Radio 4's *Today* programme that dangerous paedophiles might be committed for detention under the Mental Health Act, he stressed that preventive custody could be justified only where a sufficient risk could be identified (26 December 2001).

[84] AN Groth, 'Patterns of Sexual Assault against Children and Adolescents' in AW Burgess, AN Groth, LL Holmstrom and SM Sgroi, *Sexual Assault of Children and Adolescents* (Lexington, Mass; Lexington Books, 1978).

[85] TCN Gibbens, KL Soothill and C Way, 'Child Molesters' in DJ West, (ed) *Sex Offenders in the Criminal Justice System* (Cropwood, Cambridge Institute of Criminology, 1980); RA Knight and RA, Prentky, 'Classifying Sexual Offenders; the Development and Corroboration of Models' in WL Marshall, DR Laws and HE Barbaree, *The Handbook of Sexual Assault: Issues Theories and Treatment of the Offender* (New York, Plenum, 1990); B Simon, LMJ Sales, A Kaszmiak and M Khan, 'Characteristics of Child Molesters: Implications for the Fixated-Regressed Dichotomy' (1992) 7 *Journal of Interpersonal Violence* 211.

Whether or not some child molesters are exclusively paedophile, evidence of such a tendency was highly probative in *Thompson*. The case ultimately turned on the likelihood of a homosexual paedophile, by coincidence, arriving at the specified time and place and being mistakenly selected by the victims as the man who molested them. But courts deal with that issue entirely on the basis of unscientific assumptions about the prevalence of paedophilia in the community.

USING PROFILE EVIDENCE

We have seen in Rosemary West's case that a personality which, to a layman, seems excessively deviant may have its own evidential value.[86] It is commonly assumed that fire setting is pathological; it is noteworthy that offences of criminal damage by fire must be charged as arson and are subject to a greater penalty than other kinds[87] of criminal damage. Also, in *Calladine*,[88] the Court of Appeal said that in arson cases psychiatric reports should be called for as a matter of course, so that the mental element in the perpetration of the offence may be judged before sentence is passed. Certainly adult fire setters suffer more frequently than other delinquents from mental illness, especially in the case of serial arsonists,[89] and, even amongst those with a financial motive, a very high incidence of personality disorders is likely.[90] A previous record for offences of arson could have probative value; it might be relevant to rebut the defence of accident.[91] In cases of disputed identification, previous offences of arson would be probative if the identification was not itself a product of the police rounding up the 'usual suspects', in which case the criminal record would not reduce the risk of error. Admitting the evidence would not, and should not, inevitably mean that the defendant would be convicted. Disposition evidence rarely amounts to sufficient evidence in itself to justify a conviction.

It has been argued that to admit profile evidence into criminal trials may mislead the finders of fact, since a profile deals in generalities, not the guilt of an individual. Mair rightly points out that whilst histories of indecent exposure, obscene phone calls, and voyeurism may be associated with sexual offending, we need to know how frequently they occur in the history (especially the adolescent history) of non-offenders.[92] But Ormerod has suggested that this is not a problem if an

---

[86] Presumably Beggs' fixation with goring the legs of young men while they slept was not sufficiently deviant.

[87] Criminal Damage Act 1981 ss 1(3); 4(1).

[88] *The Times* 3 December 1975.

[89] DM Barnett and M Spitzer, 'Pathological Fire-Setters 1951–1991' (1994) 34 *Medicine, Science and Law*.

[90] NDC Lewis and H Yarnell, *Pathological firesetting*, (New York, Coolidge Foundation, 1951); JMW Bradford, 'Arson; a Clinical Study' (1982) 27 *Canadian Journal Psychiatry* 188; KJB Rix, 'A Psychiatric Study of Adult Arsonists' (1994) 34 *Medicine, Science and Law* 21.

[91] *R v Gray* (1866) 4 F & F 1102; *Dossett* (1846) 2 C 7 K 306.

[92] KJ Mair, 'Can a Profile Prove a Sex Offender Guilty?' (1995) 3 *Expert Evidence* 139.

expert merely gives evidence of an opinion, for instance, that such a personality is consistent with the defendant's guilt.[93] The defence might want to show that the defendant does not fit the profile of that kind of offender. Courts have shown little enthusiasm for this kind of evidence, however. In *State v Cavallo*,[94] defence profile evidence was excluded on the ground that there was no proof that rapists have particular mental characteristics, or that psychiatrists could, by examination of a person, determine the presence or absence of these characteristics. And profiling does not enjoy universal support amongst the ranks of psychologists. Professor Gudjonsson writes:

> Profiling is neither a readily identifiable nor a homogeneous entity, and its status is properly regarded as a professional sideline not amounting to a true science.[95]

Attribution theory and the fundamental attribution error suggest that decision-makers will be inclined to overstress the role of the defendant's bad character as a factor in the case. Once aware of a history of behaving in a similar way, they will be ready to infer intent.[96] Whether or not similar fact evidence does cause prejudice has not been established, although it is clear that it increases the probability of a finding of guilt. It was seen in chapter five that there is some psychological data suggesting that it increases the chance of conviction in joined trials.[97] On the other hand, results were ambiguous in a study that presented mock jurors with a hypothetical case in which a man was accused of the manslaughter of a child in his care. The defendant was alleged to have beaten the child on other occasions. In one version of the experiment, the judge gave the correct direction, that this evidence was not to be used to show that he had such a cruel and sadistic nature that he was probably guilty of this offence; it was relevant for the limited purpose of deciding the issue of nexus or connection in relation to his defence of accident. Where the direction was given, the number of guilty verdicts was lower than where no warning was given, or where the similar fact evidence was not used at all.[98] Nonetheless, the conviction rate was much higher than experts predicted. These results suggest that the jurors were so ready to convict this defendant that the similar fact evidence, warning or not, had little effect.[99]

---

[93] DC Ormerod, 'Evidential Implications of Psychological Profiling' (1996) *Criminal Law Review*.

[94] (1982) 88 NJ 508; 443 A (2d) 1020.

[95] GH Gudjonsson and G Copson, 'The Role of the Expert in Criminal Investigation' in JL Jackson and DA Bekerian, (eds) *Offender Profiling: Theory, Research and Practice* (Chichester, Wiley, 2000).

[96] Conversely, the effect could be that the inference drawn from a good character is that such a person cannot have intended the outcome. Either way, there is a risk that the jury might under-estimate situational factors: D McGillis, 'Attribution and the Law: Convergence between Legal and Psychological Concepts' (1978) 2 *Law and Human Behavior* 289.

[97] And see S Tanford and SD Penrod, 'Social Inference Processes in Juror Judgments of Multiple-Offence Trials' (1984) 47 *Journal of Personality and Social Psychology* 749.

[98] In which case only weak circumstantial evidence remained.

[99] EG Schaefer and KL Hansen, 'Similar Fact Evidence and Limited Use Instructions. an Empirical Investigation' (1990) 14 *Criminal Law Journal* 157.

Evidence of the Defendant's Criminal Record

The case law on similar fact evidence conjures up a nightmare world of serial killers and child molesters. More conventional criminal histories are routinely concealed from fact-finders in the Anglo-American trial.[100] At present, the legal system operates an uneasy compromise between the fear of such knowledge instilling prejudice, and the need to avail courts of relevant evidence. There is a risk that those with criminal records are targeted early on in police investigations. It has been suggested that police are over-reliant on criminal record — relying on a 'usual suspects' approach.[101] This may have the effect of creating a 'typology' or stereotype, criminalising sections of the population such as the young unemployed, or young blacks in expensive cars. At trial, previous misconduct may be used to establish guilt only where it is admissible as part of the prosecutor's case under the similar facts principle discussed above. Such cases are comparatively unusual. Also, prosecutors are not allowed, in general, to cross-examine accused persons on their criminal records in order to discredit them. The defence, however, may forfeit their 'shield' by means of the tactics they employ. For example, they may put the defendant's character in issue, or attack the character of a prosecution witness.[102] The court may then choose to permit cross-examination of the defendant on his or her criminal record, the relevance of the previous convictions being confined strictly to the issue of the defendant's credibility as a witness.[103] Details of the surrounding circumstances of the offence are not to be revealed.[104] Fact-finders are left to resolve the logical problem of relating, for example, previous convictions for actual bodily harm to the question of how believable the defendant is when denying an allegation of fraud. In *Winfield*,[105] the defendant was charged with indecent assault. A defence witness gave evidence of his good character in matters of sexual morality. It was held in the House of Lords that it was perfectly proper to question the witness on the matter of Winfield's previous convictions for offences of dishonesty, since a man's character is 'indivisible'.

The struggle juries and magistrates may have in relating criminal record to the issue of the defendant's credibility in some cases was recognised by the Court of Appeal in *Watts*.[106] The defendant was on trial for indecent assault. He lost his shield and was cross-examined on his previous convictions for sex offences against children. Lord Lane, then Lord Chief Justice, felt that the questions should

---

[100] Although this is far from controversial: Law Commission, *Evidence in Criminal Proceedings: Previous Misconduct of a Defendant Consultation Paper No 141* (HMSO 1996); Law Commission *Evidence of Bad Character in Criminal Proceedings* Law Com No 273 Cm 5257 (London, HMSO, 2001). R Auld, *Criminal Courts Review* (HMSO, 2001) para. 11.112–11.120. See also Criminal Justice Bill 2003.

[101] Soothill, Way and, Gibbens, above n.54.

[102] S.1(f)(ii) Criminal Evidence Act 1898.

[103] *Selvey v DPP* [1970] AC 304. The court may exercise its disecretion against the prosecutor.

[104] McLeod [1994] 3 All ER 254.

[105] [1939] 4 All ER 164.

[106] [1983] 3 All ER 101.

not have been allowed because they seemed to have little bearing on the credibility issue, and created the risk that the jury would take the convictions as evidence of guilt. But in the later case of *Powell*,[107] Lord Lane LCJ criticised his own decision in *Watts*, since it took no note of the 'indivisibility' of the defendant's character. Thus Powell, who was accused of living off immoral earnings, was held to have been rightly cross-examined on previous offences of allowing premises to be used for the purposes of prostitution. Yet here also the similarity of the previous offences to the present charge created a clear risk that the jury would infer propensity to commit that kind of offence and therefore guilt. However, we have seen in chapter four that witnesses other than the defendant are regularly cross-examined on their previous convictions, irrespective of their nature, in order to discredit them. Jurors therefore routinely face the unenviable task of determining, for example, whether a record for drink-driving means that they should not believe what the witness has said in evidence.

Juries must be instructed that previous convictions admitted once the shield has been lost are relevant only to the defendant's credibility. A previous conviction for perjury would appear to have the most direct relevance to that issue. However, a judicial admonishment to jurors to use the criminal record only for the purpose of assessing the credibility of the defendant seems to be as ineffective in relation to perjury convictions as it is for other kinds of criminal history.[108] In their study, Hans and Doob[109] found virtually no discussion of credibility amongst their mock jurors. Their results, however, may be have limited applicability to real trials. The mock jurors had to base their judgment on written transcripts, rather than the demeanour and personality of a live witness. Informing them of the criminal record of a person whom they cannot see or hear may distort the verdict. Also, in some of the scenarios used in the simulations, the previous offending was, in some instances, arguably probative of guilt, and could have been used as similar fact evidence in a real trial. For example, in one of their vignettes, the victim of a burglary supplied identification evidence. The accused's previous conviction was for burglary. His girlfriend supplied an alibi. He had been arrested because he was in the vicinity of the offence, and was carrying a similar amount of money to that stolen. The issue for the jurors therefore was, how likely is the eyewitness to have mistakenly identified a person who is carrying the correct amount of money, whose alibi is supplied by his girlfriend, and who is a convicted burglar? Some lawyers would exclude the conviction as more prejudicial than probative, but would not deny that it has at least some probative value on the issue of guilt. Wagenaar[110] also claims that fact finders use criminal history for illegitimate purposes. But, again, some of

---

[107] [1986] 1 All ER 193.
[108] RL Wissler and MJ Saks, 'On the Inefficacy of Limiting Instructions where Jurors use Credibility Evidence to Decide on Guilt' (1985) 9 *Law and Human Behavior* 37.
[109] VP Hans and AN Doob, 'Section 12 of the Canada Evidence Act and the Deliberations of Simulated Juries' (1975) 18 *Criminal Law Quarterly* 235.
[110] WA Wagenaar, PJ van Koppen, and HM Crombag, *Anchored Narratives: the Psychology of Criminal Evidence* (Hemel Hempstead, Harvester Wheatsheaf, 1993).

the misconduct evidence he describes could quite reasonably be used on the issue of guilt. One of the cases he cites involved a series of offences which appear to have been committed by the same person. The accused had been identified in respect of one of these, as in *Black*.[111] Tanford and Cox found that prior perjury convictions in a civil trial increased findings of liability and lowered credibility ratings. It also produced the prohibited propensity reasoning.[112] But there was no increase in liability if the jurors were warned to disregard the previous conviction altogether. Thus it seems that juries are not incapable of following instructions, but cannot manage the 'forbidden reasoning' that demands that they operate the dichotomy which rigidly separates the issue of a defendant's guilt from that of the credibility of a defendant who claims in court not to be guilty. Since many lawyers regard this distinction as illusory, fact-finders' confusion is not surprising.

It has proved difficult to devise a more coherent criterion to identify where previous convictions have genuine relevance.[113] A simpler approach would be to inform the finders of fact of the criminal records of all defendants at the outset of the trial, with such warnings on the matter of prejudice as may be appropriate.[114] But would this be unfair to defendants? Empirical evidence is inconclusive as to whether knowledge of previous convictions disposes fact-finders more readily to convict. Hans and Doob's methodology is unsatisfactory. Research at the London School of Economics[115] in the 1970s found a decreased tendency to convict if the previous offence was dissimilar to the current charge. This study created conditions close to those of a real trial, using tape recordings recreated from a transcript. Similar results using similar methods were obtained in the Oxford Jury Study conducted by Sally Lloyd-Bostock;[116] a previous conviction dissimilar in nature to the offence charged meant the defendant was less likely to be convicted than if not told of any previous convictions at all.[117] In the New Zealand jury study, evidence of previous convictions was admitted in ten cases. In only three of these did the jurors report that any weight was attached to it. In two of the other cases they thought it weakened the prosecution case, by suggesting desperation.[118] This is consistent with Bennett and Feldman's finding that the most important factor in a verdict is a plausible narrative. In the trials they studied, the defendant's characteristics came into play only when it became 'impossible not to resort to

---

[111] Above n.36.

[112] S Tanford and M Cox, 'Decision Processes in Civil Cases: the Impact of Impeachment Evidence' (1987) 12 *Social Behavior* 165.

[113] Law Commission, *Consultation Paper* n. 100; Law Commission, *Evidence of Bad Character*, n.100.

[114] Auld, above n. 100 para.8.112–8.120.

[115] AP Sealy and WR Cornish, 'Juries and their Verdicts' (1973) 36 *Modern Law Review* 496.

[116] S Lloyd-Bostock, 'The Effects on Jurors of Hearing about the Defendant's Previous Convictions: a Simulation Study' [2000] *Criminal Law Review* 734, also Law Commission, *Consultation Paper* n.100, Appendix D.

[117] Cf Sealy and Cornish, above n. 115 and Oxford magistrates: S Lloyd-Bostock, *The Effect on Magistrates of Knowing a Defendant's Criminal Record*, Law Commission *Evidence of Bad Character*, above n.100 Appendix A.

[118] Law Commission of New Zealand, *Juries in Criminal Trials*, Report 69, (Wellington, Law Commission of New Zealand, 2001) paras. 6.12–6.16.

these bits of data as documentation for central issues in the trial'.[119] However, the Oxford study found that both magistrates and juries are slightly more likely to convict in cases where the previous convictions are similar in nature to the current offence.[120] This could be explained simply as recognition that a defendant's history of offences of a similar kind 'statistically and logically suggests that he is more likely than those without such a record to commit such offences again'.[121]

The tendency to use the criminal record as an indicator of guilt is pronounced only in two instances. The Oxford Study found that juries appear to be very much affected and therefore more likely to convict, irrespective of the nature of the charge, where there is a previous conviction for indecent assault on a child. It should be noted, however, that the summing-up the mock jurors were given could have been far more robust and specific on the issue of prejudice. The Study found, however, that if magistrates are aware of previous sexual offences against children, they are more likely to convict only where the trial concerns a similar offence. Yet they react strongly in cases where the defendant has a previous conviction for wounding with intent, contrary to section 18 Offences Against the Person Act 1861. Participating magistrates used this as an indicator of guilt in trials for all offences, including crimes of dishonesty. Professor Lloyd-Bostock suggests that the explanation for magisterial hostility to section 18 offenders may be that they know the true nature of the offence, specifically, that it is reserved for really serious violence, usually where a weapon is involved.[122] Certainly, experienced magistrates have dealt with a great many people who have committed acts of violence, and many know their histories, and that of their families.[123] While it does not follow as a matter of logic that defendants with violent histories are more likely than others to be lying or guilty of offences of dishonesty, it may nevertheless be correct as a matter of empirical fact to believe them to be more likely than others to produce false alibis, or to be disposed to commit a variety of crimes. The Oxford results may, in fact, provide a valuable insight into the apparent division of opinion between laymen and lawyers about the significance of criminal histories. It is possible that they employ entirely dissimilar reasoning processes. Lawyers try to construct a logical syllogism in which the bad character of the defendant plays a part in one of the propositions. Fact finders make an assessment of the defendant's character based on their knowledge and experience of the world, and reason empirically on the question of the likelihood of such a person committing a subsequent offence in the manner suggested by the prosecution.

To reveal criminal record in some cases and not others may create the worst of all worlds. Fact-finders may assume that defendants who do not raise evidence of their own good character are trying to conceal their previous convictions.

---

[119] WL Bennett, and MS Feldman, *Reconstructing Reality in the Courtroom* (London, Tavistock, 1981) 165 This is supported by the New Zealand research.

[120] S Lloyd-Bostock, above n.116; S Lloyd-Bostock, above n.117.

[121] Auld, above n.100, para. 11.118.

[122] S Lloyd-Bostock, above n 117, para, A. 36.

[123] P Darbyshire, 'Previous Misconduct and Magistrates' Courts: some Tales from the Real World' (1997) *Criminal Law Review* 105.

Leaving courts to guess what these previous convictions might be could cause more harm than the truth would have done.[124] A measure of such speculation was reported in the New Zealand study. Conjecture was based to some extent on the other evidence, or if there were no clue there, on the race or status of the defendant. Jurors claimed that they attached no weight to any speculation that occurred.[125] Experienced magistrates know the rules on the admissibility of previous convictions, and so, if no evidence of good character is adduced by the defence, will generally assume that the accused has a criminal record.[126] This is unfortunate, since sometimes the explanation for an advocate's failure to mention the defendant's good character is pure oversight.[127] Where defence lawyers are aware that the nature of their case inevitably will cost the client his or her shield, they may mention the previous convictions themselves, pre-empting the prosecution and hoping to 'steal their thunder' and defuse the issue. Research suggests that the tactic is effective, and reduces the likelihood of conviction, but not to the level of cases where the criminal record is not revealed at all.[128] Clearly, the way the defence do this is crucial; there may be some histories for which are impossible to create positive 'spin'.

In this context, courts' readiness to generalise from past instances to the present case could be explained as an application of the co-variation principle combined with the fundamental attribution error. Such reasoning may work in the defendant's favour when the jury is invited to draw the inference of a lack of criminal propensity from evidence of unrelated but admirable aspects of the defendant's character. Some enthusiasts for community service orders believe that a convicted offender who wants to go on helping people on expiration of the order must have stopped committing burglaries. However, to give fact-finders negative information may not cause disproportionate prejudice, and would make judicial instructions less unintelligible. To eliminate uncertainty and arbitrariness, a rational system might routinely mention the defendant's previous convictions at the outset of a trial in as unsensational a fashion as possible.

A PREDILECTION TO CRIME

We see the fundamental attributional bias towards internal causes in operation elsewhere in the criminal justice system. It colours judicial reasoning in cases in which the admissibility of evidence depends on whether the police procured or encouraged the commission of the crime. To some extent, the issue in cases where a 'honey-trap' is provided is whether or not the defendant's criminal tendencies are so entrenched

---

[124] Auld, above n.100 para. 11.118.
[125] W Young, N Cameron and Y Tinsley, *Juries in Criminal Trials*, Law Commission of New Zealand Preliminary Paper 37, Vol 2, (Wellington, New Zealand, 1999), paras. 6.12–6.16.
[126] Derbyshire, above n.123.
[127] M McConville, J Hodgson, L Bridges and A Pavlovic, *Standing Accused* (Oxford, Oxford University Press, 1994) 216: J Vennard, *Contested Trials in Magistrates' Courts* Home Office Research Study No 71 (London, Home Office, 1982); Darbyshire, above n.123.
[128] KD Williams, MJ Bourgeois and RT Croyle, 'The Effects of Stealing Thunder in Criminal and Civil Trials' (1993) 17 *Law and Human Behavior* 597.

that it can be reasonably assumed that he or she would have committed offences in any event. In many common law jurisdictions, entrapment evidence, where the police apparently lure a suspect into committing a crime, has become a major ethical issue.[129] In the United States, 'virtue-testing', or pressuring people into committing crime, has led the Supreme Court to require in each case evidence that the defendant had a predisposition to commit the criminal act, irrespective of the approach by the government agent.[130] For this purpose, the level of inducement is balanced against the court's assumptions about the nature of criminality. Some English cases adopt a similar approach.[131] However, the conviction was upheld in *Shannon*,[132] where a young actor was induced by a journalist posing as an Arab sheikh to obtain drugs for him. Offers of glittering opportunities were dangled in front of him. But it was made clear that the sheikh was already disappointed in him because he had not brought a gift in the shape of a 'joint'. The Canadian Supreme Court prefers an objective approach that concentrates on the behaviour of the alleged *agent provocateur*.[133] Their approach at least avoids having to speculate to what extent the value of the prize inspired the defendant's reaction.

In *Williams v DPP*,[134] plain-clothes officers left an insecure and unattended van in a busy street. It contained dummy cigarette cartons. The defendants were seen lingering near to the van, and eventually they removed the cigarette cartons. The magistrates found as facts that the police plan had not been directed at the defendants in particular, and that they approached the van voluntarily. On appeal to the Divisional Court, Wright J held that the police had not been acting as *agents provocateurs*; they had done nothing to force, persuade, encourage or coerce the defendants to do as they did; the situation was similar to the case of a 'heroic WPC' who might linger, acting as bait, in an area in which sex attacks have occurred. The analogy is far from being exact. In a case like *Williams* it is less clear that the enticement has not increased the local crime rate rather than help reduce it. Nevertheless, such practices were approved in *Dawes v DPP*,[135] where the enticement was a powerful car which, in fact, was a 'rat-trap', locking in anyone who got into it. The Divisional Court thought there was nothing objectionable about this kind of lure, as long as the suspect, who is effectively under arrest once the doors lock, is informed of the fact within a reasonable time. There is no *agent provocateur* effect, either, in cases where child volunteers are sent in to test whether shopkeepers will sell them fireworks, alcohol, cigarettes or lottery tickets.[136] In all these cases, it is

---

[129] G Robertson, 'Entrapment Evidence: Manna from Heaven or Fruit of the Poisoned Tree?' (1994) *Criminal Law Review* 805.

[130] *Sorrells v US* 287 US 435 (1932); *Jacobson v US* (1992) 503 US 540.

[131] *Ameer and Lucas* [1977] *Criminal Law Review* 104.

[132] (1980) 71 Cr App R 192.

[133] Robertson, above n.129.

[134] [1993] 3 All ER 365.

[135] [1994] *Criminal Law Review* 604.

[136] *London Borough of Ealing v Woolworths plc* [1995] *Criminal Law Review* 58. Cf *Marshall and Downes* [1998] 3 All ER 683, under-age agents were asked to buy alcohol in order to obtain evidence against shop-keepers suspected of breaching the regulations.

assumed that the defendant's disposition, rather than the circumstances of the particular situation, that has led to the commission of the offence.

Yet in the context of sentencing, it is widely accepted that there is no reliable method of predicting future criminality. In a sample of nearly six hundred male offenders convicted of violent sex crimes, who were each examined by two psychiatrists, two psychologists, and a social worker, eight per cent of those classified as non-dangerous and released were involved in further assaults within five years. Of the 'dangerous' individuals who were released, thirty-four per cent committed further assaults — a strike rate of about a third.[137] Although it has been claimed that clinicians can identify the potentially violent individual with accuracy better than chance,[138] this is disputed,[139] partly on methodological grounds.[140] In general, a prediction accuracy of about thirty-three per cent is the best that can be expected. Of every three disordered patients predicted by psychiatrists or psychologists to be violent, one will subsequently commit a violent act and two will not.[141] Among disordered and non-disordered populations, the best predictors of future offending are age, gender, social class, and criminal history.[142] It is clear that in the 'honey-trap' cases, courts took no account of any of these factors. Even if they had, statistics suggest they would have been wrong in at least half the cases. Nor could courts claim that a propensity to reoffend can be so firmly established that police inducement played no causal role. *Williams* demonstrates the persuasive force of mere opportunity; before the defendant approached the van, the police officers watching had been forced to break their cover in order to chase away under-age children who were about to remove the cigarette cartons.

FACING POLICE PRESSURE

Staying Silent?

Few suspects have ever availed themselves during questioning of the right to silence, either in the United States[143] or the United Kingdom.[144] Under the

---

[137] HL Kozol, RJ Boucher and RF Garafalo, 'The Diagnosis and Treatment of Dangerousness' (1972) 18 *Crime and Delinquency* 371.

[138] R Blackburn, 'Risk Assessment and Prediction' in J Magure, T Mason, and A O'Kane, (eds) *Behaviour, Crime and Legal Processes* (Chichester, Wiley, 2000).

[139] D Mossman, 'Assessing Predictors of Violence: Being Accurate about Accuracy' (1994) 62 *Journal of Consulting and Clinical Psychology* 783.

[140] J Monahan, 'Risk Assessment of Violence among the Mentally Disordered: Generating Useful Knowledge' (1988) 11 *International Journal of Law and Psychiatry* 249.

[141] J Gunn and PJ Taylor, *Forensic Psychiatry: Clinical, Legal and Ethical Issues,* London, Butterworth, 1993) 627; J Monahan, 'The Prediction of Violent Behavior: Toward a Second Generation of Theory and Policy' (1984) 141 *American Journal of Psychiatry* 10.

[142] Gunn and Taylor, above n.141, 627.

[143] M Wald, R Ayers, DW Hess, M Schantz and CH Whitehouse, 'Interrogations in New Haven: the Impact of *Miranda*' (1967) 76 *Yale Law Journal* 76.

[144] Prior to Police and Criminal Evidence Act 1984: DJ Smith and J Gray, *Police and People in London vol. 4 The Police in Action* (Policy Studies Institute London, 1983); P Softley, *Police Interrogation: an*

Criminal Justice and Public Order Act 1994,[145] refusal to answer police questions entitles the jury to draw adverse inferences, including an inference of guilt. A recent Home Office study shows that the legislation is having the desired effect. The right to silence is being exercised (wholly or partly) in fewer cases than before in all police areas. Although suspects who receive legal advice are more likely than others to remain silent, they, too, are remaining silent less frequently. Black suspects used to stay silent more than white or Asian suspects, but now their figure is closer to the average.[146] Whether or not the 1999 Act will secure more criminal convictions is not yet clear. In the past, the 'No comment' interview was more often associated with conviction than acquittal, although prior to the change in the law, juries were instructed that suspects were entitled to refuse to answer questions.[147]

Before drawing an adverse inference from failure to answer police questions, the court should consider the circumstances at the time of the questioning, including the time of day, the defendant's age, experience, mental capacity, state of health, sobriety, tiredness, knowledge, personality and legal advice:

> References to 'the accused' do not mean some hypothetical, reasonable accused of ordinary phlegm and fortitude, but the actual accused with the qualities, apprehensions, knowledge and advice as he is shown to have had at the time.[148]

This approach did not appear to help the defendants in *Condron and Condron*.[149] Their solicitor had advised them to say nothing because he thought they were unfit for interview because of drug withdrawal, although the Force Medical Examiner had passed them fit for questioning. The jury were told that they were entitled to draw adverse inferences, and convicted. A major criticism of the new law is that psychologically vulnerable suspects, who really ought to remain silent, because of the risk that they may incriminate themselves unwittingly, are particularly unlikely to do so. And suspects in general have insufficient psychological strength to refuse to answer police questions, unless a solicitor advises them to remain silent:

> To remain silent in a police interview room in the face of determined questioning by an officer with legitimate authority to carry on his activity requires an abnormal exercise of will… if it does occur, the observer would be forgiven for making the fallacious assumption that the abnormal behaviour is associated with some significant cause (in this context guilt as opposed to innocence).[150]

Observational Study in Four Police Stations, Royal Commission on Criminal Procedure Research Study No. 4 (1980). After 1984: M Zander and P Henderson, *Crown Court Study*, Royal Commission on Criminal Justice Research Study 19 (HMSO, London, 1993).

[145] SS, 34–7.
[146] T Buck, R Street and D Brown, *The Right to Silence and the Impact of the Criminal Justice and Police and Criminal Evidence Act 1994* HORS 199 (London, Home Office, 2000).
[147] Zander and Henderson, above n.144.
[148] *Argent* [1997] *Criminal Law Review* 347.
[149] [1997] *Criminal Law Review* 215.
[150] B Irving, *Police Interrogation: a Case Study of Current Practice*, Royal Commission Criminal Procedure Research Study Nos. 1 and 2 (London, HMSO, 1980).

Being Tempted to Confess

Clifton Lawson, an eighteen-year-old, confessed on videotape to the brutal rape and murder of an elderly woman. He supplied details to the police that only they and the killer would know. He had an IQ of 70, the emotional maturity of a five-year-old, and 'disturbed mental conditioning'.[151] It was then discovered that fingerprints at the scene were not his. The real killer was caught and convicted. It transpired that Lawson had overheard the police and the Forensic Medical Examiner discussing details of the case. He confessed because he wanted to leave the police station and go to choir practice. Professor Gudjonsson[152] would describe this kind of confession as 'coerced-compliant'. That is a false confession motivated by the desire to escape from a highly stressful situation. The immediate gain (frequently nothing more than the need to establish some short-term certainty of future events)[153] becomes a more powerful influence on the subject's behaviour than the more uncertain long-term effects of the confession, even if the allegation concerns a serious offence. The majority of false confessions are coerced-compliant. Wagenaar agrees that common occasions for false confessions include: the suspect takes an apparently easy way out, not anticipating the long term consequences, perhaps thinking it will be possible to retract later; or, having to take the only way out because the pressure means that the suspect simply cannot carry on; or where the suspect is simply outwitted by the questioner — a likely enough event in the atmosphere of police custody, which inflicts a form of sensory deprivation.[154]

'Voluntary' confessions, in the Gudjonsson classification, are not induced by the police in any way. Highly publicised crimes are usually the target for voluntary confessions. When Charles Lindberg's baby was kidnapped and murdered in 1932, more than two hundred people offered unsolicited confessions.[155] This kind of behaviour may be motivated by a desire for notoriety, or to relieve a general feeling of guilt, or reflect an inability to distinguish fact and fantasy. Judith Ward claimed to be a member of the Irish Republican Army, and drew the attention of police officers to this supposed connection every time she got the opportunity. In the aftermaths of IRA bombings she was sometimes to be found at the scene screaming abuse at the police. She confessed to planting a bomb that blew up a coach on a motorway. At her trial, she claimed that she could not remember making the admission, and that in any event it was not true. Her appeal against conviction was allowed, partly because of expert testimony that she was a hysteric, unable to distinguish fantasy from reality.[156]

---

[151] Kassin, SM, and Wrightsman LS, *The American Jury on Trial* (New York, Hemisphere,1988) 87.
[152] GH Gudjonsson, *The Psychology of Interrogations, Confessions, and Testimony* (Chichester, Wiley, 1992).
[153] GH Gudjonsson, 'The Psychology of False Confessions' (1989) 57 *Medico-Legal Journal* 93.
[154] Wagenaar, van Koppen and Crombag, above n.110, 109–110.
[155] Kassin and Wrightsman, above n.151, 89.
[156] *Ward* [1993] 3 All ER 577.

A third category of confession in the Gudjonsson typology is 'coerced-internalised'. People who do not trust their own memory may begin to accept the suggestions of the police and become temporarily persuaded that they might have, or did indeed, commit the crime. Such a confession is more likely to be elicited by gentle, rather than aggressive interviewing. It may be retracted later on, although the subject is more likely to stick to it than is the coerced-compliant. Even if it is withdrawn later the subject's memory may be permanently distorted. Gudjonsson and MacKeith argue that interrogative suggestibility and compliance are enduring psychological characteristics relevant to erroneous testimony. During police questioning, such traits may cause false admissions to be made, and these could form the basis of a conviction. Suggestibility is a tendency to accept uncritically information communicated during questions.[157] It is greatest in people of low intelligence. According to Gudjonsson, suggestibility is to some extent inherent in the personality and can be measured by a reliable test, but it can also be aggravated by conditions. Compliance is a tendency to go along with requests of the person perceived to be in authority, even though the subject does not necessarily agree with them.[158] Acquiescence, a person's tendency to answer questions affirmatively irrespective of content, is also most common with people of low intelligence.[159] However, analysis of an individual's general personality does not give the whole picture:

> People are generally not passive recipients of suggestive influences from others — they are constantly in a dynamic relationship with their social and physical environments.[160]

Suggestibility is increased in certain situations. The ability to cope with leading questions depends upon a number of factors. One is the stressfulness of the police interrogation at the police station. Another is the subject's level of certainty about the true answer. A third is the level of suspicion or anger the interviewer inspires in the subject, reducing suggestibility. If the interviewer is trusted, suggestibility increases,[161] and if it is at a high level, even questions requiring only a 'Yes/No' answer are dangerous since, when in doubt, some people have a tendency to give affirmative answers.[162]

Experienced officers are well aware of the power of suggestion.[163] The fact that an interview is conducted perfectly properly, within legal guidelines, is no guarantee

---

[157] GH Gudjonsson, 'A New Scale of Interrogative Suggestibility' (1984) 15 *Personality and Individual Differences* 303.

[158] GH Gudjonsson, 'Compliance in an Interrogative Situation: a New Scale' (1989) 10 *Personality and Individual Differences* 535.

[159] CK Sigelman, E Budd, C Spanhel and C Schoenrock, 'When in Doubt Say Yes: Acquiescence in Interviews with Mentally Retarded Persons' (1981) 19 *Mental Retardation* 53; GH Gudjonsson, 'The Relationship between Interrogative Suggestibility and Acquiescence: Empirical Findings and Theoretical Implication' (1986) 7 *Personality and Individual Differences* 195.

[160] GH Gudjonsson and N Clark, 'Suggestibility in Police Interrogation: a Social Psychological Model' (1986) 83 *Social Behaviour* 86.

[161] *Ibid.*

[162] Gudjonsson, n.157.

[163] B Irving and IK McKenzie, *Police Interrogation* (London, Police Foundation, 1989) 169.

of the reliability of admissions obtained. Although it is clear that the experience of being held on arrest and questioned by police is inevitably intimidating and stressful,[164] courts seem to have little sympathy for defendants who cannot cope. In *Fulling*,[165] the defendant claimed that she confessed because the police had given her the distressing news that her partner had broken his promise to her and re-established a sexual relationship with another woman; this woman was being held in the cell next to her own. Fulling had in fact been talking to her without realising her identity. She said that the revelation upset her so much that she was desperate to go home. Her appeal against conviction was dismissed, since there was no illegality in the conduct of the police. In this case, the Court of Appeal declared that to prove oppression,[166] the defence must show that the police used violence. In a later case, however, known as the 'Cardiff Three', the decision was more realistic.[167] A confession was excluded because of the interrogator's hectoring manner over days of interviews. His conduct was deemed oppressive in that he ignored the suspect's denials, apparently determined to bully admissions out of him rather than ascertain his version of the facts.

The judiciary in England and Wales have recently acknowledged the vulnerability of some suspects, such as those with low or borderline IQ.[168] However, although expert evidence on the reliability of the confession will be allowed for defendants with a personality disorder or learning difficulties,[169] whether or not the confession will be excluded altogether depends upon the exercise of the trial judge's discretion. In *Kilner*,[170] the defendant had a low IQ, epilepsy, and became hysterical when he found himself in difficulties. Although there had been no misconduct by the police, the confession was not admitted at trial. In contrast, the trial judge in the case of *McKenzie*[171] did not exclude the defendant's confession. McKenzie had been arrested on suspicion of arson, which he duly admitted in interview. Unprompted, he then went on to confess to twelve murders, ten of which the police did not believe he had committed. However, they suspected that McKenzie may have committed the remaining two murders, and eventually he was put on trial for them, despite the lack of any other evidence to implicate him. He was convicted. Psychological tests showed that the defendant, who was thirty-eight years old, had an IQ of between 73 and 76. On appeal, Professor Gudjonsson gave expert evidence of McKenzie's guilt obsession, due to being sexually abused as a child, and of his suggestible and compliant personality.[172] The Court of

---

[164] Eg., B Irving and L Hilgendorf, *Police Interrogation: The Pyschological Approach*; B Irving, *Police Interrogation: A Case Study of Current Practice* Royal Commission on Criminal Procedure Research Studies Nos 1 and 2 (London, HMSO, 1980).
[165] [1987] 2 All ER 65.
[166] For the purposes of s. 76 Police and Criminal Evidence Act 1984.
[167] *Miller, Paris and Abdullahi* (1993) 97 Cr App R 99.
[168] *Silcott, Braithwaite and Raghip, The Times* 9 December 1992.
[169] *Ward* [1993] 3 All ER 577.
[170] [1976] *Criminal Law Review* 740.
[171] (1992) 96 Cr App R 98.
[172] Gudjonsson, above n.152 p243–47.

Appeal quashed the murder convictions, and held that where the prosecution case depends wholly upon a confession made by a defendant who suffers from a significant degree of mental handicap and the confession is unconvincing to the point where a jury, properly directed, could not properly convict upon it, then the judge should withdraw the case from the jury altogether.

Miscarriages of justice remain possible, should a confession from a vulnerable person be to some extent borne out by other evidence. In *Bailey*,[173] an elderly woman died in a fire. She lived in a flat adjoining the defendant's. Bailey confessed to a friend, and then to police, that she was responsible for the fire. There was no appropriate adult present at her interview with the police, who were not aware that Bailey was mentally handicapped. She later retracted the confessions she had made to the police, but then confessed again in the presence of a solicitor and a social worker. The case proceeded, despite evidence of learning disability, on the ground that the later confessions contained so much detail, and she displayed such remorse, that they could be considered reliable. However, it is possible that she learned these details from the police in earlier interviews. The only concession to her vulnerability made by the Court of Appeal was the ordering of a retrial so that the jury could be properly alerted to her disability. Gudjonsson's review of a number of instances of miscarriages of justice clearly demonstrates how reliance on confession evidence can lead to error. It is apparent that confessions are relatively easy to obtain from persons being questioned in situations of stress. In cases such as *Mackenzie* and *Ward*, English courts have confined their recognition of this to suspects of proven abnormal suggestibility. The judgment in Ward refers to personality disorders so severe as properly to be characterised as mental disorders, and even so, the jury should be directed that they do not have to accept the expert testimony.[174] In reality, however, the risk of miscarriage of justice derives not from whether an abnormality fits into some recognised category, but from its causal relationship with reliability.

In Scotland and Holland no one can be convicted on the strength of a confession alone. In all but a few United States jurisdictions, an extra-judicial confession by the defendant, without corroboration, is not considered sufficient to sustain a conviction. However, although the psychological literature appears to establish clearly that confessions are not reliable indicators of guilt, criminal justice systems rely heavily upon them. French legal culture does not recognise the psychology of false confessions at all.[175] Other systems are reluctant to change their practice. Wagenaar argues that this is because confessions supply very strong anchoring. There is often a good fit between the prosecution narrative and the confession. Yet that may be because the police are employing the narrative at the time they decide whom to interview. Denials will be disregarded because they do not fit.

---

[173] *The Times* 26 January 1995.
[174] *O'Brien, Hall and Sherwood, The Times* 16 February 2000.
[175] J Hodgson, 'Comparing Legal Cultures: the Comparativist as a Participant Observer' In D Nelken, (ed) *Contrasting Criminal Justice* (Aldershot, Ashgate, 2000).

In his study, seven disputed confessions were retracted, but were treated as if their diagnostic value was as high as before.[176] He concludes:

> To beat the confession, the retraction needs to be a narrative containing at least three components or sub-stories: (a) one should provide an explanation of why the initial confession was made, although being false; (b) one offering a likely alternative or suspect and explaining why that other person did it and/or why the suspect himself could not have done it, and (c) one that explains why the prosecution's story, that the defence counsel persuaded the defendant to retract his confession, is not true.[177]

Most retractions fail all three criteria.[178] Acquittals following confession evidence are rare.[179] The fundamental attribution error means that it is difficult to persuade fact-finders that an innocent person might confess. If defence lawyers fail to persuade judge or magistrates to exclude a confession they claim is unreliable, it will be admitted in evidence. They must then persuade the tribunal of fact not to rely on it. This may be an uphill struggle, because people are so often taken at face value.[180] In one experiment featuring mock jurors, transcripts of trials contained a confession to police. If the defendant had been threatened by the police officer, the subjects rejected the confession. But if the confession followed an offer of leniency, they tended to convict even after an explanation that the law would consider it involuntary.[181] Even police officers, who are aware of the tactics generally employed, find it hard to believe that a confession may not be true.[182]

---

[176] Wagenaar, van Koppen and Crombag, above n.110, 112.

[177] *Ibid*, 114.

[178] *Ibid*.

[179] J Baldwin and M McConville, *Confessions in Crown Court Trials* Royal Commission on Criminal Procedure Research Study No 5 (London, HMSO, 1980).

[180] R Underwager and H Wakefield, 'False Confessions and Police Deception' (1992) 10 *American Journal of Psychology* 49.

[181] EE Jones, 'The Rocky Road from Acts to Dispositions' (1979) 34 *American Psychologist* 107.

[182] T Williamson, '*Strategic Charges in Police Interrogation*' (unpublished Ph D thesis, University of Kent).

7

Laymen and Science

I N A TEST case against British Nuclear Fuels,[1] Mrs Reay sued for damages in respect of the death of her daughter, Dorothy, who had died of leukaemia at the age of ten months in 1962. The issue was whether the exposure to radiation of Dorothy's father, a worker at the defendants' plant at Sellafield, had caused her illness. A number of plaintiffs alleged that, since within populations close to nuclear re-processing plants the occurrence of childhood leukaemia and non-Hodgkin's lymphoma tended to be higher than the national average, the defendant's activities at the Sellafield plant in West Cumbria must be causally linked to the illnesses and subsequent deaths of their children from those diseases. Fifty experts in genetics, epidemiology and radiation damage gave evidence. There were half a million pages of documents. A hundred leading scientists in several countries submitted reports. Dan Brennan QC explained:

> Mr Justice French will come to a common sense conclusion. He is not likely to be bogged down by the scientific refinements. One cannot have judges spending their time analysing what scientists say and forgetting about ordinary people.[2]

Whether the judge felt flattered by this representation of his efforts is not reported. In the course of his judgment, he observed that the case essentially turned upon the legal issues of duty of care and causation,[3] but added that this inevitably involved him in a painstaking review of the scientific evidence. In the event, he decided that the epidemiological evidence was inconclusive and was substantially contradicted by the evidence of the defendant's geneticists. There can be no doubt that whether or not the judge felt confident to assess the scientific evidence, he was considerably assisted, as is any fact-finder confronted by complicated science, by the operation of the burden of proof. The plaintiffs had to prove on the balance of probabilities that exposure to radiation had caused the leukaemia. With twenty-five expert witnesses ranged on each side, convincing the court would inevitably be a difficult task.

---

[1] *Reay and Hope v British Nuclear Fuels* (1994) 5 Med LR 1.
[2] *The Times* 27 October 1992.
[3] *The Times* 27 October 1992.

ADMITTING EXPERT EVIDENCE

Expert witnesses are by no means always scientists. Experts in matters cultural or aesthetic have given evidence of their opinions in cases such as the 'Oz Trial', where the comedian, Spike Milligan, the disc jockey, John Peel and the Bishop of Woolwich discussed the merits of an allegedly obscene publication.[4] For these witnesses to have been identified as experts depended upon the perspective of the trial judge. It is for the judge in a civil or criminal case to decide both whether the expert witness operates within a viable area of expertise, and whether he or she is an expert in it. In a case where the judge is satisfied, it is possible to find accepted as an expert witness a person who has no paper qualifications and belongs to no professional body. In *Silverlock*,[5] the witness, a solicitor, studied handwriting as his hobby. It was held that his experience and expertise qualified him to assist the court in comparing handwriting. Experts must know something the judge or jury do not. The judge will decide whether or not that is the case. So, for example, if the decision rests upon what might be expected in the proper management of a business, the judge will decide whether expert help is required.[6] This *ad hoc* approach requires a decision in each individual case, in the light of its particular facts. This can be expensive and time wasting, and leads to uncertainty pre-trial.

Courts in the United States have attempted to devise criteria to measure whether a science is sufficiently well established and reliable for expert evidence to be allowed. *Frye v US*[7] employed a criterion of 'general acceptability to the scientific community'. The test was referred to with approval in the English case, *Gilfoyle*.[8] The defendant was accused of the murder of his pregnant wife, who had been found hanging in the garage at their home. He claimed that she had committed suicide. An expert produced a report claiming that she was unlikely to have done this. This 'psychological autopsy' was excluded on the ground that all the matters dealt with in it were within the experience of the jury. But the court also made the point that there were no criteria by reference to which the quality of the opinion could be tested. Yet there have been American cases concerning psychological autopsy in which the *Frye* test was not followed. It has been criticised as unduly conservative. The criterion of general acceptance discriminated against any developing science. It was also potentially misleading, since any technique is likely to be widely accepted amongst the community of scientists who use it, whatever those outside it may think. The later case of *Daubert v Merrell Dow Pharmaceuticals*[9] aimed to make the courts more flexible in response to innovation, while at the same time aware that reliability is of paramount importance. The court is enjoined by *Daubert* to consider factors such as whether the technique in question has been subjected to peer review;

[4] *R v Anderson and others* [1972] 1 QB 304.
[5] [1894] 2 QB 766.
[6] *Barings plc v Coopers and Lybrand, The Times* 7 March 2001.
[7] 293 F 1013 (DC Cir 1923).
[8] [2001] *Criminal Law Review* 312.
[9] 113 S Ct 2786 (1993).

whether it has been generally accepted, and whether the theory or technique can be or has been tested. Can a determination be made of its 'falsifiability'? this means that plausibility depends upon whether a theory or concept is capable of being shown to be false. Any proposition incapable of being verified in this way is to be treated with great suspicion by the courts. It has been said that this approach reflects more accurately than *Frye* that of scientists themselves in deciding which information to consider when deciding questions of scientific fact.[10] But this can be so only if 'science' can be clearly identified, and if those same criteria are employed by all those who practice it. The social and behavioural sciences, economics, sociology and psychology, do not fit easily into this portrait of a body of knowledge consisting of a set of propositions which have been demonstrated to hold in all circumstances. Under the *Daubert* test, American judges retain the gate-keeping role, screening evidence for unreliability. They will ultimately have to decide what counts as science and what does not.

Experts in Human Behaviour?

Experts may give evidence on matters outside the normal experience of the trier of fact. Where the issue is someone's personality or mental state,[11] admissibility turns on whether that person is or is not 'normal'. If they apparently are not, the court may avail itself of the witness's superior expertise.[12] Child witnesses, equally, may legitimately be the subject of expert evidence on the nature and development of children, since this is outside the experience of the triers of fact.[13] However, the expert witness may not offer an opinion on whether a particular witness should be believed or not even where he or she has a personality unfamiliar to lay persons,[14] although a mental illness that might affect witness credibility should be brought to the notice of the court.[15] In *Re S and B*,[16] a psychiatric social worker described a witness's tendency to fantasise. She was not allowed to say that she believed the witness's testimony (that her brother had abused his children), to be true, since this was the ultimate issue to be decided by the court. She was permitted to express the belief that the witness's claim to have been abused as a child herself was true. May J refused, in *MacKenny*,[17] to allow a psychologist to say that since the principal prosecution witness was a psychopath, he was highly likely to lie.

Exclusion of expert evidence on the ultimate issue may, paradoxically, increase the efficacy of expert opinion. According to 'reactance theory'[18] apparent

---

[10] HL Feldman, 'Science and Uncertainty in Mass Exposure Litigation' (1995) 74 *Texas Law Review* 1.
[11] *Chard* (1971) 56 Cr App R 268.
[12] *Turner* [1975] 1 All ER 70, 74.
[13] *DPP v A and BC Chewing Gum* [1968] 1 QB 159.
[14] *Toohey v MPC* [1965] AC 595.
[15] *MacKenny* (1981) 72 Cr App R 78.
[16] *The Independent* June 1 1990.
[17] (1981) 72 Cr App R 78.
[18] See chapter five.

encroachment into jury territory may be counter-productive. In a transcript-based mock trial, expert evidence on the issue of insanity had a strong effect on the jurors' perception, but was more instrumental if the expert did not give an opinion on the ultimate issue.[19] The rule, however, can force experts into an unsatisfactory no-man's-land between giving an opinion on the ultimate issue in the case, and giving evidence so lacking in specificity that it can be dismissed as irrelevant. For example, the defendant in *Hunt*[20] had been physically, sexually and mentally abused by her alcoholic stepfather. At fourteen, she had had a sexual relationship with her mother's boyfriend. At her criminal trial she raised the defence of duress. The defence wished to call a psychiatrist to testify that if a woman from infancy to adolescence effectively has been 'trained' to fear and obey men who seem powerful and dangerous, she can become supine and prone to be led into the role of victim. The Court of Appeal upheld the trial judge's refusal to admit this evidence, because although the witness could say that he would not have been surprised if she had reacted in this way, he could not say that she had been.

Psychiatry and psychology do not fit comfortably within the *Daubert* model of scientific knowledge. There is, within the disciplines, extensive disagreement about questions of central importance, such as methodology. Also, the fact that, for courtroom purposes, diagnosis has to be made after the event increases the risk of discrepancy. So also do the less than ideal conditions in which psychiatric and psychological assessments for the purposes of litigation tend to be made. The observation period normally available in respect of diagnoses for clinical purposes is unlikely to be available while a relatively short period of contact possibly makes it easier for a mental illness to be faked. In any event, a retrospective analysis inevitably involves guesswork. Also, it is difficult to formulate appropriate parameters for the operation of psychological tests for forensic use. The employment of psychometric tests give the court something tangible to consider, but they may suffer from poor face validity. It is often difficult to know how they were validated, and if the court seeks to counter that by asking for more test material, confidentiality may be breached.[21] To some extent, behavioural sciences represent a challenge to the power of a tribunal of fact to determine how people respond to situations. In consequence, they are particularly likely to suffer should it become apparent that experts disagree. Psychiatry seems to be regarded with suspicion. For while evidence of physical injury or disability is routinely admitted, evidence of mental disorder must amount to a 'recognised' psychiatric condition[22] if the courts are to take it seriously.[23] This suggests that judges know little of psychiatry, where a diagnostic theory is regarded as proved or disproved, not according

[19] R Rogers, RM Bagby, M Crouch and BL Cutler, 'Effects of Ultimate Opinions on Juror Perceptions of Insanity' (1990) 13 *International Journal of Law and Psychiatry* 225.

[20] (1995) 1 Cr App R 82.

[21] GH Gudjonsson, 'The Current Status of the Psychologist as an Expert Witness in Criminal Trials' (1984) 37 *Bulletin of the British Psycholgical Society* 80.

[22] *Ward* [1993] 3 All ER 577.

[23] A Buchanan and G Virgo, 'Duress and Mental Abnormality' (1999) *Criminal Law Review* 517.

to whether it is 'true', but according to whether it is useful. Modern psychiatry treats as a condition a bundle of symptoms that fit together under one umbrella. The diagnostic label enables doctors to communicate with each other, and has uses in terms of recommended treatment; it avoids any reference to cause.[24]

Judges have the power to decide whether or not a condition amounts to a recognised disorder. They will decide in which areas of psychology it is possible to have special expertise. Where knowledge appears sketchy, or opinions are not universally held, they feel free to develop their own concept of mental abnormality. Any aspect of personality which is thought to be within the daily experience of the jury will be excluded. They therefore operate their own perception of what kind of experience members of the jury will have had of a particular personality type, apparently untroubled by the risk that jurors may not all have encountered it to the same extent, and may not have interpreted it in the same way.[25] Obscure or recently identified conditions are less likely than familiar ones to be regarded as genuine fields of expertise. In *Reynolds*,[26] the court rejected expert evidence on a person who allegedly could not separate fantasy from reality. In *Weightman*,[27] the same fate befell expert evidence on the nature of a histrionic personality disorder. Low intelligence has not been dealt with in a consistent way. The Court of Appeal treated as normal a man with an IQ of 72, so that evidence on the issue of his alleged recklessness was excluded,[28] but later upheld expert evidence admitted to demonstrate the psychological effect of interview conditions on a teenager with a mental age of seven and an IQ of between 70 and 80.[29] In *Roberts*[30], a defendant who was deaf pleaded provocation. The Court of Appeal held that the jury could assess the likely effect of his disability on his mental state in stressful circumstances; no amount of medical evidence would further enlighten them. A more flexible approach is discernible in *Strudwick*,[31] where the mother of a three-year-old child was jointly accused with her co-habitee of cruelty and murder. The prosecution argued that since she did nothing to protect her child from him, she must have encouraged the assaults. The defence wished to call psychological and psychiatric evidence that she had been abused herself, causing an irrational expectancy that her child would survive; an emotional blanking out had made her incapable of reacting to the violence in her home. The defence argued that if they were not able to adduce this evidence, her behaviour would appear completely heartless. An expert witness was required to support her explanation. The Court

[24] J Wing, *Reasoning about Madness* (Oxford, OUP, 1978).
[25] MT MacCrimmon, 'Fact Determination: Common Sense Knowledge, Judicial Notice and Social Science Evidence' in S Doran and J Jackson, (eds) *The Judicial Role in Criminal Proceedings* (Oxford, Hart Publishing, 2000).
[26] [1989] *Criminal Law Review* 220.
[27] (1990) 92 Cr App R 291.
[28] *Masih* [1986] *Criminal Law Review* 393.
[29] *Silcott and others* [1987] *Criminal Law Review* 765; [1988] Crim LR 293.
[30] [1990] *Criminal Law Review* 122.
[31] (1993) 99 Cr App R 326.

of Appeal held that the expert evidence was not necessarily inadmissible, although the mother did not suffer from a mental illness.

> The law is in a state of development in this area. There may well be other mental conditions about which a jury might require expert assistance to understand and evaluate their effects on the issues in a case.[32]

However, in this case the testimony would have made no difference to the outcome, as she had lied on a wide range of issues.

Lawyers characteristically utilise scientific categories developed for one purpose for a completely different one. For example, the defence of duress depends upon establishing that the defendant was subjected to threats that would have intimidated a 'sober person of reasonable firmness'. That equation takes account of any individual physical or psychiatric disability. But lesser mental disorders are of no significance in this context. In *Hegarty*,[33] the Court of Appeal upheld the exclusion of evidence of the defendant's emotional instability, because a sober person of reasonable firmness is not 'emotionally unstable' or in a 'grossly elevated neurotic state'. They were equally restrictive in *Horne*,[34] disallowing evidence that the defendant was unusually pliant and vulnerable to pressure. Yet evidence of psychiatric illness is allowed, despite the fact that attaching a label to a condition cannot identify a particular level of distress or loss of function.[35] In their insistence on a distinction between psychiatric illness and mere mental distress, lawyers want to operate an unrealistic dichotomy.[36] In psychiatry the difference is a matter of degree rather than kind, and as medical knowledge advances, changes over time.

> Medical expertise lies along a line between the predictive technological know-how of the physical science and the loose generalisations of social science practice.[37]

Psychology is more vulnerable than psychiatry to being excluded by judges in the exercise of their 'gate-keeping' function. Evidence given by experts in behavioural or social science is not easily accommodated within the *Daubert* test for admissibility. Behavioural science theories may be inherently inconsistent with *Daubert* criteria such as falsifiability and error rate.[38] The requirement for study falsifiability

---

[32] Farquharson LJ at 331.

[33] [1994] *Criminal Law Review* 353.

[34] [1994] *Criminal Law Review* 584.

[35] Buchanan and Virgo, above n. 23.

[36] Law Commission *Liability for Psychiatric Illness* Report, Law Com No 249 (London, HMSO, 1998) para.3.27.

[37] R Smith, 'Expertise and Causal Attribution in Deciding between Crime and Mental Disorder' (1985) 15 *Social Studies of Science* 67.

[38] JT Richardson, GP Ginsburg, S Gatowski and S Dobbin, 'The Problem of Applying *Daubert* to Psychological Syndrome Evidence' (1995) 79(1) *Judicature* 10.

is not appropriate to social sciences: 'we correctly refuse to abuse a child for the sake of research'.[39] Controlled experiments are virtually impossible. Aware of this, many American judges have, as a result, sidestepped *Daubert* on the grounds that the test does not apply to 'soft' science, such as economics, psychology, or sociology.[40] Hence, they have admitted evidence of false confessions and suggestible personalities, posttraumatic stress disorder and repressed memory syndrome. Meanwhile, a Canadian court held that expert evidence should be adduced to dispel any jury myths about battered women. In *Lavallee*[41], the defendant shot her partner in the back but pleaded self-defence. He had been violent over a long period. An expert witness testified that 'learned helplessness' had caused the defendant to see no opportunity to escape, and therefore to believe that she could not otherwise help herself.

Battered woman syndrome is said to establish a causal relationship between the pattern of abuse suffered by the defendant, her psychological reactions to it and her perception of her subsequent conduct. Its critics object that evidence of learned helplessness makes facts asserted by the defendant appear more likely, while the only party who can refute them is dead.[42] Redmayne questions the wisdom of adducing evidence of battered woman syndrome, given its controversial status. A simpler way to dispel misapprehension would be to provide the bare statistical evidence of the number of women who do not leave violent relationships. The position would be clearly demonstrated, and the court would be spared from having to grapple with largely untested hypotheses about women's reasons for remaining.[43] Redmayne may over-estimate juror readiness to absorb information about domestic violence. In Ewing's sample of trials where psychological self-defence was raised, convictions for some form of homicide were returned in more than seventy per cent of cases.[44] This may be partly explained by a jury assumption that the defendant should have left home to escape violence. The assumption seems to survive even expert evidence that explains that a battered woman could be persuaded to stay by a promise to reform, that she could believe that deadly force was the only way to protect herself, and that she could believe that her husband would kill her.[45] Juries tend to be influenced more by the circumstances in which the woman kills her abuser than whether or not they heard expert evidence on battered wife syndrome. Factors such as whether or not the killing took place during or after a direct confrontation with the victim, whether he was asleep and

[39] MH Graham, 'The *Daubert* Dilemma: At Last a Viable Solution' (1998) 2 *International Journal of Evidence and Proof* 211.
[40] R Slovenko, 'The *Daubert* Sequelae' (1998) 2 *International Journal of Evidence and Proof* 190.
[41] (1990) 55 CCC (3d) 97.
[42] RP Mosteller, 'Syndromes and Politics in Criminal Trials and Evidence Law' (1996) 46 *Duke Law Journal* 461.
[43] M Redmayne, *Expert Evidence and Criminal Justice* (Oxford, Oxford University Press, 2001) 185.
[44] CP Ewing, *Battered Women who Kill: Psychological Self-Defence as Legal Justification* (Lexington, MA. Heath, 1987).
[45] M Dodge and E Green, 'Jurors and Expert Conceptions of Battered Women' (1991) 6 *Victims and Violence* 271.

the level of violence he employed are the most significant contributors to the outcome. In non-confrontational situations, acquittals are significantly less likely.[46]

The reception of 'syndrome evidence' has not met with universal approval. For instance, controversy surrounds the reception in rape trials of evidence of rape trauma syndrome. This is offered to demonstrate that the complainant's behaviour is consistent with her allegation that she was raped. Critics suggest that while the alleged syndrome is based on inconclusive research, it could nonetheless cause great prejudice to the defendant. It has not been established whether rape trauma syndrome is a subset of post-traumatic stress disorder. It lacks specificity, in that many kinds of behaviour appear to fall within its compass; the victim may be afraid to be indoors, or she may be afraid to go out of doors, depending on where the rape took place. Notwithstanding considerable scepticism, evidence of rape trauma syndrome has been admitted in some courts in the United States. Some American judges, however, allow it only if the defence argue that the complainant's behaviour suggests that she has not been raped. Given the adverse effect on the fact-finder where a rape complainant displays no emotion,[47] expert evidence to prevent her calmness from being misconstrued may be advisable.[48] Brekke[49] conducted an experiment with mock jurors who listened to an audiotape of a re-enactment of rape trial. Some heard expert testimony linking rape trauma syndrome to the specific case, others heard an expert witness describe rape trauma syndrome generally, and others heard no rape trauma syndrome evidence at all. They were more likely to convict in the former case. The authors suggest that since the evidence did not affect the defendant's credibility ratings, it did not cause undue prejudice against him. Instead, the evidence countered the potential effect of rape myths in the minds of the jurors.

It has been suggested that over-willingness to accept syndrome evidence has led to miscarriages of justice. Repressed memory syndrome has been a target for criticism; it has been said that according to the falsifiability criterion, claims for repressed memory are not based on valid science.[50] Yet there are psychiatric disorders, such as multiple personality disorder and attention-deficit hyperactivity disorder, which are listed in professional diagnostic manuals[51] but equally could be said to be based on shaky ground.[52] In *Borawick v Shay*,[53] the controversy surrounding

---

[46] Although verdicts associated with mental disorder may be more likely: NJ Finkel, KH Meister, DM Lightfoot, 'The Self-Defense Defense and Community Sentiment' (1991) 15 *Law and Human Behavior* 585.

[47] See chapter four.

[48] PA Frazier and E Borgida, 'Rape Trauma Syndrome; a Review of Case Law and Psychological Research' (1992) 16 *Law and Human Behavior* 293.

[49] N Brekke and E Borgida, 'Expert Psychological Testimony in Rape Trials: a Social Cognitive Analysis' (1988) 55 *Journal of Personality and Social Psychology* 372.

[50] Richardson, Ginsburg, Gatowski and Dobbin, above n. 38.

[51] Eg, American Psychiatric Association, *Diagnostic and Statistical Manual* (DSM III and DSM IV (American Psychiatric Association, Washington DC, 1980, 1994).

[52] Richardson, Ginsburg, Gatowski and Dobbin, above n. 38.

[53] 842 F Supp 1501 (D Conn 1994).

repressed memory theory, in terms of reliability and of general acceptance, was discussed at length. The testimony was disallowed. There was no discussion of the falsifiability issue. In *State v Cressey*,[54] falsifiability was considered in relation to child sexual abuse accommodation syndrome. The court noted that evaluations of abuse victims deal almost exclusively with vague psychological profiles and symptoms, and unquantifiable evaluation results. Similarly, in *State v Foret*[55] the Louisiana Supreme Court noted that the untestability of child sexual abuse accommodation syndrome stemmed from its 'very nature as an opinion as to the causes of human behaviour'.[56] Yet in *Ohio v Martens*,[57] psychological evidence of rape trauma syndrome was allowed on the basis that *Daubert* does not require general acceptance in the scientific community; the court did not consider the issues of falsifiability and potential error rate.

Mosteller fears that courts are being bombarded with an escalating number of new conditions, such as 'urban survival syndrome', which could be described as 'trash syndromes'.[58] He suggests that judicial willingness to entertain them derives partly from the increasing impact of political reactions to the abuse of women and children. The word 'syndrome' itself has little or no specialist meaning. Ignoring the weaknesses of the research on which even a syndrome as well known as battered woman syndrome is based, courts simply react to an increasing perception of domestic violence as a social problem. Even so, he suggests, the alternative is to leave the jurors to their own 'untutored biases', and they may be inferior to even incomplete scientific examination.[59] The *Daubert* test cannot supply a solution to this problem. To apply it strictly would deprive fact-finders of relevant bodies of knowledge. To abandon any kind or critical screening process in relation to expert evidence on behavioural issues would expose courts to the risk that plausible 'junk science' would affect decision-making. Renaker suggests that evidence which serves a scientific knowledge purpose (a category which would include only evidence which complies with *Daubert*) should be distinguished from 'specialist knowledge', which is based on experience. This category would include the nature of drug trafficking and comparison of handwriting. In cases involving battered woman syndrome, for example, the evidence would have the beneficial effect of countering any jury prejudice, but would not be masquerading as a proven science. This is, effectively, the strategy of American judges.[60] But if 'junk science' is to be excluded, judges will have to be able to identify genuine experience and knowledge. American and British judges appear to have found no alternative, where 'soft science' is concerned, to reliance on their own intuitive assessment of the alleged field of expertise.

---

[54] 628 A 2d 696, 700 (NH 1993).
[55] 628 So 2d 1116 (La) 1993.
[56] At 1125.
[57] 629 NE 2d 462 (Ohio App 3 Disc 1993).
[58] Mosteller above n.42.
[59] *Ibid.*
[60] TS Renaker, 'Evidentiary Legerdemain: Deciding when *Daubert* should apply to Social Science Evidence' (1996) 84 *California Law Review* 1657.

The Objectivity of Science

There is substantial evidence that experts who operate in an adversarial system run a risk of becoming biased in favour of the party instructing them. This may be less marked in an inquisitorial system, although, Redmayne points out, even in France, experts are initially consulted by the police or prosecutor.[61] It has been said that

> for whatever reason, whether consciously or unconsciously, the fact is that expert witnesses instructed on behalf of the parties to litigation often tend to espouse the cause of those instructing them to a greater or lesser extent, on occasion becoming more partisan than the parties.[62]

A Lord Chief Justice remarked, 'I have myself, when at the Bar, been asked more than once in conference with an expert, "What do you want me to say?"'[63] In contrast, Lord Bingham records only one clear instance of an expert witness 'consciously and deliberately attempting to mislead a tribunal'.[64] The most notorious example of bias in a civil case is *Vernon v Bosley (No 2)*,[65] in which mental health professionals were severely criticised by the Court of Appeal. The case originally sprang from the tragic deaths of Mr Vernon's two daughters. The defendant, the children's nanny, admitted negligence but disputed the scale of damages sought.[66] The dispute centred on the plaintiff's claim that post-traumatic stress disorder had rendered him incapable not only of working, but of looking after himself. This contention was supported by expert evidence from a clinical psychologist and a consultant psychiatrist. The trial involved a mass of detailed evidence, and so the judge, Sedley J, delayed giving judgment. In the meantime, Mr Vernon, who was engaged in a matrimonial dispute, called the same two expert witnesses to give evidence in the Family Court that he was capable of looking after his surviving children. They testified that he was much recovered from his severe depression. However, neither Miss Bosley's lawyers nor Sedley J were informed of this. Damages were accordingly assessed at £1.3 million. At the appeal stage the matter became known, and the experts modified their evidence yet again. The Court of Appeal, plainly appalled by the readiness of these experts to 'present the plaintiff's condition on different dates in different proceedings in the light that seemed most helpful to the immediate cause', ruled that expert witnesses have a continuing duty

---

[61] Redmayne, above n. 43, p 206.

[62] *Abbey National Mortgages plc v Key Surveyors Nationwide Ltd* [1996] 3 All ER 184, Sir Thomas Bingham at 191.

[63] Lord Taylor of Gosforth, *The Lund Lecture*, delivered to the British Academy of Forensic Science November 1994 (1995) 35 *Medicine Science and Law* 3.

[64] T Bingham, *The Business of Judging: Selected Essays and Speeches* (Oxford, Oxford University Press, 2000).

[65] [1997] 1 All ER 614.

[66] *Vernon v Bosley (No 1)* [1997] 1 All ER 577.

to disclose a change of opinion, even after evidence has been given in court, if it is so fundamental as to alter a material fact on which a client's case is based.[67]

Judges in civil cases have recently taken steps to emphasise the overriding duty of the expert witness, which is to the court,[68] particularly in cases concerning the welfare of children.[69] Here it has been spelled out that not only should opinions presented to the court be entirely honest, but the underlying evidence should be properly researched.[70] If insufficient data is available to support a conclusion, the witness must say so. Hypothetical opinions must be clearly presented as such. All material must be made available to other expert witnesses in the case.[71] The 'brittle bones cases' during the 1980s and 1990s had caused judges to look closely at the role of experts in cases involving children. Dr Paterson, a biochemist who had studied bone pathology, gave evidence in a number of cases of suspected child abuse. He testified that fractures in certain young children were caused by brittle bone syndrome. The fact that no more fractures occurred once they were removed from their homes was explained on the basis that the disorder had been only temporary. He failed to say that it this theory was controversial. The cases culminated in a decision by Wall J, who heard expert evidence seriously doubting the validity of the theory. Henceforth Dr Paterson's views must be treated with the 'greatest caution and reserve'.[72] Wall J went on to say that it is the duty of expert witnesses to express their opinions within the particular area of their expertise. It should be made clear whenever a theory is merely hypothetical. If it is controversial, this also should be explained to the court, which should be presented with any material which contradicts the hypothesis. If there is overwhelming evidence of non-accidental injury, any expert witness who offers an innocent explanation has a heavy duty to ensure that he has considered carefully all available material.

There have been some disturbing examples of experts identifying themselves with the prosecution side at the expense of objectivity, most notoriously, in the case of Dr Skuse, whose evidence against the Birmingham Six and the Maguire Family has since been discredited.[73] In Australia, prosecution scientists appear similarly to have been carried away by the partisan atmosphere, in the case of 'the dingo baby' case.[74] The adversarial outlook apparently shared by many expert witnesses may derive from the lawyers who employ them. It has been claimed that

---

[67] *Vernon v Bosley (No 2)* [1997] 1 All ER 614, per Thorpe LJ at 647; see chapter two.
[68] *Whitehouse v Jordan* [1981] 1 WLR 246; *Stevens v Gullis, The Times* 6 October 1999. The Civil Procedure Rules make this explicit.
[69] *Re R (a minor) (expert evidence)* [1991] 1 FLR 293.
[70] In other varieties of case, opponents must rely on cross-examination to discredit expert evidence.
[71] *Re AB (child abuse) (expert witness)* [1995] 1 FLR No 2 181.
[72] *Ibid.*
[73] Sir John May, Return to an Address of the Honourable the House of Commons Dated 30 June 1994 *for a Report of the Inquiry into the Circumstances Surrounding the Convictions arising out of the Bomb Attacks on Guildford and Woolwich in 1974: Final Report* (London, HMSO 1994).
[74] TR Morling, *Report of the Royal Commission of Inquiry into the Chamberlain Convictions* (Darwin, Government Printer 1987).

it is common for solicitors to apply improper pressure on experts.[75] Sheppard and Vidmar found that experts gave more biased testimony following interviews with adversarial attorneys than if they were interviewed in a non-adversarial way before they gave evidence.[76] The opinion of mental health professionals was found, in another study, to vary according to which side retained them.[77] For example, in a case of alleged psychiatric injury following a major disaster, the plaintiff's psychiatrists found sixty-nine per cent of the adults to be suffering from severe impairment, with no hope of recovery. Defence psychiatrists found only nineteen per cent to be suffering to that degree.[78] Given that the clinicians involved did not depend upon court appearances to earn a living, it seemed that the reason for the disagreement was that they identified themselves with the party instructing them. A slide into adversarial thinking, once hired by one side or the other, may in fact be inevitable given the human tendency to select evidence that confirms a hypothesis.[79] Expert witnesses in adversarial proceedings, having been instructed by party, are invariably required to do this. But polarised attitudes can harden to the extent that they are not dependent upon being instructed for the purposes of a particular case. One psychiatrist wrote:

> The defence function to present their client's case in the most favourable light within the rules of evidence: failure to do so would be a great disservice to their client, and a defence expert who insists on the disclosure of damaging evidence would rightly be dropped from the case.[80]

The adversarial trial may thus be seen as an institutional source of pressure upon the scientists who participate. Whether or not this distorts the outcome of the trial is debatable. Redmayne suggests that the highly motivated critical scrutiny conducted by the opposition may be more testing than inquisitorial procedures would be.[81]

OVERRULING THE EXPERT

Courts may reject even unanimous expert opinion in homicide cases where the defence is diminished responsibility.[82] The jury's own assessment of the defendant's

---

[75] *Access to Justice: final report by Lord Woolf MR, to the Lord Chancellor on the civil justice system in England and Wales,* (HMSO, London, 1996) para.13.25.

[76] BH Sheppard and N Vidmar, 'Adversary Pretrial Procedures and Testimonial Evidence: Effects of Lawyers' Roles and Machiavellianism' (1980) 39 Journal of *Personality and Social Psychology* 320.

[77] RK Otto, 'Bias and expert testimony of mental health professionals in adversarial proceedings: a preliminary investigation' (1989) 7 *Behavioral Sciences and the Law* 267.

[78] J Zusman, 'Primary Prevention' in A Freedman, H Kaplan and B Sadock, (eds) *Comprehensive Textbook of Psychiatry II* (Baltimore, The Williams and Wilkins Company, 1975).

[79] JE Tschirgi, 'Sensible Reasoning: a Hypothesis about Hypotheses' (1980) 51 *Child Development* 1.

[80] Dr Philip Joseph, Letter to the Editor, (1994) 6 *Journal of Forensic Psychiatry* 221.

[81] Redmayne, above n. 43, 23–4.

[82] *Walton v R* [1978] 1 All ER 542. See above chapter three.

mental state therefore prevails over that of the professionals. It may be based on little more than the defendant's performance in court, the circumstances of the killings and signs of rationality at the material time. There is evidence to show that mock jurors in simulated insanity trials are influenced by the defendant's evidence (even in transcript-based simulations) as well as expert evidence.[83] In cases of alleged medical negligence, one of the issues is whether the defendant complied with accepted medical practice, established by proof of the consensus within the profession. In most cases, the fact that an opinion is held by distinguished experts in the field would demonstrate that the opinion is reasonable. However, in a rare case, if it could be demonstrated that the professional opinion is not capable of withstanding logical analysis, the judge is entitled to hold that it is not a reasonable view. This could happen where there are lacunae in professional practice.[84]

Sometimes expert evidence is rejected because of the plausibility of the narrative offered by the opposing side. The trier of fact may be able to construct a historical narrative account of the dispute, which indicates a clear trend in favour of one party or another. In the Canadian case, *Farrell v Snell*,[85] a surgeon had continued to operate on the plaintiff's eye despite noticing a haemorrhage in it. The defendant's medical evidence was that it was could not be proved that this was the cause of the plaintiff's loss of sight in that eye. In reply the court said, 'Causation need not be determined by scientific precision. It is...essentially a practical question of fact which can best be answered by ordinary common sense'.[86] 'Common sense' again was the determining factor where a doctor who was to perform an abortion miscalculated the date of conception, and the abortion failed. The baby born in due course was severely disabled. Although science could not accurately ascertain the cause of the disabilities, common sense dictated that the level of coincidence suggested fault in the defendant.[87] In *Harper v Nasser*,[88] the plaintiff claimed damages for loss of earnings following a car accident. She had worked effectively before the car accident, but not afterwards. The defendant called an expert witness who said that poor work for the first six months following the accident was attributable to it, but after that, her poor earnings were the consequence of a neurotic condition that predated the accident. The expert testimony was rejected on the grounds of logical inconsistency; the plaintiff had been a success before the accident and was so again by the time of trial.[89] In *Page v Smith*,[90] the plaintiff took to his bed within hours of a car accident, which in itself had been trivial. He claimed that the immediate reoccurrence of the chronic fatigue syndrome from

---

[83] Rogers, Bagby, Crouch and Cutler above, n. 19.
[84] *Bolitho v Hackney Heath Authority* [1992] 4 All ER 77.
[85] (1990) 72 DLR 4th 289.
[86] At 306, quoting *Alphacell v Woodward* [1972] 2 All ER 475, Lord Salmon 490.
[87] *Cherry v Borsman* (1991) 75 DLR 4th 668.
[88] Lexis March 1 1991; quoted in T Ward, 'Psychiatric Evidence and Judicial Fact-Finding' (1999) 3 *International Journal of Evidence and Proof* 180.
[89] Ward, *ibid.*
[90] [1995] 2 All ER 736: see chapter 2.

which he had suffered in the past was attributable to the accident. Otter J agreed that coincidence was an improbable explanation.

Fact-finders are entitled to prefer their own assessment of a witness's condition, based on demeanour, to the evidence of an expert. Sedley J's decision in *Vernon v Bosley*[91] rested partly on the plaintiff's demeanour. There were signs of psychological disorder, confirming, in the judge's mind, the finding of 'obsessional psychological state' by the plaintiff's experts. This, together with a 'masterly reconstruction' of Mr Vernon's biography,[92] reinforced the opinion of the plaintiff's expert witnesses. The Court of Appeal confirmed that it was for the judge, not the expert, to construct the story and compare it with medical knowledge as presented at the trial. In the case of a mother who allegedly suffered from Munchausen's Syndrome by Proxy, and who had been abusing her child,[93] Wall J relied heavily on the 'basic honesty and straightforwardness' of the delivery of her testimony. He duly overruled an expert opinion that occasional contact between them could cause psychological morbidity in the child. He declared: 'In my judgment, the risk of psychological morbidity is reduced rather than increased by continuing contact during which the mother has the opportunity to show herself kind and loving'.[94] However, in a recent case, the Court of Appeal held that Thorpe J was not entitled to reject wholesale the unanimous opinion of three expert witnesses that a father's personality had been so damaged by his own boyhood experiences that he was unsuitable to be his child's primary carer following the mother's death. The judge was entitled to depart from the experts' opinion on issues of future placement, and even, perhaps on the parent-child attachment, although he should give his reasons for that. However, it was not open to him to conclude on the basis of impressions of the father in the witness box, that the experts were wrong about his damaged core personality and continuing psychological instability.[95]

Personality of the Expert

How is a choice between rival experts made? There is some evidence that the more inaccessible scientific evidence becomes, the more a jury relies on the witness's personality.[96] This could afford supremacy to the 'superficial expert or charlatan' who offers 'the most confident and comprehensive answer'.[97] An expert witness may merely be repeating the findings of other scientists who are not in court,[98]

---

[91] Above n. 66.
[92] Ward, above n.88, 188.
[93] *Re DH* (1994) 2 FCR 3: see chapter four.
[94] *Ibid.*, Wall J at 34.
[95] *In Re M* (2002) *The Times* 24 July.
[96] JL Cooper, EA Barnett and HL Sukel, 'Complex Scientific Testimony: how do Jurors make Decisions?' (1996) 70 *Law and Human Behavior* 379.
[97] Bingham, above n. 64, 18.
[98] *H v Schering Chemicals* [1983] 1 All ER 849.

and whose demeanour cannot be examined. Nevertheless, judges consider the impression made by the witness in court significant:

> Members of the jury, the resolution of scientific argument of this sort is difficult, particularly difficult for a jury of lay people. The only way you can resolve these differences is by your impression of the witnesses. Use any technological knowledge that you have, but in the end you will judge it primarily by your impression of the witnesses, and secondly, perhaps by a comparison of their relevant experience.[99]

The force of the testimony inevitably depends on the charm, charisma, confidence, appearance and presentation of the expert, plus his or her ability to stand up to cross-examination. The failure of the defence expert witness at the trial of the Maguire Seven to do this played a significant role in the miscarriage of justice that ensued.[100] In *Abeda v Gray*,[101] the issue was whether a car accident had triggered the plaintiff's schizophrenia. The judge at first instance preferred the evidence of the defendant's expert witness on the question, but he gave no reason for this. The Court of Appeal inferred that he must have based this on his 'impression' of the expert witness, and declined to interfere. In *Pickford v ICI*,[102] the House of Lords upheld the judge's finding on the cause of a typist's disabling condition in her hands, stressing the importance of his assessment of the expert witness's demeanour. Here competence is measured not only in terms of confidence and fluency, but in the prevailing stereotype of the scientist: 'Usually, I like my expert to be around 50 years old, have some grey in his hair, wear a tweedy jacket and smoke a pipe'.[103]

Wagenaar argues that prosecution expert witnesses may be assumed to have superior status or experience, a reaction which might be exacerbated in the case of a scientist employed by the Government as a forensic specialist. This can also give the impression that the prosecution expert serves justice, while the defence expert is simply a 'hired gun'. Curiously, apparent neutrality in the expert does not appear to inspire confidence. In an experiment where the jurors watched a video re-enactment of a rape trial in which the issue was consent, the disputed evidence concerned rape trauma syndrome. The jurors, far from giving more credence to this evidence if it came from an expert who declared that he was paid by the court, gave it more weight if it came from an expert who admitted he was retained by the prosecution.[104] Those jurors were more ready to convict, and remembered

---

[99] Bridge J direction to the jury at the trial of the Birmingham Six; quoted in R Nobles and D Schiff, 'Miscarriages of Justice: a Systems Approach' (1995) 58 *Modern Law Review* 299.

[100] Sir John May, above n. 73. See J McEwan, *Evidence and the Adversarial Process*, 2nd edn. (Oxford, Hart Publishing, 1998) 162.

[101] (1997) 40 BMLR 116.

[102] [1998] 1 WLR 1189.

[103] H Hillenbrand, 'The Effective Use of Expert Witnesses' (1987) *BRIEF*, Autumn, 48.

[104] NJ Brekke, PJ Enko, G Clavet and E Seelar, 'Of Juries and Court-Appointed Experts, the Impact of Nonadversarial Versus Adversarial Testimony' (1991) 15 *Law and Human Behavior* 451.

his evidence better, although it was less balanced, perhaps because it was less circumscribed and littered with caveats. Where the court has no reasonable ground to prefer the evidence of one expert to another, the opportunity exists to accept whatever opinion fits its purpose best, anchoring its choice on the authority of the preferred expert.[105] As an illustration, Wagenaar cites the case of John Demjanjuk, accused in Israel of war crimes. Five eyewitnesses claimed that they recognised him, although many years had passed. The defence called an expert witness who explained the potential weaknesses of this evidence. The court rejected this, employing the 'questionable anchor' of the 'known fact' that in such conditions witnesses cannot make a mistake.[106]

COURTS AND SCIENCE

We have seen that, where experts give evidence in court, lay persons and judges, as the ultimate adjudicators of fact, may have to distinguish biased from objective opinion. They may have to choose between opposing opinions on the same issue, delivered by experts who practice in different fields, one of which is based on pure research and the other on experience. To perform these tasks, fact-finders may have to wrestle with the mysteries of

> chemical engineering, metallurgy, soil-mechanics, brain surgery, naval architecture, computer technology, nuclear radiation, oil refining, navigation, mining engineering, combustion and the international currency markets.[107]

Advocates at least have the advantage of long informal discussions with the expert witness to clarify the scientific context.[108] In the absence of such an opportunity, is it possible for lay persons to make a rational decision within such fields of expertise? Judges who hold public enquiries into disasters such as a financial collapse or an outbreak of disease in cattle are helped by scientific expert assessors. But in a conventional court of law, judge, jury or magistrate struggle alone to make what sense they can of the scientific evidence before them. Nevertheless, Belfast jurors in Jackson's survey reported high levels of comprehension of expert testimony. They also found judicial interventions and requests for elucidation helpful when an expert witness was giving evidence.[109] Similarly the New Zealand jury survey found jurors in general to be confident that they understood the expert evidence.[110]

---

[105] WA Wagenaar, PJ van Koppen, and HM Crombag, *Anchored Narratives: the Psychology of Criminal Evidence* (Hemel Hempstead, Harvester Wheatsheaf, 1993) 179.
[106] *Ibid.* 174.
[107] Bingham above, n. 64, 19.
[108] *Ibid.* 20.
[109] J Jackson, 'Juror Decision-Making in the Trial Process', in G Davies, S Lloyd-Bostock, K MacMurran, and C Wilson, (eds) *Psychology Law and Criminal Justice* (Berlin, de Gruyter, 1996).
[110] W Young, N Cameron and Y Tinsley *Juries in Criminal Trials: Part II, New Zealand Law Commission Preliminary Paper* 37, Wellington, New Zealand 1999, para 3.14: M Zander and P Henderson,

Some lawyers are sceptical; there have been cases in the United States where it has been argued that the jury was so out of its depth that the trial amounted to denial of due process. In *Re Japanese Electronic Products Antitrust Litigation*,[111] the case involved expert evidence on economic and technical electronic matters. It was held that the trial should be heard by a judge rather than a jury, for the right to jury trial must give way to the right to due process where the civil case is too complex for a jury to decide in a proper manner. For although the law does not demand scientific precision of jurors, it does contemplate a resolution of each issue on the basis of a fair and reasonable assessment of the evidence. This might not be possible because of the length of the trial or because of conceptually difficult factual issues. Would judges really cope better? In *Brown v Board of Education*,[112] the Supreme Court relied on empirical studies which suggested that segregated schools inflict psychological harm on black schoolchildren. These had been criticised elsewhere on methodological grounds.[113] In cases of uncertainty in science, a court relies heavily on any scientific consensus, and the incidence of the burden of proof. Yet the consensus may itself be based on inadequate information. In mass tort cases, the evidence is generally ambiguous precisely because the product alleged to have caused harm has not been sufficiently tested. Thus the very negligence complained of (marketing a product which has not been thoroughly tested) hampers claimants from pursuing their case. If scientists are undecided, judges and juries are unlikely to find the claimants' case unproven. Since the scientific evidence of causation is generally still at the developmental stage, such cases are frequently lost, because the burden of proof operates against the claimants. The difficulty of proof in these cases hardly encourages manufacturers to be careful.[114]

Carol Jones has demonstrated the ambivalence of the attitude of lawyers to scientists.[115] Law tends to treat science or expertise as an autonomous, objective entity which has authority independent of the institutional settings in which it is used. The convenient myth of scientific certainty[116] may be seen in *Daubert* in the Supreme Court's use of the phrase 'scientific knowledge', where the reality is merely 'scientific belief'. Wagenaar confirms that too often courts discuss the evidence of two conflicting scientists as an inquiry into which is 'right'.[117] It is curious that lawyers assume an objective scientific reality, given that legal culture accommodates two conflicting but plausible versions of the law, produced from

Crown Court Study, Royal Commission on Criminal Justice Research Study 19, (HMSO, London, 1993).

[111] 631 F 2d 1069 (3d Cir 1980).
[112] 347 US 483 (1954).
[113] S Brewer, 'Scientific Expert Testimony and Intellectual Due Process' (1998) 107 *Yale Law Journal* 1535.
[114] Feldman above, n.10.
[115] CA Jones, *Expert Witnesses: Science, Medicine and the Practice of Law* (Oxford, Clarendon, 1994).
[116] B Wynne, 'Establishing the Rules of Laws: Constructing Expert Authority' in R Smith and B Wynne, (eds) *Expert Evidence: Interpreting Science in the Law* (London, Routledge, 1989).
[117] Wagenaar, van Koppen, and Crombag, n. 105, 180.

the same original sources. An apparent conflict of view between scientists is less a matter of different interpretations of a body of literature than a question of which body of literature is most applicable to the case.[118] Jones suggests that scientists should share some of the blame for the reification of science in which lawyers indulge, because they also are prone to suggest that finding the right answer is merely a matter of employing correct procedure. The finders of fact, who cannot escape the responsibility of reaching a decision notwithstanding fundamental conflicts in the scientific evidence before them, may strive to extract certainty from doubt. Meanwhile, partisan interest demands that lawyers manipulate scientists and their opinions. To this end, the expert is turned into a collaborator in adversarial strategies; but when error leads to a miscarriage of justice, the experts are retrospectively accused of bias and viciously scapegoated for 'failing to live up to the idealised vision of the man of science' lawyers promulgate.[119] She argues that there is

> an inbuilt tension between the lawyer's wish to discredit an expert in a particular case and his wish to preserve the overall currency of expert evidence.[120]

The duplicity of the advocate may be seen in a standard cross-examination technique. Counsel accuses the expert witness of dealing in probabilities rather than certainties; if the expert replies that nothing is ever a hundred per cent certain, the response is to sneer, 'We always thought scientists dealt in facts'. Expert witnesses are often blamed for the failures of the adversarial system, as in the case of Dr Clift in Scotland in 1972.[121] He was accused of withholding evidence, failing to disclose that samples he had tested contained mixtures of fluids, and failing to disclose the victim's blood group. But the information had been in his original report, subsequent to which he was not asked for that information again.

Damn Lies and Statistics

The predilection of lawyers to insist upon the certainty of science may have led to a gross over-estimation of the reliability of DNA, which has, on occasion, been invested with the quality of virtual infallibility. Yet, like any other forensic evidence, it depends upon correct laboratory procedures being followed.[122] Contamination with other material must throw any conclusion into serious doubt. Meanwhile, the significance of results obtained must be understood.

---

[118] *Ibid.*
[119] Jones, above n.115, 269.
[120] *Ibid.* at 270.
[121] Referred to in R Smith, 'Forensic Psychology, Scientific Expertise and the Criminal Law' in R Smith and B Wynne, (eds) *Expert Evidence: Interpreting Science in the Law* (London, Routledge, 1989).
[122] See description of the process in *Doheny and Adams* [1997] 1 Cr App R 369 per Phillips LJ at 372.

Advocates, judges and even experts themselves have fallen into error, so that the probative force of a DNA match was presented to a jury as follows: 'the likelihood of [the source] being any other man but Andrew Deen is one in three million'.[123] Here the court is plunged into the deep and treacherous waters of statistical probability. The difficulty may be seen in the controversy surrounding the trial in 1999 of Sally Clark, a solicitor accused of murdering her two sons, on separate occasions, whilst they were very small babies. Professor Sir Roy Meadow, a paediatrician, not a statistician, testified that the chance of two cot deaths occurring in one family was one in seventy-three million. The Royal Statistical Society subsequently threw this figure into doubt.[124] Although the Court of Appeal accepted that the statistic was wrong, the error was thought to be of minimal significance, and had not affected the jury verdict.[125] The case highlights the problem that not every scientist has expertise in statistics. 'The mistake has been to assume that an expert in blood is also an expert on probability, and unfortunately, many are not'.[126] It may in a particular case be clear to the finders of fact where the greater expertise in the field resides. If it is not, reliance on common sense to resolve conflicting testimony may prove dangerous.

Propositions, which are consistent, but appear otherwise to laymen, include the following:

a)   The probability that an unknown person taken from the population would have the same profile as the defendant is 1 in a billion

b)   The probability that there is another person in the population with the same profile as the defendant is 1 in 50.[127]

Intuitive assumptions rarely produce accurate predictions of likely outcome. An everyday example of a common mistake on probabilities is known as the 'Gambler's Fallacy'. The probability that a tossed coin will land Heads or Tails, or that the ball in a roulette wheel will land in a red or black square, remains at 50:50 even after the coin has come down Heads several times in succession, or after a long run of black on the roulette wheel. Yet most people will assume that the probability of the coin now landing on Tails, or the ball now landing in red, has increased. In addition, the 'Mind Projection Error' causes observers to assume

---

[123] *Deen* (1994) *The Times* 10 January. Evidence from the expert witness, himself guilty of the 'Prosecutor's Fallacy' (below).

[124] (2001) *The Times* 23 October.

[125] *Clark* 2 October 2000 www.lexis-nexis.com/professional. Court of Appeal (CD); see now the appellate judgment above chapter 1, n. 79; B Mahendra, 'Science and Uncertainty in the Miscarriage of Justice' [2001] *New Law Journal* 1686. The other evidence against Clark consisted of little more than some superficial similarities in the domestic circumstances in which the two babies died, together with some tentative medical evidence.

[126] B Robertson and GA Vignaux, 'Expert Evidence: Law, Practice and Probability' (1992) 12 *Oxford Journal Legal Studies* 392.

[127] IW Evell, LA Foreman, G Jackson and JA Lambert, 'DNA Profiling: a Discussion of the Issues' (2000) *Criminal Law Review* 341.

that the uncertainty they have about whether a tossed coin will land on Heads is a quality of the coin tossed, rather than of their own uncertainty about which side it will land on.[128] The representativeness heuristic makes the layman insensitive to base-rate information. Saks and Kidd[129] give the example of asking whether John is an engineer or a lawyer. If told that John is a member of a group comprising thirty lawyers and seventy engineers, most people will correctly say it is thirty per cent likely that he is a lawyer. But if told he is well-read, active in politics and argumentative, the estimate of probability shifts to ninety per cent. This is a powerful and misleading heuristic bias. Saks and Kidd asked experimental subjects to imagine betting on a) drawing a red marble from a bag containing fifty per cent red, and fifty per cent white, marbles; or b) drawing a red marble seven times in succession, given replacement, from a bag containing ninety per cent red, and ten per cent white, marbles, or c) drawing a red marble at least once in seven successive tries, given replacement, from a bag containing ten per cent red, and ninety per cent white, marbles. The subjects thought b), the least likely, was the safest bet. It seems that, in judging the likelihood of an outcome involving a series of interconnected events, people will overestimate the probability to a significant degree. If the probability of each event on its own is high, they disregard the conjunctive events. Saks and Kidd conclude that heuristical reasoning will prevail over the advice of statisticians.

A fallacy that has caused courts to go astray in the past is known to statisticians as 'transposing the conditional', and to lawyers, because of its effect, as 'The Prosecutor's Fallacy'. If the court is told that only one person in a million will have a DNA profile which matches that of the crime stain, and that the defendant has a DNA profile which matches the crime stain, it is liable to conclude, wrongly, that there is a million to one probability that the defendant left the crime stain and is guilty. In fact, if one in a million has matching DNA, the defendant will be one of perhaps twenty-six men in the United Kingdom who share that characteristic. If nothing more is known, the statistical probability of guilt is twenty-six to one against. Hence, the court must move on to consider any other evidence that bears on the guilt or innocence of the accused, and adjust the probability accordingly. If he has a good alibi, the probability of his guilt diminishes accordingly. If he was at the scene of the crime, it will increase dramatically on the basis of the unlikelihood of two men with such a rare characteristic in common being at the same place by coincidence.[130]

The Court of Appeal has been forced to quash convictions where the Prosecutor's Fallacy affected consideration of DNA evidence, as in *Deen*,[131] where

---

[128] B Robertson and GA Vignaux, 'Probability: the Logic of the Law' (1993) 13 *Oxford Journal Legal Studies* 457.

[129] MJ Saks and RF Kidd, 'Human Information Processing and Adjudication: Trial by Heuristics' (1980–1981) 15 *Law and Society Review* 123.

[130] Cf DJ Baldwin and P Donnelly, 'The Prosecutor's Fallacy and DNA evidence' (1984) *Criminal Law Review* 711.

[131] *The Times* 10 January 1994.

it infected the testimony of the expert witness himself. The Lord Chief Justice observed, 'It makes it very difficult, even if the scientist gets it right, and the judge gets it right — what on earth does an ordinary jury make of it? How does a jury understand probability?'[132] In *Doheny and Adams*,[133] the defendant Doheny resembled, but only in some respects, a description given by an eyewitness. He had the opportunity to pass the house where the offence took place. The Court of Appeal quashed his conviction because of doubt as to the correct figure for the random occurrence ratio — the frequency with which the matching DNA characteristics are likely to be found in the population at large, showing how many other men could have matched the sample, The Court made it clear that a scientist introducing evidence of a DNA comparison should explain not only his methodology, but also the 'random occurrence ratio'. It may be appropriate to indicate how many people with matching characteristics are likely to be found in the United Kingdom or in a more limited relevant sub-group, in this instance, Caucasian sexually active males in the Manchester area. The expert witness should not be asked his opinion as to whether it was the defendant who left the crime stain, nor should he use terminology that may lead the jury to believe that he is expressing such an opinion. The Court gave an example of how the jury should be directed:

> Members of the jury, if you accept the scientific evidence called by the Crown, that indicates that there are probably only four or five white males in the United Kingdom from whom that semen stain could have come. The defendant is one of them. The decision you have to reach on all the evidence is whether you are sure that it was the defendant who left the stain or whether it is possible that it was one of that other small group of men who share the same DNA characteristics.[134]

It is curious that although an expert witness producing DNA evidence must give a detailed explanation of its statistical significance, it seems that other areas of forensic science, in which identification is accepted without demur, have avoided these issues. No such requirement appears to attach to fingerprint, or even ear print, evidence.[135] Evidence of an ear print as a 'unique match' was accepted at a murder trial in Leeds Crown Court[136] with little in the way of peer review of

---

[132] above n. 123.

[133] [1997] 1 Cr App R 369.

[134] Criticised by Evell, Foreman, Jackson and Lambert, n 127, because it assumes that the random occurrence ratio is a frequency, whereas it is a relative frequency. The probability of a match varies according to whether the population contains the defendant's family or not, or whether it contains a mixture of ethnic groups.

[135] Evell, Foreman, Jackson and Lambert, n 127.

[136] The conviction was quashed and a retrial ordered by the Court of Appeal in the light of misgivings expressed by forensic experts who had not given evidence at the trial on the reliability of earprint evidence. However, there was no reason to doubt the admissibility of earprints. *Dallagher* [2002] *Criminal Law Review* 821.

scientific publications and no database to support the opinion. And even in DNA cases,

> Jurors evaluate evidence and reach a conclusion not by means of a formula, mathematical or otherwise, but by the joint application of their common sense and knowledge of the world to the evidence before them.[137]

In *Adams (Denis) No 2*,[138] the defence introduced expert evidence which explained how Bayes' Theorem might assist the jury to assess the weight to give the DNA evidence adduced by the prosecution. The Theorem involves an initial estimate by the fact-finder of the likelihood of the end proposition. As each item of proof is introduced, this estimate is recalculated on the basis of the degree to which the new evidence supports or contradicts the proposition to be proven. The recalculated probability is then treated as a prior assessment in processing a further item of proof, and the exercise is repeated in the light of any further items of evidence. The end result, after all adjustments have been made in accordance with received items of evidence, is a 'posterior probability'.[139] The trial judge made it clear that whether or not the jury followed this procedure depended entirely upon their decision as to whether it would assist them to reach a verdict. Or, if they preferred, they should 'use the methods which juries in this country have used for many, many years, pretty satisfactorily'.[140] They were instructed that they must agree which method they would employ. On appeal, the judge was upheld in his distinction between the statistical approach and a common sense approach, and in allowing the jury as a single unit to choose between them. But, although Bayes' Theorem is a sound and reliable methodological approach in some circumstances, Lord Bingham LCJ suggested that in jury trials it could be a recipe for confusion, misunderstanding and misjudgment, very probably among judges, as well as, almost certainly, among jurors.

It seems that in general, laymen are accused, on the one hand, of subscribing to probability fallacies that cause them to give statistical evidence insufficient weight,[141] and, on the other, of being mesmerised by statistics. 'Statistical evidence can be a veritable sorcerer in our computerised society.'[142] From their review of a number of research studies, Kaye and Koehler conclude that mock juries do not appear to overvalue probabilistic evidence, or confuse the probability of innocence with the stated infrequency of an incriminating trait. The authors enter the caveat that many of the experimental subjects are university students, who may have greater than average appreciation of probability. But should it be

---

[137] *Adams* [1996] 2 Cr App R 467.
[138] [1998] 1 Cr App R 377.
[139] MD Finkelstein and NB Fairley, 'A Bayesian Approach to Identification Evidence' (1970) 83 *Harvard Law Review* 489.
[140] *Adams (Denis) No 2*, above n.138, at 381.
[141] Saks and Kidd, above n. 129.
[142] Calif Supreme Court, *People v Collins* 68 Cal 2d 319, 320 (1968).

the case that, on the whole, moderately probative statistical evidence is undervalued rather than the reverse, the explanation is not self-evident. One possibility is that the evidence may be too abstract to have impact,[143] or there may be a lack of perceived causal relevance,[144] or it may be insufficiently specific.[145] Redmayne observes that if jurors are trying to construct a story out of the evidence, it is difficult to compare the defence story with a statistic, and this may tempt them to disregard it.[146] However, it seems that expert witnesses are not alone in having differing views as to the significance of statistical evidence; so also do the academics engaged in evaluating the ability of laymen to understand it. A major problem with the various research studies is that it is not clear that statistical propositions adopted for experimental purposes are correct.[147] Koehler suggests that jurors be given a lecture on probability and statistics which stresses the relevant concepts for the evidence they will hear.[148] Even assuming the jury understands it, however, the question remains whether all professional statisticians would agree with it. In the United States, the National Research Council found itself unable to devise acceptable guidance for the courts.[149] In the absence of an unassailably right answer, adversarial logic demands that fact-finders be presented with the rival versions of statistical theory.[150] It is not difficult to see why the Court of Appeal suggests that 'common sense' is the final recourse of a jury presented with impenetrable statistical evidence.

---

[143] RE Nisbett, E Borgida, R Crandell and H Reed, 'Popular Induction: Information is not Necessarily Informative' in JJ Carroll and JW Payne, (eds) *Cognition and Social Behavior* (Hillsdale, NJ: Erlbaum, 1976).

[144] A Tversky and D Kahnman, 'Availability: a Heuristic for Judging Frequency and Probability' (1973) 5 *Cognitive Psychology* 207.

[145] M Bar-Hillel, 'The Base Rate Fallacy in Probability Judgments' (1980) 44 *Acta Psychologica* 211.

[146] Redmayne, above n. 43.

[147] DH Kaye and JJ Koehler, 'Can Jurors Understand Probabilistic Evidence?' (1991) 154 *Journal Royal Statistical Society* 75.

[148] JJ Koehler, 'Probabilities in the Courtroom: an Evaluation of the Objectives and Policies' in DK Kagehiro and WS Laufer, (eds) *Handbook of Psychology and Law* (New York, Springer-Verlag, 1991).

[149] B Robertson and GA Vignaux, 'Why the NRC Report on DNA is wrong' [1992] *New Law Journal* 1619.

[150] EJ Imwinkelreid, 'The Next Step in Conceptualizing the Presentation of Expert Evidence as Education: the Case for Didactic Trial Procedures' (1997) 1 *International Journal of Evidence and Proof* 128.

8

The Impact of Psychology on Law

T HIS CHAPTER EXAMINES some areas of law where the work of psychologists has had significant impact. To lawyers the reforms may seem radical. To many psychologists, the changes made do not go nearly far enough.

THE EVIDENCE OF THE EYEWITNESS

The status of the eyewitness as the best and most reliable source of evidence has been severely undermined. In the United States, a study of post-1900 wrongful convictions indicated that misidentification was a significant factor in fifty-two per cent of the cases.[1] In England and Wales, the Devlin Report[2] made the legal profession suddenly aware of the voluminous psychological literature on eyewitness recall and identification evidence. The implications were serious. The error rate recorded in psychological experiments on description accuracy varied between sixty-five and seventy-five per cent, and was increased by lapse of time.[3] Although recognising someone is easier than describing them, accuracy remains alarmingly low, averaging, across the multiplicity of studies, between thirty-five and sixty per cent.[4] Good observation conditions and prolonged observation periods make little difference.[5] The memory of eyewitnesses appears to be easily compromised by stereotypes which can become absorbed into the memory,[6] and by suggestion.[7] At the same time, it is difficult to obtain spontaneous descriptions

---

[1] A Rattman, 'Convicted but Innocent' (1988) 12 *Law and Human Behavior* 283.
[2] *Report of the Departmental Committee on Evidence of Identification* Cmnd 338 (London, HMSO, 1976).
[3] MP Toglia, TM Shlecter and DS Chevalier, 'Memory for Direct and Indirectly Experienced Events' (1992) 6 *Applied Cognitive Psychology* 293; BL Cutler and SD Penrod, *Mistaken Identification: the Eyewitness, Psychology and the Law* (Cambridge, Cambridge University Press, 1995); J Shepherd, J Ellis and G Davies, *Identification Evidence: a Psychological Evaluation* (Aberdeen University Press, 1982); PN Shapiro and SD Penrod, 'Meta-Analysis of Facial Identification Studies' (1986) 100 *Psychological Bulletin* 139.
[4] Shepherd, Ellis and Davies, above n.3: BR Clifford and R Bull, *Psychology of Person Identification* (London, Routledge and Kegan Paul, 1988); BR Clifford, 'Eyewitness Testimony; the Bridging of a Credibility Gap' in D Farrington, K Hawkins and S Lloyd-Bostock, (eds) *Psychology, Law and Legal Process* (London, Macmillan, 1979).
[5] Shepherd, Ellis and Davies, above n. 3.
[6] FC Bartlett, *Remembering: a Study* (London, Cambridge University Press, 1932).
[7] EF Loftus, 'Shifting Human Color Memory' (1977) 5 *Memory and Cognition* 696.

from an eyewitness without leading questions.[8] So while suggestive or leading questioning may reduce the number of omissions, the overall number of errors may increase.[9]

Identification parades provide only limited safeguards against wrongful identifications. If a parade is held at which the real actor is not present, there is a one-third likelihood of the eyewitness selecting a volunteer.[10] It appears that in the anxiety to choose someone, the eyewitness will select the line-up member who, compared with the other members of the line-up, most resembles the culprit.[11] If there is a familiar face in the line-up, it may be confused for that of the offender, the witness forgetting where it was in fact seen on earlier occasions. This is known as the 'transference effect'. Similar mistakes can be made where the person the witness saw resembled someone familiar, such as a well-known figure.[12] The fact that a witness has confidence in the identification is no indicator that it is right.[13] Eyewitnesses become more confident, of course, if they become aware that others have identified the same suspect. In 1984 Ronald Cotton was convicted in the United States of rape. The victim, Jennifer Thompson, picked him from a line-up in utter conviction that she recognised him, saying that he had a very distinctive nose. Once she became aware that the soles on Cotton's shoes matched the attacker's footprint her certainty was increased, and was unaffected by seeing the real rapist at Cotton's trial. The jury verdict in turn reinforced her confidence to the extent that she had difficulty updating her memory after events proved her to have been wrong. Cotton was released from prison in 1995 after DNA evidence established that another man had carried out the attack.[14]

Following the Devlin Report, the Court of Appeal in *Turnbull*[15] set out guidelines which, it was hoped, would protect criminal defendants from the risk of mistaken identifications. In any case which depends wholly or substantially on the correctness of one or more identifications of the accused which the defence alleges

---

[8] R Bryden, *Identification Proceedings under Scottish Criminal Law* (1978 Cmnd 7096) 1.03; GM Davies, 'Research on Children's Testimony: Implications for Interviewing Practice in C Hollins and K Howells, (eds) *Clinical Approaches to Sex Offenders and their Victims* (Chichester, Wiley, 1991).

[9] KH Marquis and S Oskamp, 'Testimony Validity as a Function of Question Form, Atmosphere and Item Difficulty' (1972) 2 *Journal of Applied Social Psychology* 167.

[10] For example the results of MA Pigott, JC Brigham and RK Bothwell, 'A Field Study of the Relationship between Quality of Eyewitness Description and Identification Accuracy' (1990) 17 *Journal of Police Science and Administration* 84.

[11] GL Wells, 'What do you know about Eyewitness Ientification?' (1993) 8 *American Psychologist* 555 at 560.

[12] Peter Hain, now a Government minister, was, in 1975, confidently identified by a number of witnesses as the man they saw running away after a bank robbery. He was at the time very well-known through frequent appearances on television. Mr Hain had a complete alibi.

[13] GL Wells and Murray, 'Eyewitness Confidence' in Wells and EF Loftus, (eds) *Eyewitness Testimony: Psychological Perspectives* GL (Cambridge, Cambridge University Press, 1984); KA Deffenbacher and EF Loftus, 'Do Jurors share a Common Understanding Concerning Eyewitness Behavior?' (1982) 6 *Law and Human Behavior* 15.

[14] This man, Robert Poole, had confessed to the crime: A Memon and AT McDaid, 'Factors Influencing Witness Evidence' in J McGuire, T Mason and A O'Kane, (eds) *Behaviour, Crime and Legal Processes* (Chichester, Wiley, 2000).

[15] *Turnbull* [1977] 2 QB 871.

are mistaken,[16] the trial judge should warn the jury of the need for caution. The particular dangers attached to identification evidence must be explained; first, that in a number of cases over the years erroneous identifications by apparently honest witnesses have led to wrong convictions; and secondly, the substantial degree of risk that honest witnesses may be wrong in their evidence of identification.[17] The warning must be given even where the witness knows the suspect. Where the prosecution case consists of nothing more than poor quality identification evidence, such as a 'fleeting glimpse', the judge should withdraw the case from the jury unless there is evidence which goes to support the correctness of the identification. This other evidence may consist of another disputed identification; the two identifications may support each other, but only if they are of sufficient quality that a jury may be safely left to assess them.[18] This guidance takes no account of some specific identification issues which also feature in the psychological literature such as the extra levels of unreliability in identifications across races,[19] and, more debatably, across genders and age groups.[20]

How wise was the Court of Appeal to take the research findings seriously? On the basis that identification witnesses are wrong half the time, the logical response would be to acquit in every case. Yet, half these witnesses are right. Some individuals may have a good track record for recognition;[21] it would be unwise to dismiss all eyewitness evidence as equally unreliable. Also, the relationship between eyewitness confidence and accuracy is more complicated than some literature allows. There is a difference between having a confident delivery, and believing that one's identification is correct.[22] Eyewitnesses may legitimately feel confident about the accuracy of some of the details they recall while being less confident about others.[23] It is also doubtful whether it is possible to extrapolate directly from laboratory findings to real life situations. Stephenson suggests that, instead, testimony should be carefully scrutinised for plausibility, consistency and likely reliability.[24] An example is a case where the Royal Canadian Mounted Police interviewed a

---

[16] [1976] 3 All ER 549.

[17] *Reid v R* (1990) 90 Cr App R 121.

[18] *Weeder* [1980] CLR 645; two independent witnesses identified D. The judge must warn the jury that even a number of honest witnesses may be mistaken.

[19] JW Shepherd, JB Deregoswski and MD Ellis, 'A cross-cultural study of recognition memory for faces' (1974) *International Journal of Psychology* 9205, but see RCL Lindsay and GL Wells, 'What do we really know about Cross-Race Identification Evidence?' in S Lloyd-Bostock and BR Clifford, (eds) *Evaluating Witness Evidence* (Chichester, Wiley, 1983); J Cross, J Cross and J Daly, 'Sex, Race, Age and Beauty as Factors in the Recognition of Faces' (1971) 10 *Perception and Psychophysics* 393.

[20] NL Jalbert and J Getting, 'Race and Gender Issues in Facial Recognition' in F Lösel, D Bender and T Bleisener, (eds) *Psychology and Law: International Perspective* (New York, de Gruyter, 1992); Shapiro and Penrod, above n.3.

[21] Cutler and Penrod, above n.3.

[22] M King, (1986) *Psychology in or out of Court* (London, Pergamon, 1986) 37.

[23] GM Stephenson, 'Accuracy and Confidence in Testimony: a Critical Review and Some Fresh Evidence' in DJ Muller, AF Blackman and A Chapman, (eds) *Psychology and Law* (Chichester, Wiley, 1984) 229.

[24] GM Stephenson, *The Psychology of Criminal Justice*, (Oxford, Blackwell, 1992) 161.

number of eyewitnesses following an armed robbery and fatal shooting in the street; thirteen were interviewed four or five months later for research purposes.[25] In the early interviews, there was a strikingly high rate of accuracy. In the later interviews, accuracy did not decrease, but new information, also accurate, was offered. The witnesses resisted misleading suggestions by the interviewer. The recall of those who suffered the most stress was not adversely affected by the trauma. However, lacking any objective measure of the accuracy of these witnesses, the researchers had to rely on consistency of accounts, on the assumption that a large measure of agreement between them represents the truth. But these witnesses may have contaminated each other's memory.

Legal systems are still struggling to accommodate scientists' doubts about eyewitness reliability. In England, Barry George was convicted in 2002 of the murder of the television presenter, Jill Dando. An eyewitness, SM, positively identified him as the man she saw four hours before the murder, in the street where it took place. SM only glanced at the man, a low quality identification. Three other witnesses saw a man running along the street shortly after the murder. These were also low-quality identifications, based on a 'fleeting glimpse'. In rejecting George's appeal against conviction,[26] the Court of Appeal missed the opportunity to clarify *Turnbull* by explaining exactly how poor quality identifications might support each other. For it was far from certain that SM's identification and the three later ones related to the same man. The thin logic of mutual support collapses if there is no means of establishing that the relevant identifications relate to the same person. Although judges are enjoined in *Turnbull* to recognise that several honest witnesses may be mistaken, the Court of Appeal still seem to think that there is safety in numbers. In reality, there is a risk of serious injustice. Patrick Murphy was identified as the perpetrator of a crime by three witnesses. A miscarriage of justice was avoided only because he was able to produce eleven alibi witnesses from a meeting of Alcoholics Anonymous.[27] *Turnbull* should be extended to ensure that a case is stopped and prevented from going to the jury if all the identifications are of poor quality.

Although a *Turnbull* direction should be given every time a case that turns on a disputed identification, it is not clear from the ensuing case law whether this applies where the defendant admits being present at the scene of the crime, but denies involvement in it. There is reason to believe that a warning should be given. It has been discovered that attentionally salient information is given disproportionate weighting by eyewitnesses. For example if the observer sees a group of people amongst whom one stands out because of his clothes, or because he is nearer, the observer is likely to judge him to have played a greater causal role.[28] This risk of bias

---

[25] JC Yuille and JL Cutshall, 'A Field Study of Eyewitness Memory of a Crime' (1986) 71 *Journal of Applied Psychology* 291.

[26] *George (Barry Michael)*, *The Times* 30 August 2002.

[27] PB Ainsworth, *Psychology, Law and Eyewitness Testimony* (Chichester, Wiley, 1998) 80.

[28] L McArthur, 'What Grabs You? The Role of Attention in Impression Formation and Causal Attribution' in ET Higgins, CP Herman and MP Zanna, (eds) *Social Cognition: the Ontario Symposium* Vol 1 (Hillsdale, New Jersey, Erlbaum, 1981).

has not been appreciated by the judiciary. In the following two appeals, the defence argued that the central issue was a disputed identification. In *Thornton*,[29] the host of a wedding reception was punched and kicked by several persons he did not see. It was agreed that agreed that Thornton was present, but he denied any part in the attack. Two witnesses testified that he had been involved in the assault. The Court of Appeal held that the conflict here concerned identification, and therefore a warning should have been given. In *Slater*,[30] the defendant admitted being present at a club, but denied involvement in a violent assault. He was a man of striking appearance, described as almost spherical, 'six feet tall and very broad'. On appeal, it was held that since all the witnesses described the attacker in such terms, the case did not turn on a disputed identification. No warning was necessary. The Court of Appeal was clearly unaware of the risk that observers might accurately recall the appearance of someone so unusual, but incorrectly recall what he did.

Legal concern about the reliability of eyewitnesses is not reflected in the case of other kinds of recognition, such as voice recognition. The detailed guidelines[31] on the conduct of a visual identification parade have no equivalent of a voice identification parade, nor, indeed, is there any statutory obligation to hold one.[32] Yet accuracy appears to be lower than that for visual identification, although some voices are more memorable than others.[33] Again, witness confidence is no indicator of accuracy.[34] In *Hersey*,[35] a shopkeeper selected the defendant's voice, believing it to be that of a man who robbed him. Hersey and eleven volunteers each read out a passage from an earlier interviewer, and, allegedly, only Hersey read so that it made sense. The Court suggested that a Turnbull-style warning should be given, but did not identify the kind of factors that might affect the reliability of voice recognition.[36] Instead, the suggestion was made that expert evidence on the difficulties of voice recognition might be helpful.[37] It is not clear why it was thought that this was particularly necessary in voice recognition cases.

Psychologists have failed to devise a method of training to make identifications more accurate.[38] The training and experience of police officers might be thought to be more thorough than anything that could be devised in a laboratory setting, but they are no better than civilians at recognising faces.[39] They can recall more

[29] [1995] 1 Cr App R 578.
[30] [1995] 1 Cr App R 584.
[31] Police and Criminal Evidence Act and Codes of Practice.
[32] D Ormerod, 'Sounds Familiar?' Voice Identification Evidence [2001] *Criminal Law Review* 595.
[33] AD Yarmey and E Matthys 'Voice Evidence of an Abductor' (1992) 6 *Applied Cognitive Psychology*.
[34] LR Wallandael, A Surace, DB Parsons and M Brown, 'Ear Witness' Voice Recognition: Factors Affecting Accuracy and Impact on Jurors' (1994) 8 *Applied Cognitive Psychology* 661.
[35] [1998] *Criminal Law Review* 281.
[36] For suggestions as to appropriate warning see D Ormerod, above n. 32.
[37] For nature of the expert see *Robb* (1991) 93 Cr App R 161; *O'Doherty* (2002) *The Times* 3 June.
[38] RS Malpass, 'Training in Face Recognition' in G Davies, H Ellis and J Shepherd, (eds) *Perceiving and Remembering Faces* (London, Academic Press, 1981) HM Woodhead, AD Baddely and DCV Simmonds, 'On Training People to Recognise Faces' (1979) 22 *Ergonomics* 33.
[39] JC Yuille, 'Research and Teaching with Police: a Canadian example' (1984) 71 *International Review of Applied Psychology* 291; AD Yarmey, 'Police as Witnesses' (1999) *Expert Evidence* 237.

descriptive facts and scene details, but are no more accurate in relation to sequential action facts.[40] Although they are not superior eyewitnesses, police officers are convincing ones. Over half the legal professionals and law students in one study believed their evidence.[41] The Court of Appeal appears equally confident in them. In *Ramsden*,[42] a police officer saw the suspect for about three seconds over a distance of about ten yards. The Court of Appeal agreed with the trial judge that his identification carried more weight than an ordinary witness's. The Court even went so far as to approve a passage in Archbold[43] which argued that anyone who has been involved in the criminal justice system, whether police officer, advocate, or judge, is likely to have a greater appreciation of the importance of identification and, accordingly, to look for some particular identifying feature. In *Williams (John)*,[44] a police constable saw two men walking to a car. He saw them from a moving vehicle for a couple of seconds. The recorder, at Williams' trial for burglary, refused to stop the case although there was no other evidential support for the identification of the defendant. The Court of Appeal agreed that the officer's identification could be regarded as more reliable than a layman's; his suspicions had been aroused, and he made a particular effort to memorise the suspect's appearance.

Although the rationale of *Turnbull* is that judges must instruct jurors as to the weakness of eyewitness evidence, they themselves appear to give it excessive weight. Wagenaar reports that in cases where identification is an issue, judges give less attention than they should to the basic legal issues of act and intention.[45] Uninstructed, jurors seem to be impressed by identification evidence, particularly if there is more than one witness.[46] British police still believe that eyewitnesses are accurate and reliable most of the time.[47] Lay people are not intuitively aware of the factors that affect the reliability of identification evidence.[48] A judicial warning appears not to moderate juror enthusiasm for eyewitness evidence,[49] so courts in the United States have attempted to amplify its effect by allowing expert testimony to explain the unreliability of identifications.[50] This is very rare in England,[51] although experts are allowed to give evidence in voice

---

[40] PB Ainsworth, 'Incident Perception by British Police Officers' 1981 5 *Law and Human Behavior* 231.
[41] BR Clifford, 'Police as Eyewitnesses' (1972) 22 *New Society* 176.
[42] [1991] *Criminal Law Review* 295.
[43] PJ Richardson, *Archbold: Criminal Pleading and Practice* (London, Sweet and Maxwell, 2001) para. 14.25.
[44] *The Times* 7 October 1994.
[45] WA Wagenaar, PJ van Koppen, and HM Crombag, *Anchored Narratives: the Psychology of Criminal Evidence* (Hemel Hempstead, Harvester Wheatsheaf, 1993) 119.
[46] GL Wells and MR Leippe, 'How do Triers of Fact infer the Accuracy of Eyewitness Identification? Using Memory for Peripheral Detail can be Misleading' (1981) 66 *Journal of Applied Psychology* 682.
[47] M Kebbel and R Milne, 'Police Officer's Perceptions of Eyewitness Performance in Forensic Investigations' (1998) 138 *Journal of Social Psychology* 22.
[48] BS Cutler and SD Penrod, *Mistaken Identification: the EyeWitness, Psychology and the Law* (Cambridge, Cambridge University Press, 1995) 171–209.
[49] See chapter five.
[50] Also in Australia: *Smith* [1987] VR 907.
[51] GH Gudjonsson, 'Psychology and Assessment' in R Bull and D Carson, *Psychology in Legal Contexts* (Chichester, Wiley, 1995) 62. Redmayne suggests that it would be inadmissible: M Redmayne, *Expert Evidence and Criminal Justice* (Oxford, Oxford University Press, 2001) 187.

identification cases.[52] Expert evidence may not be the answer, however. Although it increases juror scepticism about the reliability of the witness, the trial may not be more effective. In a study of mock jurors where half the subjects heard psychological evidence on the weakness of identifications and the other half did not, the first half were more reluctant to believe the identification witness. But they were no better at discriminating between accurate and inaccurate testimony.[53] It seems that the expert evidence used was too non-specific; what was needed was a more individualised opinion as to who was most likely to be reliable — the very ground into which experts are not allowed to tread.

Although judges are aware that most people find it much more difficult to describe than to recognise, they nevertheless tend to call attention to the testimony of witnesses whose initial description is inconsistent with the person they picked out at the identification parade.[54] Intuitive notions are clearly difficult to displace. Reinforcing *Turnbull* by introducing a corroboration requirement might be advisable, but if several weak identifications can support each other, a substantial risk of error remains. Given an accuracy rate of only 50:50, the possibility that several eyewitnesses have identified the wrong person is alarmingly high.

FACILITATING WITNESS TESTIMONY

During the last twenty years, it has become increasingly apparent that no criminal justice system can afford to ignore the interests of victims and other witnesses. Court procedures across the world have been modified to facilitate their testimony.[55] The difficulty for Anglo-American systems has been to preserve the presumption that an accused person is innocent, whilst protecting vulnerable witnesses from the rigours of oral adversarial proceedings. There are people with comprehension and communications difficulties who cannot participate in an oral procedure without acute difficulty, and possibly, the risk of psychological damage.[56] The most clearly identifiable witnesses in this category are children; in many cases where they are called upon to give evidence, they have been the victims of crime. Doubts about the unreliability of child witnesses, and consequent insistence on corroborative evidence,[57] were swept away in England[58] and Canada[59] in the same year, making it possible to convict entirely on the basis of one child's evidence.

---

[52] *Robb* (1991) 93 Cr App R 161 below.
[53] GL Wells, RCL Lindsay and JP Tousignant, 'Effects of Expert Psychological Advice on Testimony' (1980) 4 *Law and Human Behaviour* 275.
[54] Ainsworth above n.27, 65.
[55] JR Spencer, G Nicholson, R Flin and R Bull, (eds) *Children's Evidence in Legal Proceedings* (University of Cambridge, 1990).
[56] *Barriers to Justice* (Mencap National Centre, 1997).
[57] See chapter four.
[58] Criminal Justice Act 1988 s.34.
[59] An Act to Amend the Criminal Code and the Canada Evidence Act, SC 1987, c24515, effective 1 January 1988.

Prosecutions which once would have been abandoned were taken forward.[60] However, some judges continue to stress the 'inherent frailty of children's testimony'.[61] In the past, child witnesses were regarded with such suspicion that young children were not even competent to give evidence. Children could give sworn evidence on oath only if they understood the religious significance of the oath. If they did not, they could give unsworn evidence, as long as they did understand the normal social obligation to tell the truth. In practice, this tended to mean that evidence from children younger than eight years old (unsworn), or ten years old (sworn) was rejected. Where the normal social obligation was not understood, the child was not able to give evidence at all. Judges used to question all child witnesses as a preliminary matter in order to ascertain whether they understood the importance of the oath. This often led to a quasi-theological discussion more reminiscent of a confirmation class. In *Hayes*,[62] however, it was held that if a child acknowledges the particular importance of telling the truth in court, that is more significant in determining competence than belief in the 'divine sanction'.

The cultural resistance to children's evidence stemmed partly from a fear that they would fabricate evidence, either in the belief that it will please a particular adult, or as a result of spite or fantasy. Lawyers can provide any amount of anecdotal evidence of a child who sought either attention or revenge against the intrusion of a stepparent into the family[63]. There are psychologists who have also observed that children often have different concerns from adults. Children may go to extreme lengths to cover up behaviour for which they fear rebuke — for instance playing with children disapproved of by their parents, or accepting sweets from strangers, having been told not to do it — because they are unaware of the triviality of the incident about which they are concerned in comparison with the story they are telling.[64] But to operate a strict test for competency affords ideal protection for child abusers; the younger the child they abuse, the less likely it is that a successful prosecution can be taken place. Here, psychology has provided ammunition for those who argued for changes to ensure that the legal system protects the victims of abuse.[65] For there is evidence that even small children can give a coherent account of abuse committed against them,[66] although they lack the sophisticated conceptual apparatus of adult witnesses.[67] They may make mistakes

---

[60] L Sasm, D Wolfe and K Gowdey, 'Children and the Courts in Canada' in B Bottoms and G Goodman, *International Perspectives on Child Abuse and Children's Testimony* (London, Sage, 1996).

[61] N Bala, 'Child Witnesses in the Canadian Criminal Courts: Recognizing their Capacities and Needs' (1999) 5 *Psychiatry, Psychology and Law* 323.

[62] As in *Hayes* [1977] 2 All ER 288.

[63] G Williams, 'Child Witnesses' in P Smith, (ed) *Essays in Honour of J. C. Smith* (London, Butterworths, 1987).

[64] A Trankell, 'Was Lars Sexually Assaulted? a Study on the Reliability of Witnesses and of Experts' (1961) 56 *Journal of Abnormal Psychology* 385.

[65] See JR Spencer and R Flin, *The Evidence of Children,: the Law and the Psychology* (London, Blackstone, 1993).

[66] D Jones, 'The Evidence of a Three-Year-Old Child' (1987) *Criminal Law Review* 677.

[67] G Davies, Y Stevenson-Robb and R Flin, 'The Reliability of Children's Testimony' (1986) 11 *International Practitioner* 81.

because of misunderstanding of a situation or weaknesses in recall. Some instances of unfounded allegation may have been adult-instigated.[68] Research into the suggestibility of child witnesses is inconclusive. While some studies found children to be more susceptible to suggestion than adults,[69] conflicting research results suggest that situational factors have more effect than the age of the subject.[70] There are obvious methodological problems confronting any researcher seeking to assess the veracity of child witnesses in abuse cases. Nevertheless, Jones and McGraw,[71] who surveyed three hundred and seventy-six reports by children of sexual abuse made to the Social Services Department in Denver, Colorado, during 1983, estimated that only about two per cent were false.

The 1980s and the 1990s saw an increased awareness that children were not being protected by the legal system and should not be singled out for disbelief. The public debate took place across the western world.[72] In England and Wales, legislation simplified the competency test. Children under the age of fourteen will not be required to take the oath,[73] so judges will no longer have to quiz them on its meaning. It had become apparent that an oral exchange with the judge in the courtroom is not the best method of estimating a child's level of sophistication, although most judges did their best to make the child feel relaxed. Also, there was a distinct problem of subjectivity, since different judges appear to have different expectations of the abilities of children of particular ages.[74] Under reforms of 1999, all witnesses, including children are *prima facie* competent[75] to give evidence. However, they are nevertheless not competent to give evidence in criminal proceedings if it should appear to the court that they are not able to (a) understand questions put to them, and (b) give answers which can be understood.[76] 'It is a matter of [the judge's] perception of the child's understanding demonstrated in the course of ordinary discourse'.[77] There is no lower age limit. The Court of

---

[68] Spencer and Flin, above n.65, 323.

[69] B Marin, D Holmes, M Guth and P Kovac, 'The Potential of Children as Eyewitnesses' (1979) 3 *Law and Human Behaviour* 295; RL Cohen and MA Harnick, 'The Susceptibility of Child Witnesses to Suggestion' (1980) 4 *Law and Human Behavior* 295; Cf. GS Goodman and RS Reed, 'Age Differences in Eyewitness Testimony' (1986) 10 *Law and Human Behavior* 317.

[70] GS Goodman, C Aman and J Hirschman, 'Child Sexual and Physical Abuse' in S Ceci, M Toglia and D Ross, (eds) *Children's Eyewitness Memory* (New York, Springer-Verlag, 1987); G Davies, 'Research on Children's Testimony: Implications for Interviewing Practice' in C Hollins and K Howells, (eds) *Clinical Approaches to Sex Offenders and their Victims* (Chichester, Wiley, 1991); K Saywitz, GS Goodman, E Nichols and S Moan, 'Children's Memory for a Genital Examination' (1989) Paper presented to the Society for Research on Child Development, Kansas City, USA.

[71] DP Jones and JM McGraw, 'Reliable and Fictitious Accounts of Sexual Abuse in Children' (1987) 2 *Journal of Interpersonal Violence* 27.

[72] Spencer, Nicholson, Flin and Bull, above n. 55.

[73] Youth Justice and Criminal Evidence Act 1999, s.55.

[74] K Murray, *Live Television Link: an Evaluation of its use by Child Witnesses in Scottish Criminal Trials* (Edinburgh Scottish Office Central Research Unit 1995).

[75] Youth Justice and Criminal Evidence Act 1999 s.53(1). Formal competency requirements were abolished also in Canada and Australia: Reid Howie Associates, *Vulnerable and Intimidated Witnesses: a Review of Provisions in Other Jurisdictions,* (Edinburgh, Scottish Executive Central Research Unit, 2002).

[76] S.53(3).

[77] *Hampshire*, [1995] 2 All ER 1019, Auld J at 1026.

Appeal will not interfere if the trial judge rules a four- or five- year-old child as competent.[78]

The same presumption of competence now applies to anyone suffering from mental illness or learning disability. Witnesses in this category historically have been regarded with suspicion by the criminal justice system. Research for the charity, Mencap, indicates that people with learning disabilities are far more likely than other adults to be the victims of sexual offences, assault, robbery or personal theft. Nevertheless, crimes against them have been particularly likely to be ignored, partly because of misunderstanding; there have been cases where officers have erroneously thought a person with communication difficulties was drunk, and others where he or she appeared to be simply obstructive.[79] An acute disability might be seen as a reason for taking no action, either at investigation or prosecution level, on the grounds that the witness would not be able to cope with court proceedings.[80] Parliament has responded by introducing two categories of witness, sworn and unsworn, a dichotomy redolent of the old child witness provisions. Adult witnesses now may give evidence unsworn, if of mental disability so severe that they do not understand the significance of the oath. The provision is in familiar terms. To be sworn, the witness must have sufficient appreciation of the solemnity of the occasion and of the particular responsibility to tell the truth which is involved in taking an oath.[81] The prospect looms of the kind of metaphysical seminar on the meaning of truth that children used to undergo. The net result of this reform is that adult witnesses will now fall into one of two separate groups; those who give evidence on oath, and those who give evidence unsworn. The value of this is said to be that it will allow the court to receive evidence that in the past has been denied it. The risk remains, however, that the new power to receive evidence unsworn will merely tempt judges to downgrade evidence which once was given on oath without much thought being given to the matter. A 'two-tier' system automatically suggests that unsworn witnesses are less credible than sworn witnesses.

Assisting Recall and Delivery

The insistence on oral evidence requires that witnesses are physically present in court. They must testify from memory to matters of which they have direct knowledge. The law to some extent recognises the difficulty of recalling details long after the event, and allows witnesses to refresh their memories from any contemporaneous notes they may have taken.[82] This is of no assistance to anyone

---

[78] Cf. *DPP v M* [1997] 2 All ER 749.
[79] Mencap, above n. 56.
[80] A Sanders, J Creaton, S Bird and L Weber, *Victims with Learning Disabilities — Regulating the Criminal Justice System*, Centre for Criminological Research Occasional Paper No 17, (University of Oxford, 1997).
[81] S.55(2).
[82] *Virgo* (1978) 67 Cr App R 23.

unable to make or to read contemporaneous notes. Neither is the rule that witnesses may refresh their memory from their witness statement before going into court[83] or, with leave of the judge, during their testimony.[84] The problem would not be solved by having the statement read aloud to the witness, who may have problems with concentration. Also, statements tend to be written in police language, and may be confusing. The passage of time has a particularly serious effect on the spontaneous recall of young children.[85] They can give far more accurate and detailed accounts close in time to the events.[86]

Many legal systems have acted on these findings to minimise dependency on a child's oral testimony at a criminal trial. Canada, Western Australia, Scotland, Hong Kong and most of the United States of America[87] have experimented with a videotaped interview to use in lieu of a child's evidence in chief.[88] They have also tried to reduce stress through the introduction of closed circuit television. In England and Wales, live television links were introduced for child witnesses in Crown Court trials for certain offences in 1988.[89] Certain children have been allowed to tell their story by way of a videotaped interview from 1991.[90] Interviews conducted on videotape should take place made as early as possible, in a pleasant environment in order to obtain the fullest account possible and reduce stress. The Government now plans to make the videotaped interview available for all categories of child witnesses, and for vulnerable witnesses generally. The Youth Justice and Criminal Evidence Act 1999 extends the category of vulnerable witness to include not only children, but a diverse range of adults, and provides a wide variety of special measures[91] to make it easier for them to give evidence in court. Adults with communication or comprehension difficulties are included. The purpose is to ensure that their evidence is not lost should they be unable to

---

[83] *Richardson* (1971) 55 Cr App R 244.

[84] If they did not in fact read them outside the court, *Da Silva* [1990] 1 WLR 31; and even where the statement has been read previously, see *R v South Ribble Stipendiary Magistrate ex p Cochrane, The Times* 24 June 1996.

[85] A Baddley, *Your Memory: a User's Guide* (Harmondsworth, Penguin, 1983); HR Dent and GM Stephenson, 'Identification Evidence: Experimental Investigations of Factors Affecting the Reliability of Juvenile and Adult Witnesses' in ID Farrington, K Hawkins and S Lloyd-Bostock, (eds) *Psychology, Law and Legal Process* (London, Macmillan, 1979).

[86] *Report of the Advisory Group on Video Evidence*, (Pigot Report) (Home Office, 1989).

[87] The accused's right to confrontation may give way to hearsay evidence which appears reliable: *Ohio v Roberts* 448 US 56 (1980). Many states allow it if the child is likely to suffer significant emotional harm as a result of testifying in court; *Perez v Florida* 536 So 2d. 206 (1988); *Idaho v Giles* 772 P 2d 191 (1989).

[88] Reid Howie Associates, n.75.

[89] S.32A Criminal Justice Act 1988 as amended by s.54 Criminal Justice Act 1991 and s.62 Criminal Procedure and Investigations Act 1996.

[90] S.54 Criminal Justice Act 1991.

[91] As well as the videotaped interview, special measures include ordering the use of screens (s.23), and video cross examination (s.28). Initally recommended for child witnesses in the Pigot Report, n. 86. The most revolutionary of the special measures, this would be conducted before the trial begins, and, combined with the videotaped interview, would remove from the witness any need to attend court or worry about trial dates. The provision has yet to be implemented. See also interpreters and aids to communication (ss.20,30).

cope with court procedures. It is thought, also, that if investigators are aware that special measures are available, they will be more confident about proceeding with a prosecution.

Producing an appropriate definition of witnesses with mental disability has proved problematic. To base the test on IQ would have ignored a range of relevant factors such as cognitive capacity, the ability to concentrate, and speech development. It was decided to combine a definition based on mental disorder within the meaning of the Mental Health Act 1983 with a flexible approach. This takes account of individual circumstances, such as whether the witness has a significant impairment of intelligence and social functioning, or a physical disability or is suffering from a physical disorder.[92] In any event, any person who would suffer fear or distress in connection with testifying in court[93] is eligible for special measures, irrespective of any disability being proved. The court should take account of factors that might affect witnesses' susceptibility to fear or distress, such as their age, social and cultural background, and ethnic origins.[94] There is a presumption in favour of special measures for complainants in sexual cases.[95] Since it was found that some child witnesses for whom special measures had been used resented it, and would have preferred to give evidence in a conventional manner, the Act requires that the witnesses' own preference must be considered. Some victims feel it necessary to confront their attacker in a court of law.[96] Not every person with a disability will wish to be regarded as a vulnerable witness.[97]

Evaluation

The videotaped interview for child witnesses has been available to criminal courts cases for over ten years. It has not been an unqualified success. Since it serves, in effect, as the child's evidence in chief, the use of leading questions has to be kept to a minimum.[98] The approved questioning style is modelled upon Professor Yuille's 'step-wise' approach,[99] emphasising spontaneity. In fact, it is very difficult to conduct an interview without leading; most advocates require a great deal of practice. The danger is that the interviewer will resort to closed, single-response type questions, a style which is very unhelpful to a child, despite exhortations in the

---

[92] S.16(1)(b); s.16 (2).
[93] S.17(1).
[94] S.17(2).
[95] S.17(4).
[96] J Plotnikoff and R Woolfson, *Prosecuting Child Abuse* (London, Blackstone, 1995) pp 96–7.
[97] *Report of the Interdepartmental Working Group on the Treatment of Vulnerable or Intimidated Witnesses in the Criminal Justice System* (London, Home Office, 1998) 3.8. Importance of witness's views, *ibid.*, 3.26 C Palmer, 'Still Vulnerable After All These Years' (1996) *Criminal Law Review* 633.
[98] *Memorandum of Good Practice on Videorecorded Interviews with Child Witnesses for Criminal Proceedings* (Home Office, Department of Health, 1992).
[99] J Yuille, R Hunter, R Joffe and J Zaparnink, 'Interviewing Children in Child Sexual Abuse Cases' in G Goodman and B Bottoms, (eds) *Child Victims, Child Witnesses* (New York, Guilford, 1993).

guidance to ask open-ended questions.[100] The burden of producing this interview evidence has been placed on the police officers and social workers who comprise local Child Protection Units, who are forced into operating and communicating like lawyers. A Home Office study found many interviews being rejected by trial judges because of breaches of the guidelines, including 'inappropriate comfort' or encouragement during the course of the interview with a distressed child.[101] Interviewing teams, some members of which are responsible for the child's welfare and may know a great deal about the child's family background, are thus faced with a dilemma. Should the child's immediate welfare or the requirements of a future court of trial, be their chief concern? The Crown Prosecution Service's Inspectorate consider that an increasing proportion of interviews is being conducted the approved manner, although editing is still required in fifty-four per cent of videotapes offered to the court.[102]

Now that the use of videotaped interviews is to be extended to other kinds of vulnerable witness, it seems that interviewers from the child protection units will be expected to conduct interviews with people with mental illness or learning disability. The assumption is that the communication skills appropriate to children will serve equally well with these witnesses. The supposition that a child or family specialist will have the appropriate skills and experience for this 'very different group' is wrong.[103] Their training relates in particular to sexual offences, and is poor preparation for dealing with a group who, typically, are victim to a whole range of crimes.[104] The view that a low mental age is the same as thinking like a child is a common one. But expressing learning disability in terms of mental age 'does not clearly portray the difficulties that individual will have in terms of giving evidence'.[105] There are major differences even between different kinds of disability. For example, autism can be combined with very accurate recall of detail.[106] Another problem is that these witnesses must be identified in order that a special measures interview can be conducted. Police officers are not good at recognising mild learning disability,[107] and so some police forces are providing special training for selected officers.

Using videotaped interviews does appear to reduce the levels of stress suffered by children who gave evidence by that means, as does the live link.[108] At present, few children are receiving the benefit of videotaping, although many videotape

[100] G Davies, C Wilson, R Mitchell and J Milson, *Videotaping Children's Evidence: an Evaluation* (London, Home Office, 1995).
[101] *Ibid.*
[102] Crown Prosecution Service Inspectorate, *The Inspectorate's Report on Cases Involving Child Witnesses* 1/98 (London Crown Prosecution Service, 1998).
[103] Mencap above n. 56.
[104] Sanders, Creaton, Bird and Weber, above n.80, 20.
[105] Mencap, above n.56.
[106] Sanders, Creaton, Bird and Weber, above n.80.
[107] *Ibid.*
[108] G Davies and E Noon, *An Evaluation of the Live Link for Child Witnesses* (London, Home Office, 1991) 133.

interviews exist.[109] There are practical problems that affect the admissibility of some of the interviews, but also some conservativism seems to persist in the legal profession. Out of one thousand, six hundred and twenty-one trials involving children in England and Wales, only six hundred and forty applications were made to use videotaped evidence in chief. Part of the problem may be that prosecutors prefer to have the child present in the courtroom.[110] Some have expressed the view that testimony from an image on a screen lacks the emotional power of a living child in the witness box,[111] and that children who are very calm may not convince the jury that they have been the victims of abuse.[112] This also may explain why the live link was employed in only sixteen out of forty-one cases in which it was available.[113] Thus, the 1999 Youth Justice and Criminal Evidence Act provides that the court may raise the matter irrespective of the views of prosecuting counsel,[114] and that there is a presumption in favour of special measures for child witnesses.[115] Whether it is more difficult to obtain a conviction where a child is seen only on screen is unclear. In the United States, mock jurors showed some reluctance to believe a child giving evidence by way of closed circuit television.[116] However, real jurors in Western Australia understood the reasons for and did not feel disadvantaged by its use.[117] No variance in conviction rates was found in New South Wales where closed circuit television was used.[118] Wilson and Davies[119] report no significant outcome difference whichever method of presenting evidence was used in child abuse cases. At the same time, perceptions of the credibility of the children seemed to be unaffected.

The emphasis on technology to assist vulnerable witnesses fails to recognise that many of the difficulties faced by those giving evidence in court arise from lawyer behaviour. We have seen throughout this book that advocates' tight control on the manner in testimony is delivered, with their power to lead witnesses into self-contradiction, confusion and, possibly, speechlessness, is crucial in a system so dedicated to assessment of witness demeanour. The apparent reluctance of adversarial systems to impose checks upon advocate power in relation to testimony,

---

[109] Between October 1992 and June 1993, 14,912 interviews were taped; only 24 per cent of those were forwarded to the Crown Prosecution Service; Davies, Wilson, Mitchell and Milson, above n.100 17.

[110] C Wilson and G Davies, 'An Evaluation of the Use of Videotaped Evidence for Juvenile Witnesses in Criminal Courts in England and Wales,' (1999) 7 *European Journal on Criminal Policy and Research* 81; Social Services Inspectorate, *The Child, the Court and the Video* (London, Department of Health, 1994).

[111] SB Smith, 'The Child Witness' in *Representing Children: Current Issues in Law, Medicine and Mental Health* (National Association of Councils for Children, 1987) 13.

[112] Murray, above n.74; G Davis, L Hoyano, C Keenan L Maitland and R Morgan, *An Assessment of the Admissibility and Sufficiency of Evidence in Child Abuse Prosecutions* (London, Home Office, 1999).

[113] Plotnikoff and Woolfson, above n. 96.

[114] S.19 (1).

[115] S.16(1(a); s21(1)(a).

[116] JEB Myers, *Evidence in Child Abuse Cases* (New York, Wiley, 1997).

[117] C O'Grady, *Child Witnesses and Jury Trials; an Evaluation of the Use of Closed Circuit Television and Removable Screens in Western Australia* (Western Australia Ministry of Justice, 1996).

[118] J Cashmore, 'The Prosecution of Child Sexual Assault Cases: a Survey of NSW DPP Solicitors' (1995) 28 *Australia and New Zealand Journal of Criminology* 32.

[119] Wilson and Davies above, n. 110, 81; Murray, above n.74.

and the refusal to accept that little may be learnt from the performance of a witness in the courtroom, shows that considerable distance still remains between the perspectives of psychology and law. An example of the reluctance of lawyers to let go of traditional attitudes to testimony may be seen in the failure to include defendants in the category of vulnerable witnesses eligible for special measures even if they are juveniles, or have learning disability or communication difficulties. Witnesses whose problems may be less severe, and who, in the case of juvenile crime, may in fact be older than the defendant, are thus in a favoured position. A challenge under the Human Rights Act seems inevitable.[120]

CONCLUSION

We have seen the importance of narrative affecting perceptions of foreseeability, causation, and the probative force of evidence. Within this framework, there is some evidence that finders of fact attribute responsibility according to a 'safe world' model, reminiscent of defensive attribution. At present, attribution theory itself is too blunt an instrument to enable the judgment of a court of law to be predicted with any accuracy. The contrast between internal and external locus may explain some of the underlying assumptions of the criminal law, but does not come close to accounting for individual decisions reached by tribunals of fact in civil or criminal cases. 'Attributing responsibility and the locus of cause in criminal justice may ... be a highly complex and highly subjective exercise for which attribution theory provides no more than general, unspecific principles.'[121]

Also, since psychological and legal attributions of responsibility are not identical, drawing an analogy between the disciplines is difficult. Often in psychological research the term attribution is used quite generally to refer to the mental process of organising events and interpreting a set of information. without it being intended to analyse all the concepts behind a legal fixing of responsibility.[122] To carry out research that mirrors the legal process more closely, some awareness of social context would have to be incorporated.[123] Hamilton argues that whether the actor's own motives will be taken into account by the observer, or whether the focus will be upon the blameworthy consequences, depends upon a normative evaluation upon the actor's social role. If the role is accepted, then judgment of motive will accompany the attribution of responsibility.

However, psychologists have played an important part in laying bare the unscientific nature of legal decision-making. Not before time, it is now being recognised that rational jury verdicts will be possible only when trials are conducted in full awareness of how juries organise evidence and respond to uncertainty.

[120] DJ Birch, Note on *R v Acton Youth Court* [2002] *Criminal Law Review* 76.
[121] M King, *Psychology in or out of Court* (London, Pergamon, 1986) 49.
[122] S Lloyd-Bostock, 'The Ordinary Man and the Psychology of Attributing Causes and Responsibility' (1979) 42 *Modern Law Review* 143.
[123] VL Hamilton, 'Who is Responsible? Towards a Social Psychology of Responsibility Attribution' (1978) 41 *Social Psychology* 316.

The methodological limitations of jury research have not prevented lawyers from becoming increasingly aware that some of their traditional assumptions may be mistaken. This has resulted in some, albeit cautious, legal reform. However, legal recognition of the value of psychology in the legal context has had another valuable consequence; there seems to be increasing willingness to co-operate in research. Access to real juries would allow far more scope to test theory, and to confirm or disprove laboratory findings. King accuses psychologists of lacking a theoretical base, concentrating instead of isolated laboratory experiments on narrow issues.

> What is needed is an account of the weight given by jurors individually or collectively to different items of information, or how they succeed in reconciling the conflicting opinions or facts in arriving at their decision. The problem with narrow-issue experiments is even if they successfully measure how credible a particular witness is, they cannot effectively predict the extent to which that assessment, as opposed to all the other evidence, might influence the outcome of a trial. At the same time, general theories such as just world or attribution theory tell us little or nothing about the weight given by juries to different items of information and how they resolve conflicts of interest.[124]

More work on the lines of the New Zealand jury project[125] and Waganaar's research[126] would do much to address these criticisms, and, through recognition of the importance of the story model, link the sociological with the psychological.

For example, the question of witness credibility is too complex to be addressed solely through empirical evidence derived from laboratory studies. Judgments about the veracity of witnesses depend heavily on context. In many of the experiments on lying behaviour and perceptions of dishonesty, observers are deprived of context, no narrative having been offered. It is rare, even in social situations, that the alleged lie is not part of a narrative structure. Perceptions of credibility follow the story rather than the other way round. Courts would apparently rather believe that a witness has performed a remarkable feat of memory (which lacks plausibility in itself), if it confirms a prosecution narrative. Generally, the test for lying is whether the testimony fits with other evidence, or whether it seems the witness has no reason to lie. The first method is hazardous because it promotes the selection of evidence on the basis of story plausibility. It implies verification of the story. Wagenaar records that alibis are hardly ever believed. Courts assume that friends or relations, who supply most of the alibis offered, would lie out of loyalty.[127] Experts, on the other hand, are generally believed, despite the notorious cases

---

[124] King, above n. 87.
[125] W Young, N Cameron and Y Tinsley, *Juries in Criminal Trials, Part 2*, New Zealand Law Commission Preliminary Paper 37, (Wellington, New Zealand, 1999).
[126] WA Wagenaar, PJ van Koppen, and HM Crombag, *Anchored Narratives: the Psychology of Criminal Evidence* (Hemel Hempstead, Harvester Wheatsheaf, 1993).
[127] *Ibid.*

where they were found to have misled the court.[128] Meanwhile, lawyers appear finally to be accepting the limited value of demeanour as an indicator of honesty. Reforms to the hearsay rule in the Criminal Justice Bill of 2003 indicate increased awareness that oral sworn statements in courts of law may be of less value than some-out-of-court statements made by a witness who is not able to be present. It may be many years before lawyers are able or willing to adapt questioning procedures and styles so that live witnesses can express themselves as they wish. Nevertheless, worldwide reforms to mitigate the rigours of the adversarial trial for vulnerable witnesses illustrate an increased willingness to adapt in the light of developing knowledge. As more is discovered about the work of real juries, legal systems should adapt trials to enable them to reach their verdicts in an informed and structured way. It would be a pity if, instead, the reaction were to exclude jurors from the process altogether, with no attempt to address the obstacles currently placed in their path by lawyers.

---

[128] Sir John May, Return to an Address of the Honourable the House of Commons Dated 30 June 1994 for a *Report of the Inquiry into the Circumstances Surrounding the Convictions arising out of the Bomb Attacks on Guildford and Woolwich in 1974: Final Report* (London, HMSO, 1994).

Index